The GameMaker Standard

The GameMaker Standard is the hands-on resource for creating games using the GameMaker engine. With step-by-step directions and numerous visual examples, this book teaches readers the fundamental skills and efficient procedures to help them begin creating their own games, while also offering more advanced options for seasoned game development readers who are expanding to the GameMaker format. Each chapter contains a tutorial on creating a game in a specific game genre, giving readers detailed and accurate guides to follow during their own game creation. Further features of this book include:

- Tools and methods to create a variety of games, including multi-level, two player, and RPGs
- Coverage of user interface options and GML code
- How to create a 2.5D game, and how these differ from 2D and 3D
- Pixel art creation techniques
- Industry tips and recommendations for exporting and selling personally created games

David C. Vinciguerra is the lead instructor for the Simulation and Game Development degree program at Wayne Community College. Prior to his current position he served as Co-Director of the Virtual Reality and Education Laboratory and Co-Editor for the internationally peer-reviewed journal *VR in the Schools* while teaching graduate and undergraduate virtual reality courses at East Carolina University. David lives in Pikeville, North Carolina, with his wife, Jennifer, and their daughter, Natalie.

Andrew Howell developed a love for game programming while working toward his Simulation and Game Development degree. He has developed multiple games using the GameMaker and the Unity3D game engines. During his time working in the Simulation Development Laboratory at Wayne Community College, he found teaching his skills to others enjoyable. Andrew enjoys learning new development techniques and currently resides in Goldsboro, North Carolina.

The GameMaker Standard

David Vinciguerra and Andrew Howell

CRC Press
Taylor & Francis Group
Boca Raton London New York

CRC Press is an imprint of the
Taylor & Francis Group, an **informa** business
AN A K PETERS BOOK

CRC Press
Taylor & Francis Group
6000 Broken Sound Parkway NW, Suite 300
Boca Raton, FL 33487-2742

CRC Press is an imprint of the Taylor & Francis Group, an informa business

Library of Congress Cataloging-in-Publication Data
Vinciguerra, David C.
The GameMaker standard / David C. Vinciguerra and Andrew J. Howell.
pages cm
1. GameMaker (Computer program language) 2. Computer games—Programming. I. Howell, Andrew J. II. Title.
QA76.76.C672V56 2016
794.8'1526—dc23
2015013609

ISBN: 978-1-138-85696-7 (hbk)
ISBN: 978-1-138-85697-4 (pbk)
ISBN: 978-1-315-71900-9 (ebk)

Typeset in Myriad Pro
By Apex CoVantage, LLC

Printed and bound in India by Replika Press Pvt. Ltd.

Visit the Taylor & Francis Web site at http://www.taylorandfrancis.com and the CRC Press Web site at http://www.crcpress.com

To those who have a dream and wish to make it a reality.

Contents

About the Artists

Richard Graham

Richard is a concept/illustration artist who has been drawing since he was seven years old. He learned to draw by looking over his brother's shoulder while his brother was sketching. Drawing allowed Richard to bring to life anything he could think of through art. He began by designing fictional vehicles and eventually moved on to drawing anime and cartoon characters. It was through art that he won his first trophy in an art contest. It was when Richard began selling sketches to other children in school that he began to realize how much people really loved art. He did not realize he could work as an artist for games until he saw a documentary on game design. Previously his primary focus was on being a penciler, Inker, or just a freelance artist altogether. After seeing how game designers can take an artist's work and give it life he wanted to be a part of the game design industry. Richard enjoys various art styles such as manga but his true passion is comic art and he studies the art styles of comic book artists such as Mike Mignola, Greg Capullo, Humberto Ramos, and John Romita. His mom always wanted him to do something with his art and before she passed away he promised her he would do his best to break into the art industry. It is this promise that keeps him focused on continually developing his art skills. It was in the Simulation and Game Development program at Wayne Community College that Richard was first introduced to programs such as Photoshop and tools such as drawing on a Wacom.

Whitney Joyner

Whitney first found her love for the arts when she was in middle school. A friend taught her to draw anime after which she spent her middle and high school years drawing, taking art classes, and honing her drawing skills. Because the friend mostly drew anime Whitney's art style naturally also took on the look of anime initially. As she continued to study and practice her art gradually began to morph into something more of her own, which she describes as cartoonized. Whitney discovered the field of game art by accident. She was looking into different colleges when another friend had an extra reservation to an open house at an art college. She talked to the dean who asked about some things she enjoyed and from what Whitney told her, she suggested the gaming field. She ended up checking out the Simulation and Game Development program at Wayne Community College because it was closer to home than the college she visited. She found that she really liked the idea of going into the field of game design and soon after started her path into gaming art.

Andrew Sanders

Andrew started drawing when he was about four years old. His parents said even then that he could draw pretty much anything that he could see. He focused mostly on comic book art and wanted to go into the comic book field for a while. When Andrew was in high school he had an art teacher tell him that he was drawing "wrong" so he left art for a while and went into drafting. That lead to CAD, which is what really sparked his interest in CGI work. When Wayne Community College started the Simulation and Game Development (SGD) program, it was a perfect time for him because he had just gotten out of the hospital and could not go back to work full time for a while. Prior to the SGD program, Andrew had tried to use 3ds Max, and it was pretty challenging without formal help. During his first semester at Wayne Community College, he took Maya and Game Textures and fell in love with the whole system. Since then, Andrew has never stopped working with Maya. It is by far one of his favorite things to do. He has recently started using Zbrush, which has been a great tool to work with as well. Some of Andrew's favorite things to create are vehicles, mechanical creatures, and robots.

Jennifer Vinciguerra

Jennifer Vinciguerra does a little bit of everything pretty well. One might call her a "Jill of all trades." A woman of many skills, she helped her husband, David, with this book in a variety of ways: She composed and performed the eerie violin music for the *Lost Dog* game; she designed a variety of the graphics used in *Lost Dog*, *Snail Trail*, and *Blood Vessel* and colored some of the other artists' drawings to blend them together; best of all, she most enjoyed creating all of the graphics for *Keeper of the Oracle*, particularly the landscapes. In addition to creative work, Jennifer also pitched in to proofread a bit of the technical writing and tested instructions for clarity by building some of the games as instructed in the chapters.

Jennifer holds a Bachelor of Arts degree in Geography from the University of North Carolina, which is probably why she really enjoys designing maps and landscapes for games. She also holds a Master of Science degree in Instructional Technology as well as a graduate certificate in Virtual Reality in Education and Training from East Carolina University (ECU). After working over five years as an instructional technology consultant at ECU, Jennifer opened her own Suzuki Violin studio where she currently teaches upward of 15 private students and puts to use all those years of violin lessons her parents invested in. Teaching violin allows her to spend quality time with her family, to employ her hodgepodge multimedia skills for promoting the studio, and to help her husband, David, with his exciting projects—like textbook authoring.

Acknowledgments

This book would not exist if not for the incredible team of people that contributed their time, talent, and encouragement during the creation process. Compiling this book followed a process very similar to creating games. Concept artists were needed to visualize the look of the games. 2D and 3D artists created the game visuals based on concept sketches and descriptions. Music and sound effects were created specifically for each game and beta testers and editors were needed to review materials to make sure bugs in both the games and narrative were removed. It should be noted that if any bugs still remain in the text of this book or in the games themselves it is the fault of the writers of this book alone and not those of the testers and editors who have done a phenomenal job going over each chapter and re-creating games to make sure everything is clear and working properly for the reader.

We are tremendously grateful for the patience and assistance from our families during the writing of this book, specifically in providing us the time needed to hide away and write without distractions. David would especially like to thank his wife, Jennifer, for her contributions of art, music, narrative editing, encouragement, and overall for always believing in him.

We would like to give thanks to those of you that provided ideas, technical assistance, feedback, encouragement, and contributed original artwork for this project: Richard Graham, Beth Hooks, Whitney Joyner, Glenn Royster, Andrew Sanders, Hunter Spangler (for the Lost Dog puzzle), Jaquan Walker, Alease Watkins, and Stephen Westbrook.

Additionally we would like to thank all the people involved in the review process:

Tim Bivans, Pitt Community College; Marc Tucker, Central Piedmont Community College; Stephen W. Umland, Fayetteville Technical Community College; Heather Chandler, Focal Press Game Design Workshops Series Editor; Ed Kunakemakorn, Suffolk University; and Amanda Theinert, Becker College.

Finally, we would like to thank everyone at Focal Press for their support and encouragement. Thank you, Sean Connelly (Senior Acquisitions Editor, Gaming & Animation), for envisioning this project and providing us the opportunity to be a part of it. Thank you, Anna Valutkevich (Editorial Assistant, Photography), for encouraging us, even when we missed our deadlines.

CHAPTER 1

What Is GameMaker: Studio and Who Uses It?

Learning Objectives—Upon completion of Chapter 1 readers will be able to:

- Describe what a game engine is
- Identify popular commercial games created with the GameMaker: Studio engine
- Identify which game genres GameMaker: Studio is well suited to
- Recognize the various platforms games can be exported to

Where to Start

GameMaker: Studio's user-friendly drag-and-drop interface allows both hobbyists and professionals alike to easily create video games. GameMaker: Studio allows potential designers with little or no coding experience to quickly design games and export them to various platforms. More advanced designers can make use of Game Maker Language or GML, the coding language of GameMaker: Studio, to create dynamic professional commercial products. This book will train you to use the GameMaker: Studio engine to create games in a variety of genres starting with the basic tools GameMaker: Studio provides and continuing to advanced options and techniques including using GML. The first step in our journey is to explore in more detail what GameMaker: Studio is and who uses it.

What Is GameMaker: Studio?

GameMaker: Studio is a game engine which allows users to easily create games by using drag-and-drop options and an easy-to-navigate interface. As users learn the basic steps and tools to create games they can then incorporate more advanced features into their games and customize their games further by using GML, the coding language of GameMaker: Studio. The term *game engine* is used to describe any software program which provides game creation authoring tools allowing users to create games without having to rely strictly on coding. Although games can be created using only coding, game engines allow users to skip much of the basic coding process by means of drag-and-drop options and game object property boxes in which designers can type in specific actions for objects within a game.

Who Uses GameMaker: Studio?

Although GameMaker: Studio is used by many hobbyists and students due to its user-friendly interface, it should not be considered a tool only for the novice. Many well-known commercial games have been created using GameMaker. A quick search through the games on the popular gaming website Steam, located at http://store.steampowered.com, will pull up several examples of commercially successful games created with GameMaker: Studio. An impressive list of games and comments by the designers on using GameMaker: Studio can also be located on the YoYo Games Showcase website. Included here are descriptions of a few of the games from the showcase with the designer's comments. You might find that you have already played the games mentioned, yet not realized they were created with the GameMaker: Studio engine.

Gunpoint—The game *Gunpoint* published by Suspicious Developments Ltd. is a puzzle game that allows the user to rewire each level to defeat the enemies. According to Tom Francis, designer and writer of *Gunpoint*, "The best thing about GameMaker is that it eases you into writing code. You don't need to write any to make something work, but as you gain confidence it's natural to learn how to write simple instructions as you need them. You end up coding fluently without any steep learning curve."

Hotline Miami—Jonatan Söderström and Dennis Wedin of Dennation Games, based in Sweden, released the popular game *Hotline Miami* in the fall of 2012. Söderström has stated, "I would probably not be where I am without GameMaker. It's been an amazing tool that really helped me getting into game design."

Risk of Rain—The game *Risk of Rain* developed by Duncan Drummond and Paul Morse of Hopoo Games and released on Steam in 2013 incorporates elements such as permanent death and randomly spawning enemies. On the topic of GameMaker, Drummond suggests that, "It is magic. GameMaker allows you to circumvent the difficulties of programming, allowing you to focus on more important aspects like game design and player interactions. If you're new to making games, or just want to make games fast and efficiently, GameMaker is the only option."

Super Crate Box and ***Nuclear Throne***—Rami Ismail and Jan Willem Nijman of Vlambeer, a Dutch independent game studio, created both *Super Crate Box* and *Nuclear Throne* using GameMaker. Ismail informed us that, "GameMaker is what the designer at Vlambeer has been using since he was thirteen years old. GameMaker is the development tool that allows the fastest iteration, allowing us to create games that feel great simply by iterating over everything really rapidly."

GameMaker: Studio Features

The version of GameMaker: Studio we will be using to create all of the games in this book is GameMaker: Studio Standard. GameMaker: Studio Standard is free to use and can be downloaded from the YoYo Games website at www.yoyogames.com. GameMaker: Studio Standard has all the features required to complete the games in this book with the primary restrictions including required registration, the exported game will include a "Made with GameMaker" splash screen, and games created can only be exported to the Windows platform.

There are two other versions of GameMaker: Studio: the Professional version and the Master Collection. The GameMaker: Studio Professional eliminates the need for registration and has the splash screen removed. Professional also includes additional features not present in the Standard version yet still exports only to the Windows platform. The GameMaker: Studio Master Collection contains all features and also includes multiple export options such as Mas OS X export, HTML5, Android, Xbox One, PlayStation 4, and Ubuntu Linux, among others. Each of these platform exports can be purchased separately for GameMaker: Studio Professional, allowing developers that are only looking to export one or two different platforms just those options rather than paying for everything. A full comparison list of differences between these three versions of GameMaker: Studio, as well as a complete list of the export options, can be found on the YoYo Games website mentioned earlier. In February 2015 YoYo Games was acquired by Playtech, the biggest and most successful software supplier in the real-money gaming industry, according to Nadav Goshen, Plamee Advisor, and Mor Weizer, CEO of Playtech. Playtech plans to invest more resources into improving GameMaker so it will appeal to a wider developer demographic, including the advanced developer segment.

Game Genres Ideal for GameMaker: Studio

With GameMaker: Studio Standard you are not limited to create just one particular type of game. In the following chapters we will be creating a variety of games crossing multiple game genres. In Chapter 2 we create the game *Scout*, which is a traditional Shoot 'Em Up–style game where we create an asteroid-blasting spaceship, in Chapter 3 we incorporate puzzles into a side-scroller game, and in Chapter 4 we create our first two player competitive game. Each chapter afterward explores other genres. GameMaker: Studio provides us with the options to actually create the games we have long been imagining.

Download and Install GameMaker Studio: Standard

Before starting Chapter 2: Side-Scroller Game Basics, download GameMaker: Studio Standard from the YoYo Games website (www.yoyogames.com), then install and run the software. The journey of game development is about to begin!

Resources

Steam Indie Games. "Super Crate Box." Accessed October 31, 2014. http://store.steampowered.com/app/212800/.

YoYo Games. "Cross Platform from One Codebase." Accessed March 15, 2015. https://www.yoyogames.com/studio/multiformat.

YoYo Games. "YoYo Games Is Acquired by Playtech Plc." Accessed March 15, 2015. https://www.yoyogames.com/playtech.

YoYo Games Showcase. "Gunpoint." Accessed October 31, 2014. http://www.yoyogames.com/showcase/6.

YoYo Games Showcase. "Hotline Miami." Accessed October 31, 2014. http://www.yoyogames.com/showcase/1.

YoYo Games Showcase. "Risk of Rain." Accessed October 31, 2014. http://www.yoyogames.com/showcase/15.

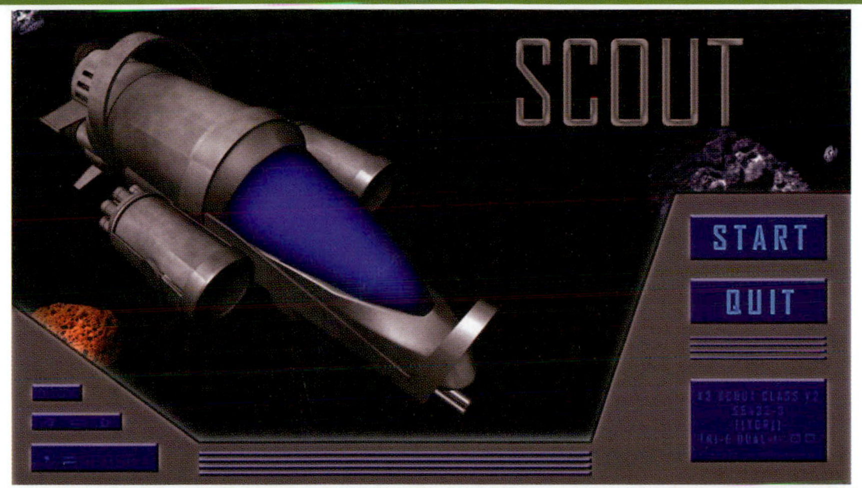

Side-Scroller Game Basics

Learning Objectives—Upon completion of Chapter 2 readers will be able to:

- Create a space-themed side-scroller game
- Identify and work with sprites
- Animate sprites using switch states and rotation techniques
- Incorporate music and sounds into their project
- Add title screens and menu options to a game
- Include power-ups that modify game objects
- Identify object spawning and randomly spawn objects on the screen
- Incorporate scoring and graphical representations of player lives
- Modify their game with additional objects, sound files, and graphics provided

Project Overview: *Scout*

Our first game is *Scout*, a classic space-themed side-scroller in which the player controls a scout class spaceship assigned to destroy approaching asteroids. A side-scrolling game is one in which the scenery moves from one side of the screen to the other with the camera following the player in the center of the screen. The player has three lives and unlimited ammo to destroy as many asteroids as they can. Each asteroid destroyed increases their score. Along the way, the player will collect power-ups which give the ship temporary special abilities. All of the graphics, sound effects, and music required to create this game can be downloaded from the

GameMaker Standard website. Graphics and sound files are commonly referred to as game assets and should be saved on your computer in a location where you can easily find them. Go to www.thegamemakerstandard.com/scout and download the Scout Game Assets zip file. Be sure to unzip all of the files and place them on your computer. After downloading the assets folder read over the updates.pdf document which contains any changes since the publication of this book. With the game assets downloaded, it is time to run the GameMaker software and get to work designing your first game.

Creating a New Project

Step 1: Click the **New** tab to create a new project.

Step 2: In the blank next to **Project Name**, type in: **Scout.** You may wish to change the project directory to some place different such as the desktop. This is where GameMaker will save your project.

Step 3: Click the **Create** button.

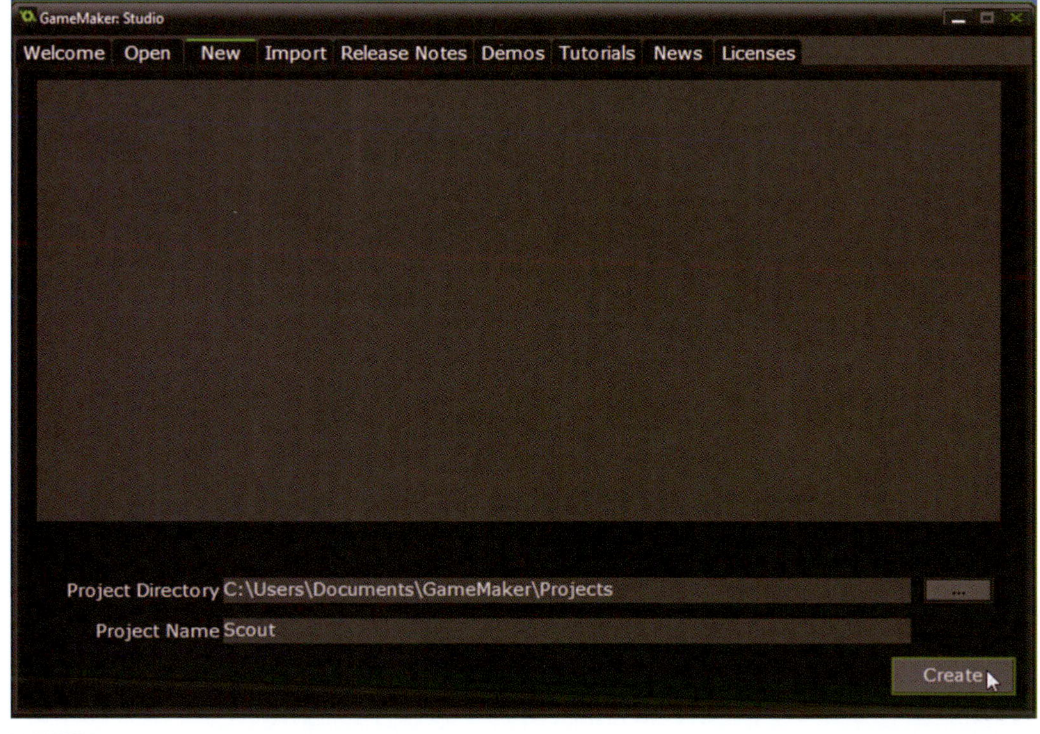

FIGURE 2.1

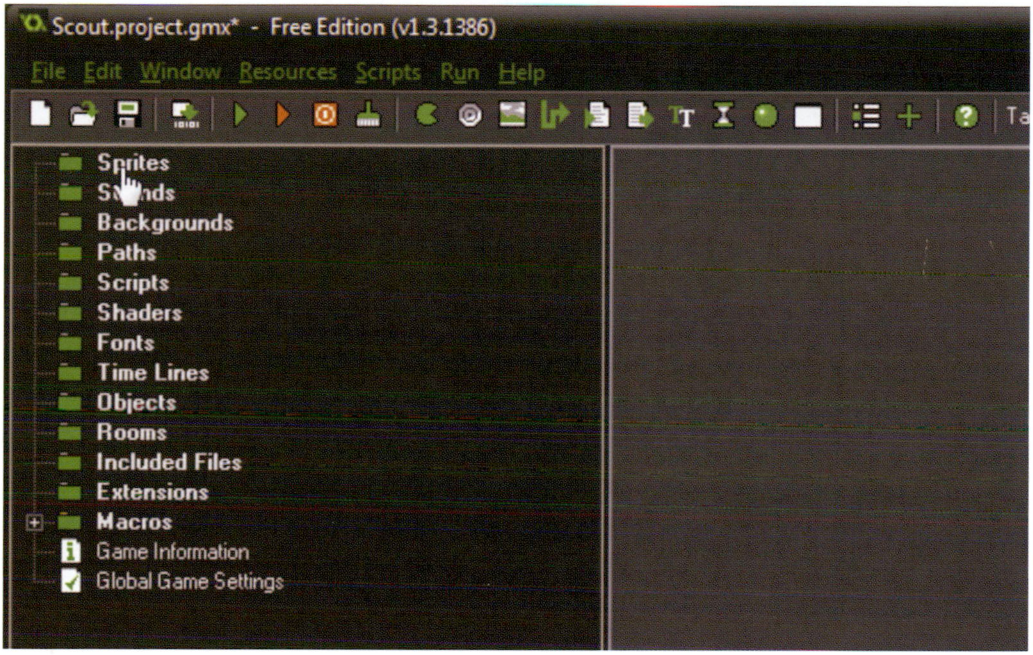

FIGURE 2.2

This opens your new project so you can now import the game assets. In the downloaded Scout Game Assets folder you will see several subfolders. The assets you will import at this point are in the Sprites, Sounds, and Backgrounds folders. The first type of asset you will add are the sprites. A sprite is any graphic used in the game, aside from background graphics.

There are a couple of ways of adding sprites. You can add each sprite individually or you can add them all at once. For this game you will add all of the sprites at once since it is the fastest option.

Should you wish to add sprites one at a time, you can right-click the Sprites folder at the top of the list then choose the Create Sprite option and import your sprites that way. Since we are adding all of our sprites at once, we can use the drag-and-drop method.

Importing Assets

Step 1: Move the GameMaker window so that it fills only half the screen. You want to be able to see the **Assets** folder we downloaded earlier in order to drag and drop the sprite files into GameMaker.

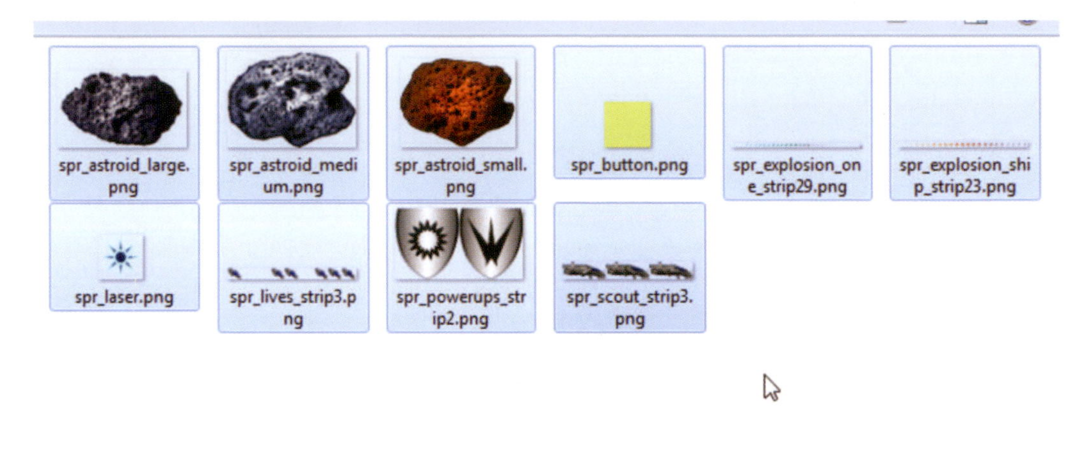

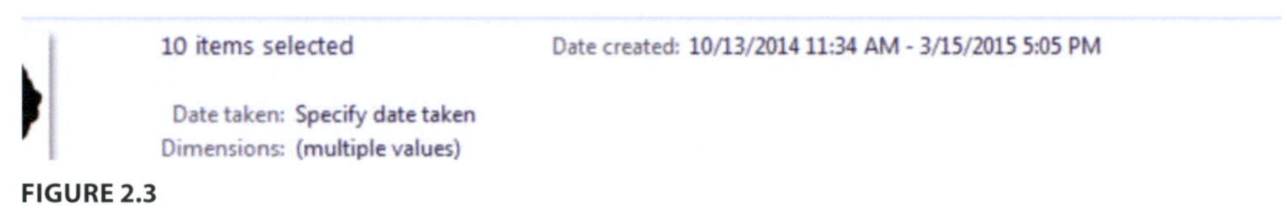

FIGURE 2.3

Step 2: Open up the **Scout_Assets Folder>Sprites** so that you can see all of the sprites. Now select all of the sprites and drag them to the grey window in the right-hand side of the GameMaker software. To select multiple files such as this, click on the first sprite, then hold down the Shift key, and select the last sprite.

Step 3: A pop-up box should now appear asking what type of resource you want to create. Choose the **Sprite** option. GameMaker may give you the option to open all the sprites at once; if so click **OK**.

Step 4: GameMaker has added the word *sprite* and a number to the file names of each of these graphics. Remove the word *sprite* and the number GameMaker added to each of these graphics. The top graphic you will see is most likely the player ship. You will see that GameMaker has added **sprite9_** at the beginning of the file name in the name blank. Highlight the text **sprite9_** and press the **delete** key. Once this is done, select the **OK** button at the bottom of this window to close it out.

Step 5: Follow the above instructions to delete the word *sprite* and the number that GameMaker added to each of these images.

Step 6: Now we can do the same thing for our backgrounds and sounds as well, although when GameMaker asks what type of resource you want to create, you will choose either **backgrounds** or **sounds** rather than **sprite** this time. Just as we did with the sprite file names, delete the word **background** or **sound** and the number GameMaker added from each file name before selecting **OK** for each item.

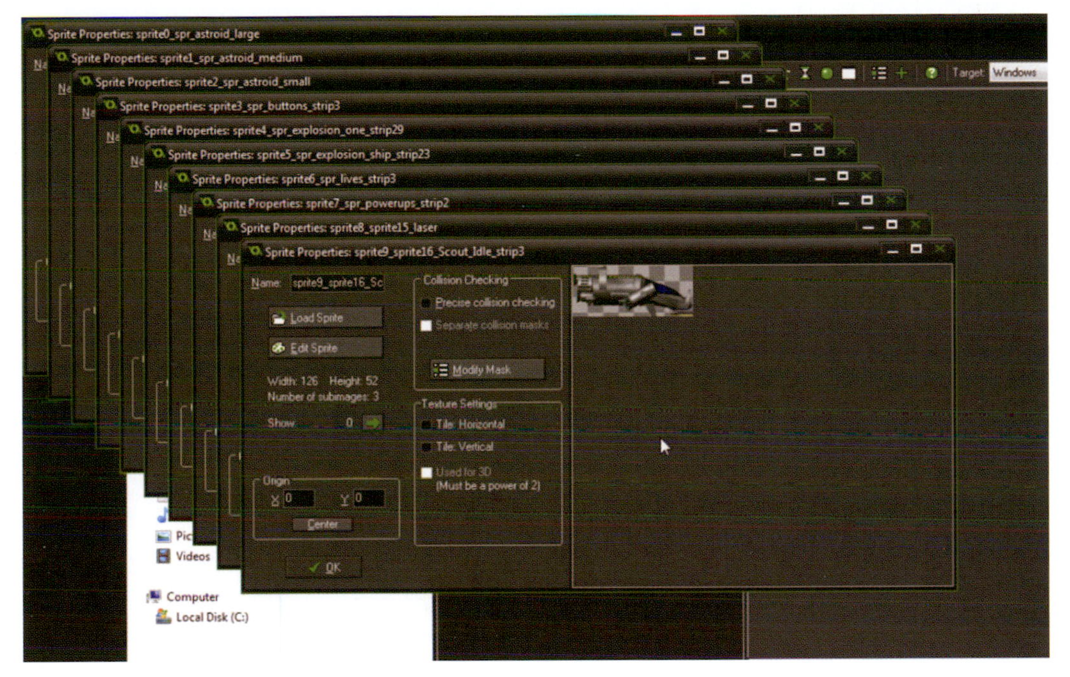

FIGURE 2.4

You will now see a list of all of these sprites under the Sprites folder, a list of all the backgrounds in the Background folder, and a list of all the sounds in the Sounds folder in the top left side of your screen.

Room Creation

GameMaker uses rooms to differentiate between different levels and screens. For this particular game, we will create three different rooms; one room for the title screen, the second for the actual game level, and the third is for the game over screen. If we were creating a game with multiple game levels, there would be a room for each additional level.

Step 1: Maximize the GameMaker screen so that it fills your entire screen.

Step 2: In the menu at the top of the window, select **Resources**. This opens a drop down box with options. Choose **Create Room**. This opens the Rooms Properties window. You can move this window around if needed so that you can still see all of the sprites on the left side of the screen.

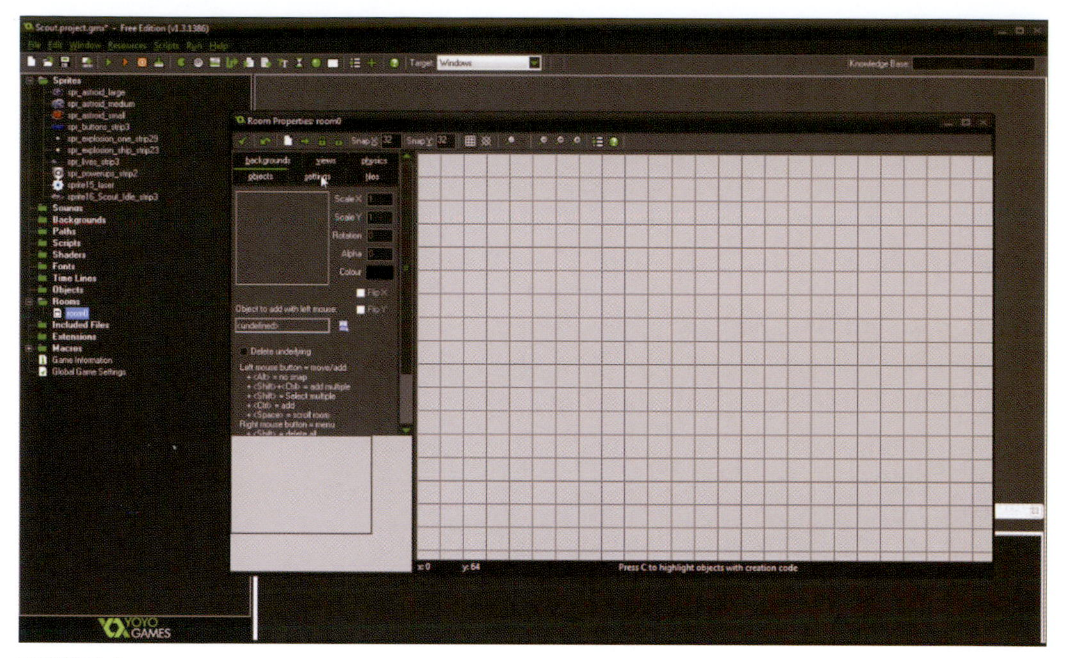

FIGURE 2.5

This room is our actual game level where all of the action occurs. We need to set the width, height, and speed for our game.

Step 3: Select the **Settings** tab and make the following changes:

- Width setting **1024**
- Height setting **576**
- Speed **30**

Step 4: Whenever you are finished making changes in one of the Properties windows in GameMaker, be sure to select the green checkmark in the top left corner of the window to save the options. We have a few more changes to make to the Room Properties, so do not click it just yet.

Adding Backgrounds

Since this game takes place in outer space, a starfield background is in order. We will be animating this background so that it scrolls from right to left continuously. This will give the illusion that the scout ship is flying through space, even though the actual scout ship sprite will not move from the left side of the screen.

Step 1: With the Room Properties window still open, select the **backgrounds** tab. There you will see a grey rectangle that has **<no background>** written inside of it. This indicates that the room does not currently have a background; let's rectify this.

Step 2: Click the small icon next to the grey rectangle to see a list of the backgrounds we have already uploaded into GameMaker. Doing so opens a drop down list with all of our background options, including the currently selected **no background** option at the top.

Step 3: Choose the background titled: **bg_starfield**. You should now see that the starfield background has been placed into the game. This particular graphic has been specifically created to fit the height and width of this game. The starfield graphic is also designed so that it can be tiled. Tiling graphics appear as one long graphic when placed side by side. The player should not notice where the first graphic ends and the next begins.

Step 4: With our backgrounds tab still selected, look to the bottom of the pane and change the **Hor.Speed** to **−2** to set the speed at which the starfield will move from right to left.

Step 5: Choose the **green checkmark** at the top left of the Rooms Properties window to close it.

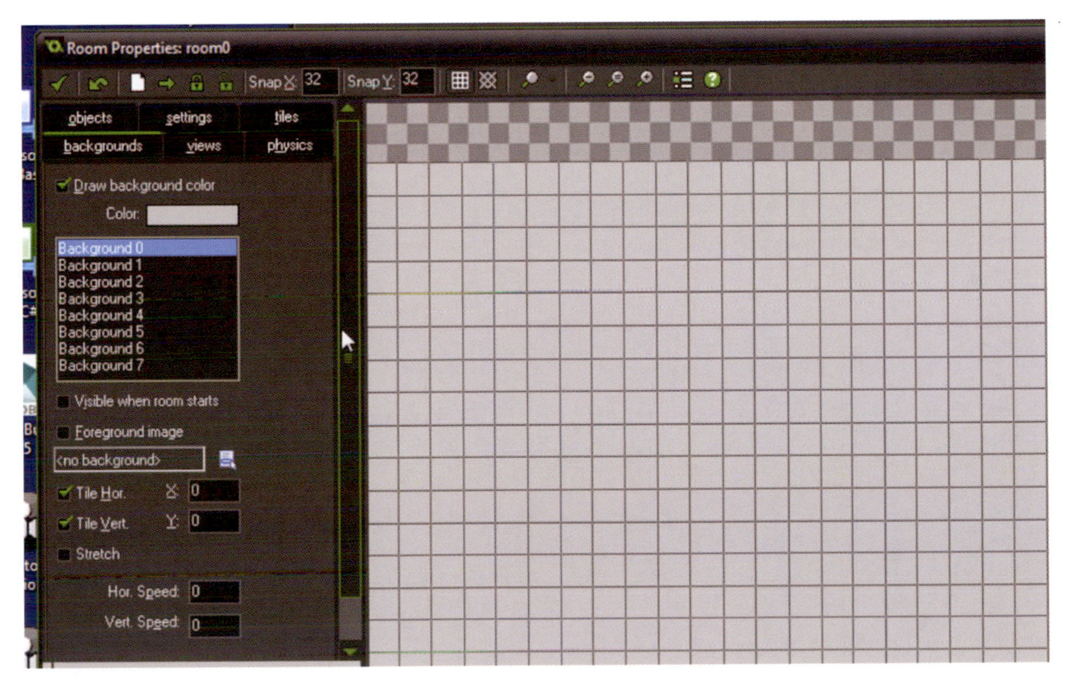

FIGURE 2.6

Test the Starfield

Now we should check to make sure our starfield is scrolling correctly. On the tool bar at the top of the GameMaker program window you will see a green triangle which looks like a play button. Any time you wish to test your game, click the green triangle and it will make a quick build of your game.

Step 1: Click the green triangle. Our game in its present state should open up and we should see a starfield that appears to be moving right to left. (It may take a moment to load the first time you run a test game. Please be patient.)

Step 2: You can close out of this game preview window by clicking on the right **x** at the top right of the game preview window.

Creating Objects

We learned earlier that sprites are graphics files. For example, in this game, the scout ship, asteroids, and power-up graphics are all sprites. However, in order for

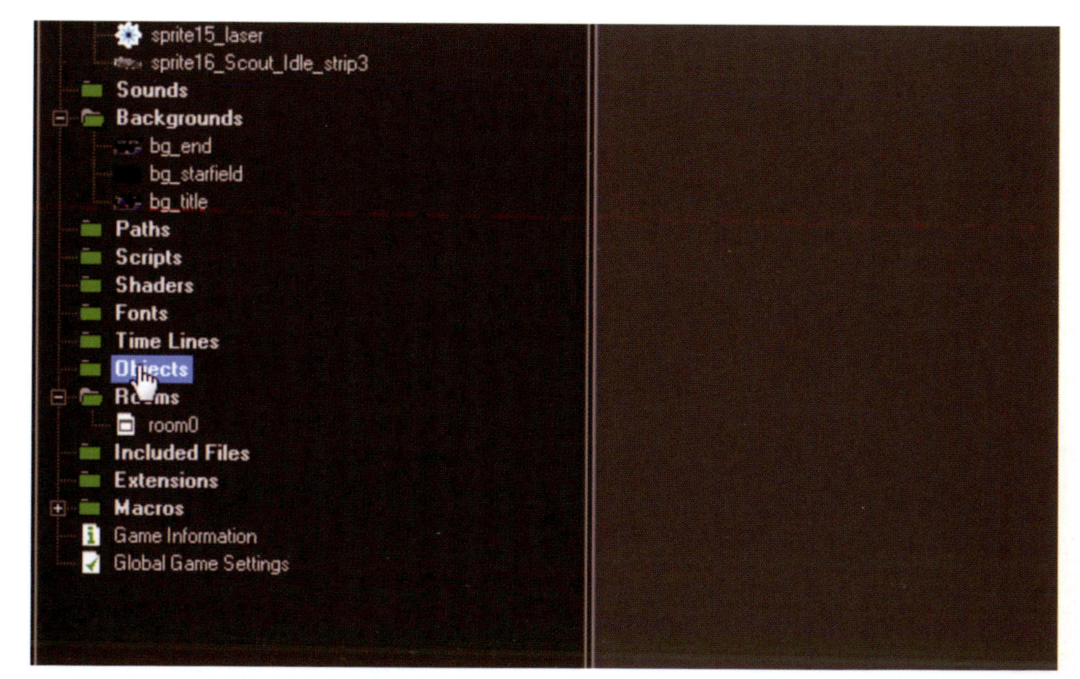

FIGURE 2.7

a sprite to have any function in the game, such as being controlled by the player or by colliding with the player ship like the asteroids, these sprites must first be added to an object. Objects allow us to tell the sprites how they should appear and act. Once a sprite has been added to an object, we can then tell the object to move up and down when the player hits certain keys on the keyboard. Or, we can tell the sprite to rotate as we will do with the asteroids. The first object we will create is our player's ship.

Step 1: Right-click the **Objects** folder in the list on the left-hand side of your screen and select **Create Object**. This opens the object Properties dialog window.

Step 2: In the **Name:** section at the top left of the window type in: **obj_scout**.

Step 3: You will notice directly below the name section that **<no sprite>** is written in the grey rectangle. This tells us that there currently is not a graphic for this object. Let's choose our hero ship idle sprite. The term *idle* refers to what a player's image looks like when the player is not pressing any keys. If this object was a person, the idle state may have a sprite of a person just standing, whereas if the player presses a certain key on the keyboard the image would change to an image or series of images of the person walking.

Step 4: Choose the icon next to the rectangle and choose: **spr_scout _strip3**.

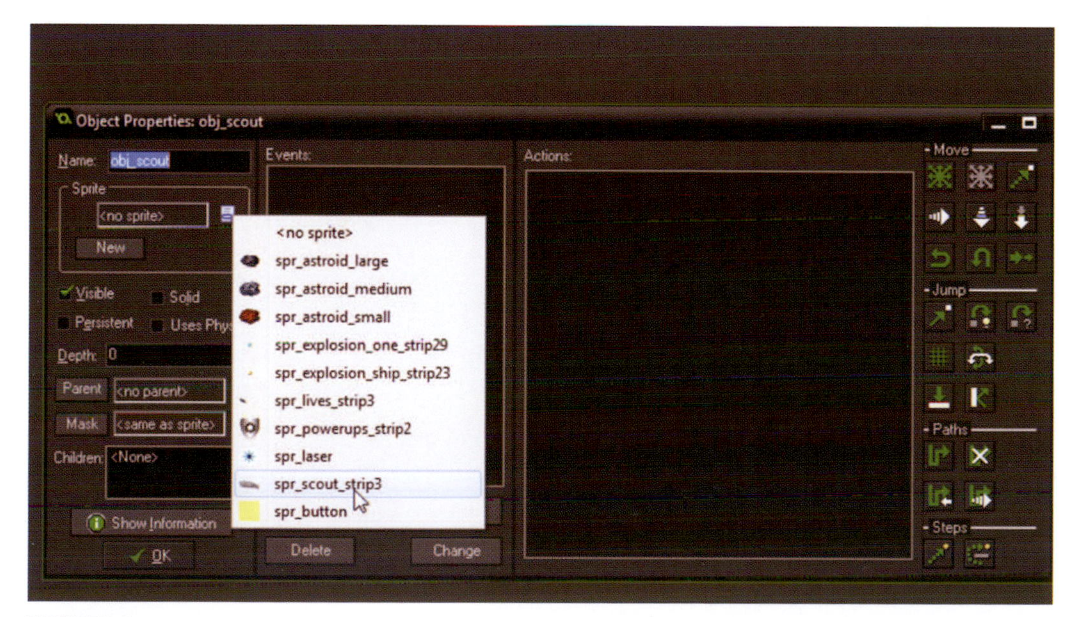

FIGURE 2.8

Creating an Event

Next, let's add an event for this object. An event tells the game which action should take place when a certain key is pressed or if a particular circumstance occurs—such as the object colliding with another. Action is what occurs if the player hits the key or the object collides with another. In this particular place, we want to create a couple of keyboard events that allow the player to move the scout ship object up and down when the player presses the arrow keys.

Step 1: Click the **Add Event** button at the bottom of the window to open up the event options.

Step 2: Choose a **Keyboard** Event and select the **<Down>** key. This will add a new **<Down>** key event in the Events window.

Step 3: Now add another **Keyboard** Event for **<Up>**.

Step 4: Look on the right side of the Object Properties window and choose the **Move** tab. (These tabs are sideways, like dividers in a notebook.)

Step 5: Look under the **Jump** submenu for the **Jump to Position** icon; it has a green arrow pointing up and to the right to a white square. Click once on this icon and drag your cursor to the Actions window. Doing so adds the **Jump to Position** Action to the Actions window and simultaneously open up the **Jump to Position** properties window so that you can input the specific details of this action.

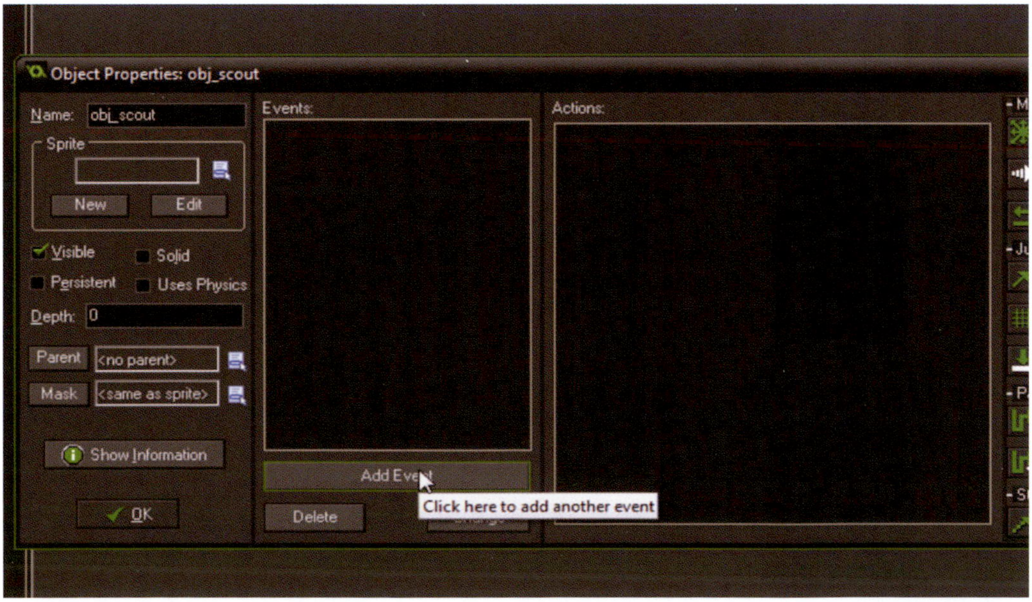

FIGURE 2.9

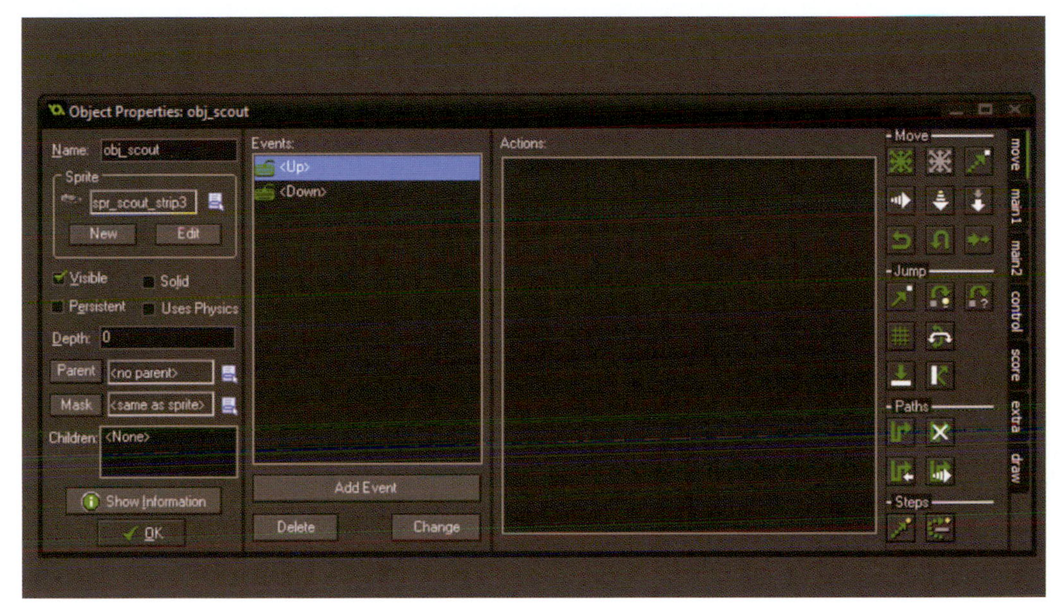

FIGURE 2.10

Our next step requires us to understand coordinates in GameMaker since we will be setting the y axis to –4. In GameMaker, **x** refers to the horizontal axis while **y** refers to the vertical axis. Thus, if an object was located in the top left-hand corner of the game screen it would be located at x = 0 and y = 0. If we were to set an object to move from x = 0 and y = 0 to x = 25 and y = 0, then we know that the object would remain at the top of the screen but move toward the right of the screen along the x axis.

Step 6: Change the **y** option to **–4** and make sure the **Applies to:** radio button is set to **Self**.

Step 7: Set the relative box so that it is checked. By checking the relative box, you are telling GameMaker that you want the object to move that number of spaces from the object's current position.

Step 8: Choose **OK** when complete to close the **Jump to Position** properties box.

Now, when the up arrow key is pressed, the ship will move upward on the screen. We need to make similar changes to the **<Down>** Event as well so that the ship will move downward when the down arrow key is pressed.

Step 9: Click the **<Down>** Event and repeat Steps 4 through 8 with one small change: This time, instead of entering **–4** as the **y** option, you want to enter **4** so the ship will move the opposite direction (down instead of up).

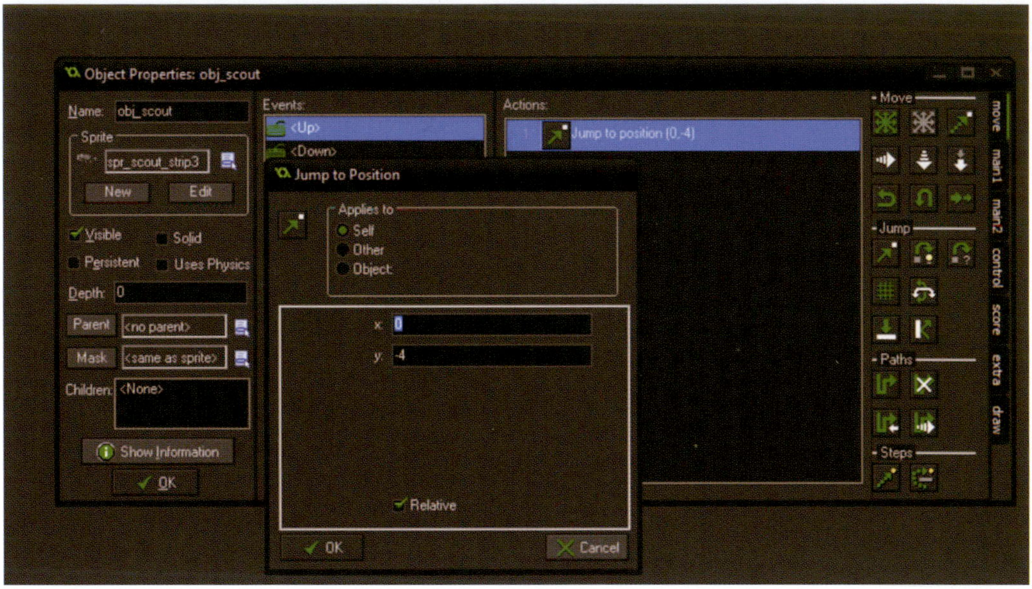

FIGURE 2.11

Changing Image States

When our player spaceship moves up, we want the image of the ship to change. In this project, we are using a strip of three different images for our hero ship, in one sprite. The idle sprite with the engine horizontal, the moving up sprite with the back of the engine pointing downward, and the moving down sprite with the back of the engine pointing upward. This change in sprites adds to the player's experience of upward or downward movement.

Step 1: In the expanding menu list on the left side of the window, locate and double-click on the **obj_scout** object. On the far right side of the Object Properties window, choose **Main1** from the tab options.

Step 2: In the **Sprite** submenu, select the **Change Sprite** icon, which looks like a green Pac-Man, and drag it into the Actions area. Doing so opens the **Change Sprite** options box.

Step 3: Make sure that **Applies to:** is set to **Self**. Then click the icon next to the sprite option to ensure the following sprite is selected: **spr_scout_strip3**. Since this is a strip of three different images, we need to identify a subimage. For the **<Up>** Event, enter **0** as the subimage. For the **<Down>** Event, enter **1** as the subimage. Enter **0** as the Speed for both the **<Up>** and **<Down>** Events.

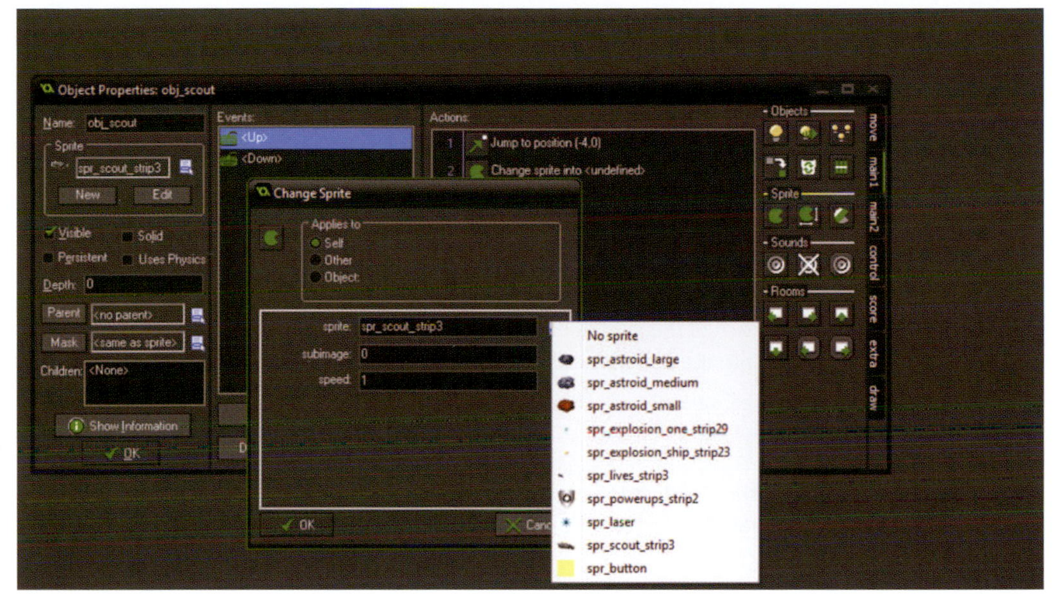

FIGURE 2.12

Step 4: From the tabs on the far right side of the Object Properties window, click the **Control**. From the **Other** submenu, locate the **Start of a Block** icon, which looks like a green triangle pointing upward. Drag the **Start of a Block** icon into the Actions area and place it above the **Jump to position [0, 4]** Action to indicate that this is the start of a block of actions.

Step 5: Drag the **End of a Block** icon, which looks like a green arrow pointing downward, underneath the **Change Sprite** Action to indicate that this is the end of the block of actions. Be sure to complete Steps 1 through 5 for both the **<Up>** and **<Down>** Events.

Step 6: Now we want to make sure that the idle image is only showing the image we want instead of other images in the strip. In the Object Properties window, click the **Add Event** button and choose **Create.** Then, on the far right side of the window, click the **Main1** tab. In the **Sprite** submenu, click the **Change Sprite** icon and drag it into the Actions area.

Step 7: In the **Change Sprite** dialogue box, ensure that **Applies to:** is set to **Self**, then set the following:

> Sprite: spr_scout_strip3
> Subimage: 2
> Speed: 0
>
> This will start the ship in the idle graphic.

Release Events

To make sure that the ship returns to the idle state after the up or down keys are pressed, we need to create events to trigger the image to return to idle.

Step 1: With the Object Properties window for the **obj_scout** ship open, click the **Add Event** button.

Step 2: Add a **Key Release <Up>** and a **Key Release <Down>** Event.

Step 3: For each of the release events, click the **Main1** tab and drag the **Change Sprite** icon into the Actions area.

Step 4: In the Change Sprite dialogue box, ensure that **Applies to:** is set to **Self** and set the following:

Sprite: spr_scout_strip3
Subimage: 2
Speed: 0

Be sure to complete Steps 3 and 4 above for both the **Release <Up>** and **Release <Down>** Events.

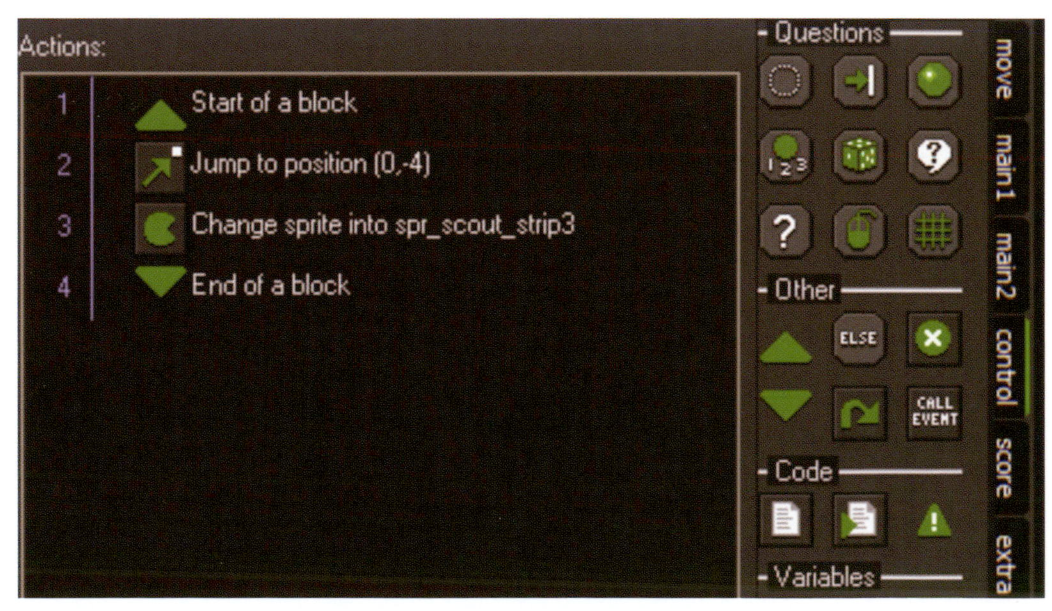

FIGURE 2.13

Adding Variables

Now it is time to add a variable. The variable tells GameMaker to check the location of the ship and stop the ship from moving up too far so it does not leave the playing area. We will also make it so that the ship cannot move down past the playable area.

Step 1: While the Control tab for the **<Up>** Event is still selected, look under the **Variables** submenu and choose the center icon named **Test Variable**. Drag it above the **Start of a Block** Action.

Step 2: In the Test Variable options box, make sure the **Applies to:** is set for **Self**.

Step 3: Type in: **y** in the variable option and the number **32** in the value option. To set the Operation, click the icon and select **greater than** for the operation. Then click **OK** to close the Test Variable option window. This will check to see where the ship is on the y axis and will not allow it to move on the y axis past the top edge of the game.

Now we need to make similar changes to the **<Down>** Event.

Step 4: Select the **<Down>** option in the Events window and drag the **Start of a Block** and **End of a Block** icons to the Actions window just as you did for the **<Up>** Event.

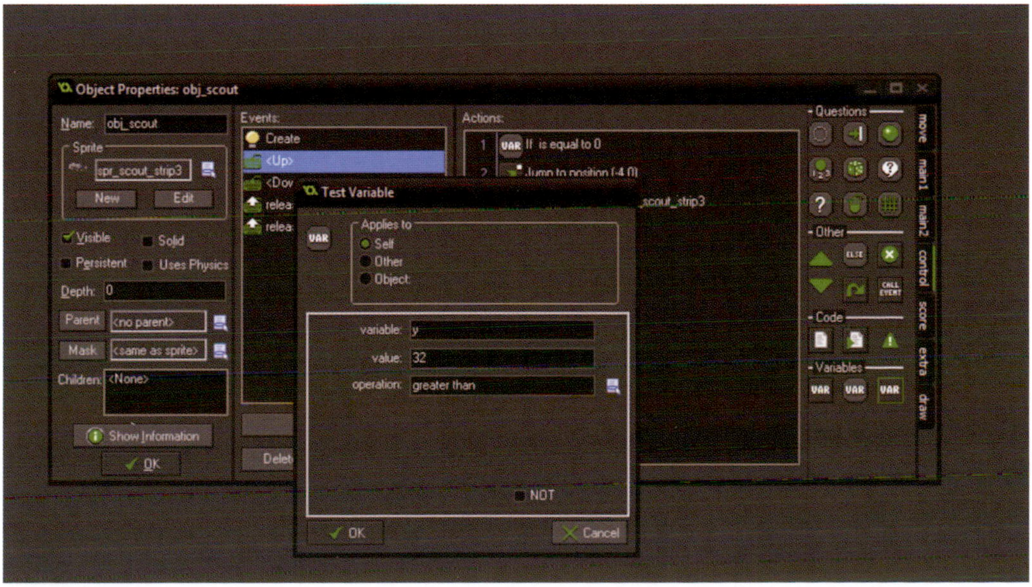

FIGURE 2.14

Step 5: Drag the **Test Variable** above the **Start of a Block** icon and set the following parameters:

Applies to: Self
Variable: y
Value: 544
Operation: less than or equal to

Step 6: Select **OK** to close the Test Variable window. Also select **OK** to close the Object Properties window.

Creating a Precise Modify Mask for Collision

Step 1: Choose the Sprite which is named: **spr_scout_strip3** and double-click to open the Sprite Properties window.

Step 2: In the Sprite Properties window that appears, find the **Origin** section and click the **Center** button.

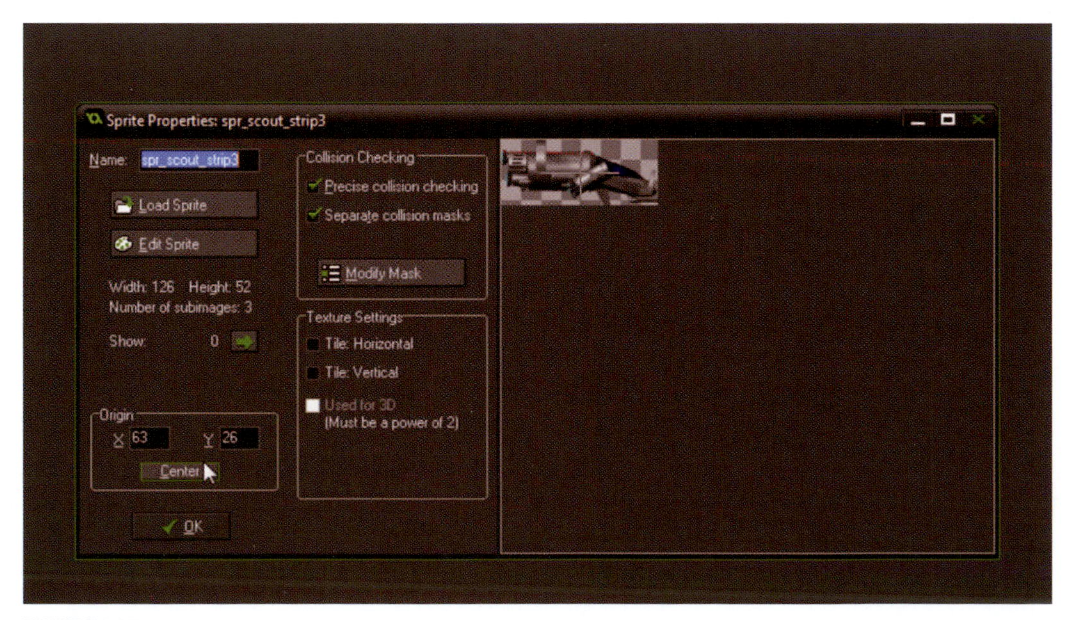

FIGURE 2.15

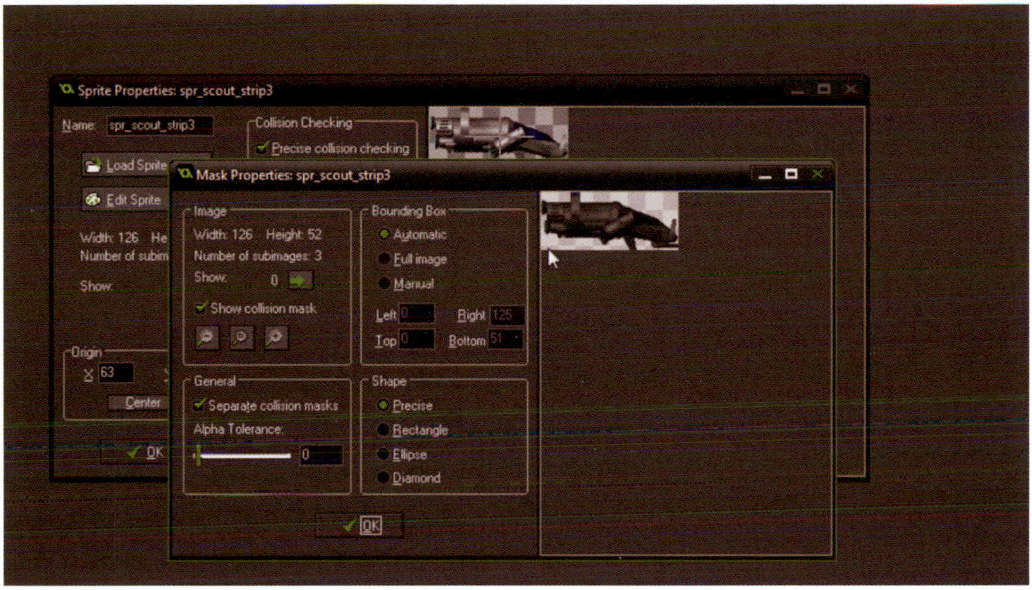

FIGURE 2.16

Step 3: In the **Collision Checking** area, select the **Modify Mask** button.

Step 4: In the Mask Properties window that appears, choose the **precise** radio button located in the **Shape** section. This will tell GameMaker where something could collide with our ship. If we had a large collision area in the shape of a square around the ship, an asteroid could hit the square and destroy the ship yet on the screen it would appear as though the asteroid missed the ship, which is not what we want.

Step 5: Keep all other options as their defaults. Select **OK** to close the Mask Properties window and **OK** to close the Sprite Properties window.

Placement of the Hero Ship Object

Step 1: Under the Rooms section on the left-hand side of the screen, double-click **room0**. This will open up the room with the starfield background.

Step 2: Next, click the **Objects** tab on the left side of the window. Click anywhere in the scene with the left mouse button to place the ship. Click and hold to drag it. Place it so that there is one column of the grid in to the left (back side) of the ship so that the ship is not touching the left wall. If you accidentally place more than one ship in your scene, you can right-click on the extra ship and choose delete to remove it. Click the **green check** button to save your changes and close the Properties window.

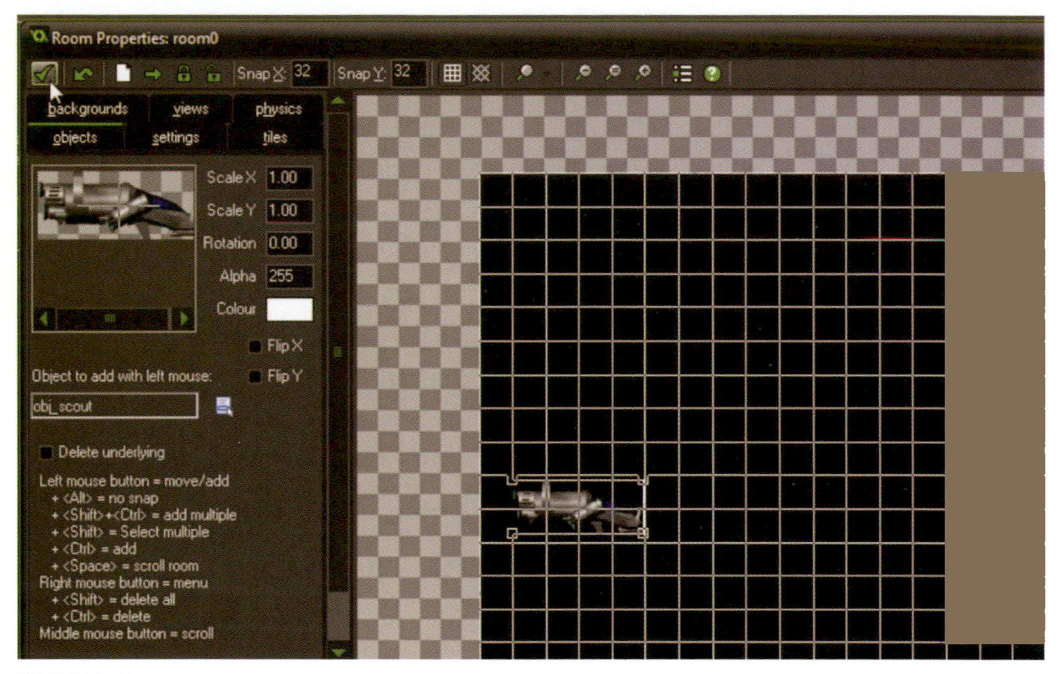

FIGURE 2.17

Now test your game. You should be able to move the player ship up and down using the up and down arrow keys on your keyboard. Notice that the navigation engines on the sides of the ship should move each time you press up or down and that the ship cannot leave the viewable area of the game. It should now look as though the player ship is flying through space.

Close out of the game preview window.

Creating the Asteroid Objects

Step 1: Select the Objects folder on the far left, right-click, and create a new object.

Step 2: Name this object: **obj_asteroid_small**.

Step 3: Choose the sprite: **spr_asteroid_small** as the image.

Step 4: Select **OK** to close the Object Properties window.

Step 5: Repeat Steps 1 through 4 to create a new object for the medium-sized asteroid and the large asteroid.

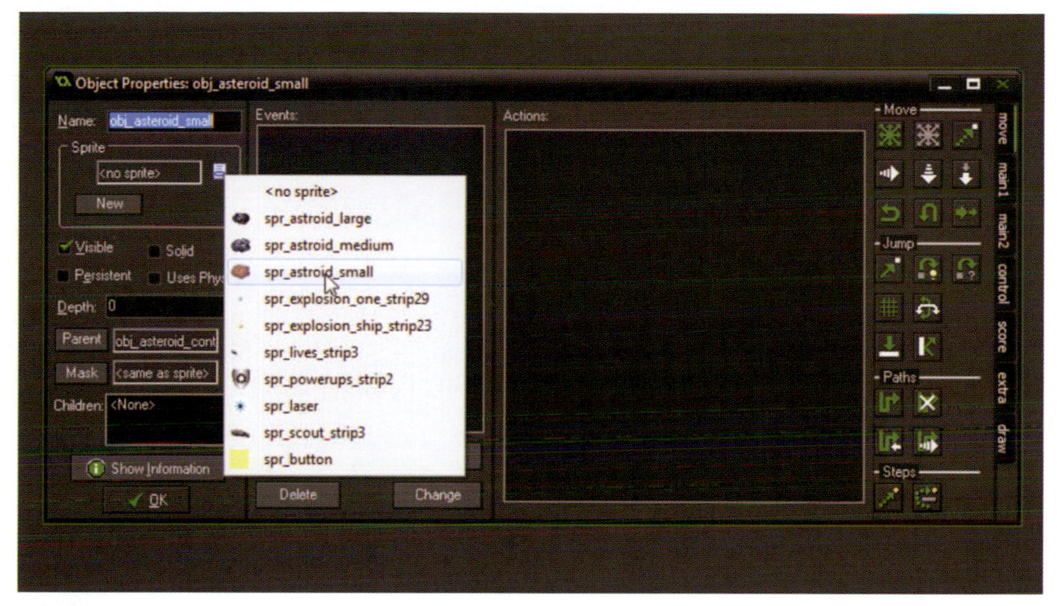

FIGURE 2.18

Adding the Asteroids to the Scene

Step 1: Under Rooms, double-click to Open **Room0** back up.

Step 2: Under the Objects tab, find the rectangle containing the text **obj_scout**. Click the icon next to it to open a list of the three asteroid objects you just created.

Step 3: Select the small asteroid. Then click on the grid to place the object in the game.

Step 4: Repeat Steps 2–3 to add the medium and large asteroids to the game.

Step 5: Once all three objects are added, select the **green check mark** to close the Room Properties window.

You can now preview your game and see the three different-sized asteroids in the game. For now it may appear that the asteroids are flying along with the ship. We will change this soon so that they will become more of a threat to the player.

Making the Asteroids Rotate

Step 1: Find the small asteroid object under the Objects folder on the left-hand side of your screen and double-click to open its Objects Properties window.

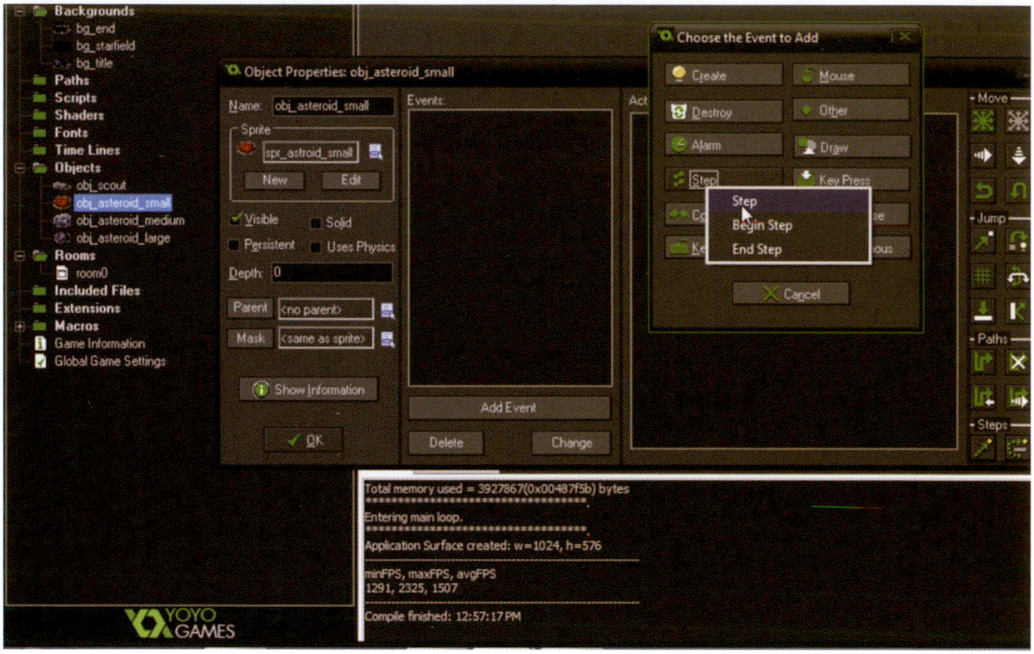

FIGURE 2.19

Step 2: Select **Add Event** and choose **Step**. Then select **Step** again from the drop down menu.

Step 3: Now go to the right side of the Properties window and choose the **Control** tab.

Step 4: Under the **Variables** submenu, select the **Set Variable** option inside the black square and drag it to the Actions window.

Step 5: In the Set Variable options window that appears, set the following:

Applies to: Self
Variable: image_angle
Value: 0.5
Relative: Checked

Step 6: Select **OK** to close the Set Variable window. Select **OK** to close the Object Properties window for the small asteroid.

Step 7: Repeat the above Steps 1 through 6 for the medium and large asteroids.

Now when you preview your game, you should see each of the asteroids moving in a large circular motion, which looks a bit odd and is not the effect we are going for. To remedy this strange motion, we need to set each of the asteroid sprite's origins to **center**.

FIGURE 2.20

Set Asteroid Sprite Origins to Center

Step 1: Under the Sprites folder select the Sprite: **spr_asteroid_large** and click the **Center** button in the Origin section.

Step 2: Adjust the modifying mask to **precise**. You may recall that we needed to do this earlier with the player's ship. Select **OK** to close the Mask Properties window. Before closing the Sprite Properties window, click the **Center** button which is located just above the **OK** button. Then select **OK**.

Step 3: Repeat these steps for the medium and small asteroids.

Now when you preview your game, you should see that the asteroids are rotating from their center point in a more natural pattern.

Creating Game Controller

Let's create a Game Controller Object. This particular object will not have a sprite so, although we will be placing it in our game, it will be invisible to the player. The Game

Controller Object will run various parts of our games such as the score, player lives, and background music. We will also use the game controller to randomly spawn the asteroids, which we will set up first.

Step 1: Select the Objects folder and choose **Create Object**. Name this new object: **obj_game_controller.**

Step 2: Choose **Add Event** and then select **Alarm** and pick **Alarm 0**. An **Alarm 0** Event will now be listed in the Events window.

Step 3: Now add another event and choose **Create**, this should place a **Create** Event above the **Alarm 0** Event in the Events window.

Step 4: The Create icon in the Events window should be highlighted to show that this is the event we are editing. Open the **Main2** tab on the right side of the window and choose the **Set Alarm** icon which looks like a circular clock.

Step 5: Drag the **set alarm** icon to the Actions window and change the number of steps to: **1**.

Step 6: Choose **OK** to close the **Set Alarm** Properties window.

Step 7: Select the **Alarm 0** Event to highlight it and make it active. Click on the **Main1** tab and under the **Objects** submenu, select and drag the **Create Moving** icon to the Actions window. The **Create Moving** icon looks like a light bulb with a green arrow to the right of it.

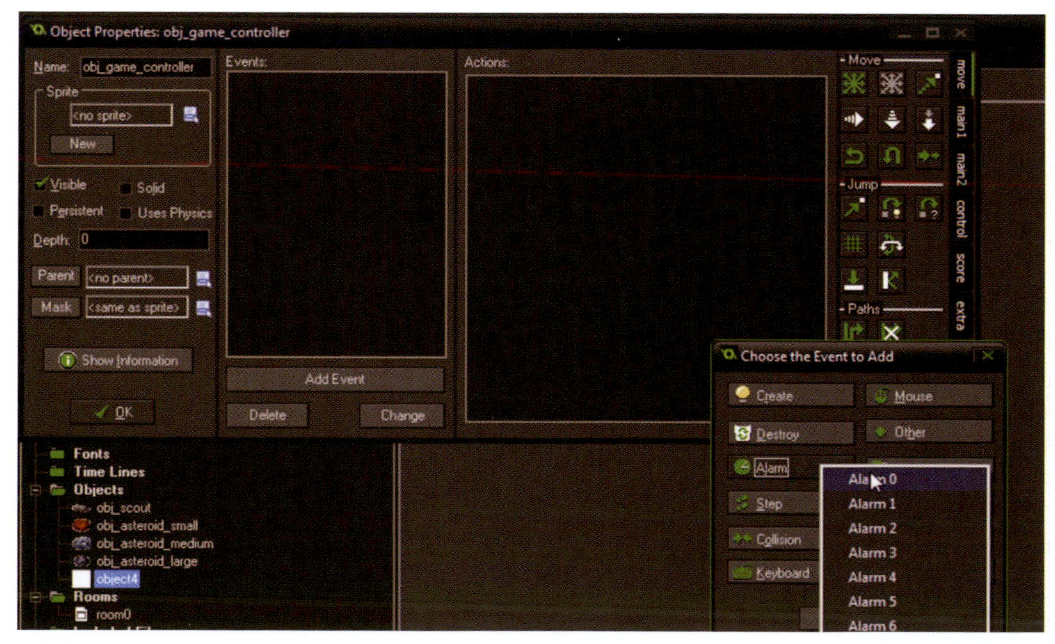

FIGURE 2.21

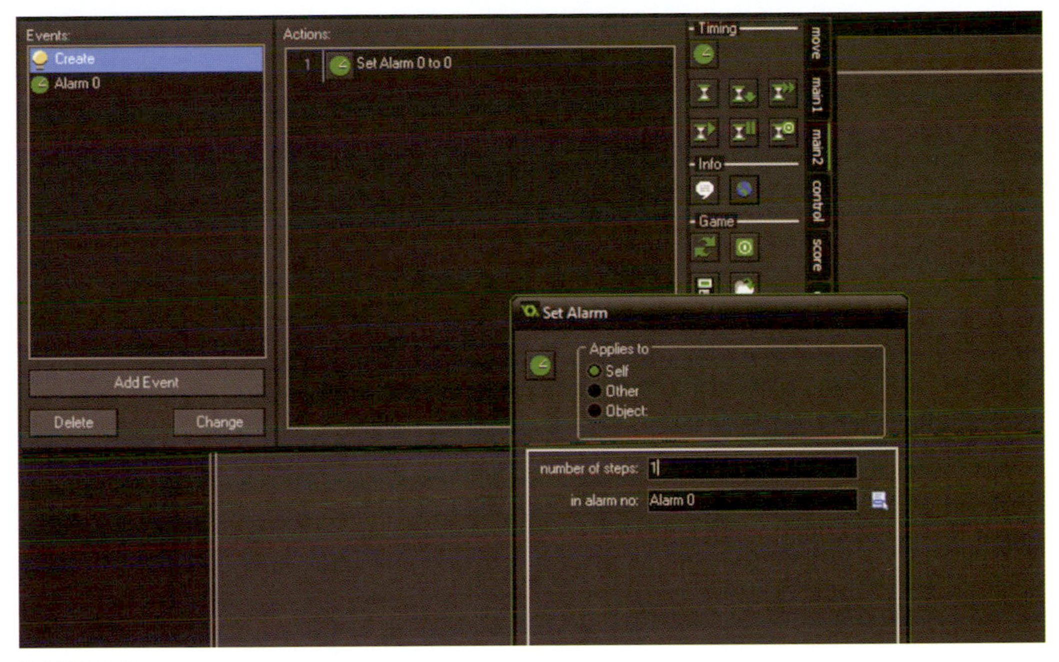

FIGURE 2.22

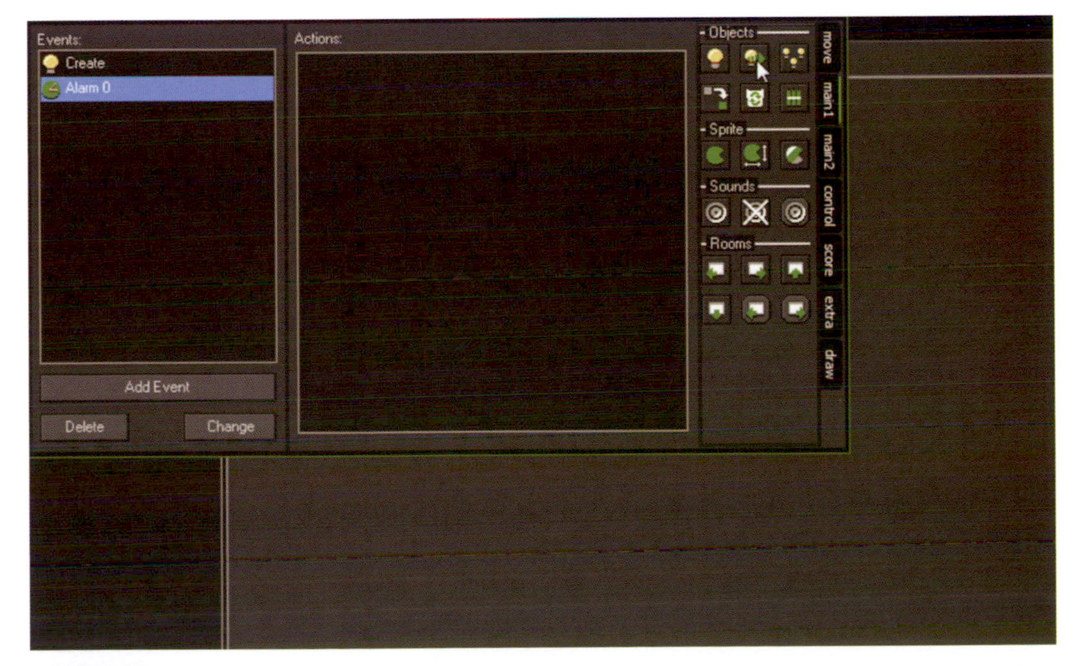

FIGURE 2.23

Step 8: In the Create Moving Properties window that appears, set the following:

Applies to: Self
Object: obj_asteroid_small
x: 1200
y: irandom(576)
Speed: 7
Direction: 180

Step 9: Then select **OK** to close the Create Moving Properties window.

The settings we just entered tell GameMaker to randomly spawn (create an instance of) the small asteroid at 1200 on the x axis, which is on the right side of the screen and anywhere on the playable area of the screen on the y axis. irandom() will pick a random whole number between 0 and the number in the parenthesis.

Step 10: With the **Alarm 0** still highlighted in the Events window, select the **Main2** tab and drag the **Set Alarm** icon so that a **Set Alarm** Action is now underneath the **Create Moving Instance** Action.

Step 11: In the Set Alarm Properties window that appears, change the number of steps to **60** and then select **OK**. Doing so sets the frequency of how often the small asteroids spawn.

Step 12: Select **OK** to close the Object Properties window.

Step 13: Open up **Room0** again and delete the three asteroids from the room.

Step 14: Click the **Objects** tab. Click the game image shown in the box and from the drop down menu, choose **obj_game_controller**. The box appears empty because no images are associated with this object. Click inside the square to select the game controller (remember it is invisible) then click anywhere on the game grid. The Game Controller will appear on the grid as a blue circle with a question mark inside of it.

Step 15: Select the **green check mark** to close the Room Properties window.

This time when you preview your game, you should find that the small asteroids are automatically spawning, rotating, and moving toward the left side of the screen. At this time, the player should be able to easily move the ship up and down and avoid all the asteroids in its path.

Spawning the Other Two Asteroids

Step 1: Under the Objects folder open up the Game Controller.

Step 2: Select **Add Event**; choose **Alarm** and pick **Alarm 1**.

Step 3: Select **Add Event**; choose **Alarm** and pick **Alarm 2**.

Step 4: Select **Alarm 1** in the Events window.

Step 5: Select the **Main1** tab and then drag the **Create Moving Instance** into the Actions window and set the following in the **Create Moving** Properties window.

Applies to: Self
Object: obj_asteroid_medium
x: 1200
y: irandom(576)
Speed: 5
Direction: 180

Step 6: Select **OK** to close the **Create Moving** Properties window.

Step 7: While Alarm 1 is still selected, right-click on the **Create Moving** Action and copy it by **right-clicking** on it and selecting **Copy**.

Step 8: Click on **Alarm 2**, and in the Actions area **right-click** and **paste** the **Create Moving** Action into the Action window.

Step 9: Double-click to open up the **Create Moving** Action you just pasted and make the following changes:

Applies to: Self
Object: obj_asteroid_large
x: 1200
y: irandom(576)
Speed: 3
Direction: 180

Step 10: Select **OK** to close the window.

Step 11: Select **Alarm 1** again so that it is highlighted.

Step 12: Click the **Main2** tab and drag the **Set Alarm** Action to the Action window. In the Properties window that appears, set the following:

Number of steps: 180
In alarm no: Alarm 1

Step 13: Click **OK** to close the window.

Step 14: With **Alarm 2** selected under Events, click on the **Main2** tab and drag the **Set Alarm** icon to the Actions window. In the Properties window set the following:

Number of steps: 360
In alarm no: Alarm 2

Step 15: Select **OK** to close the window.

Step 16: In the Events window, select the **Create** Event icon then select the **Main2** tab.

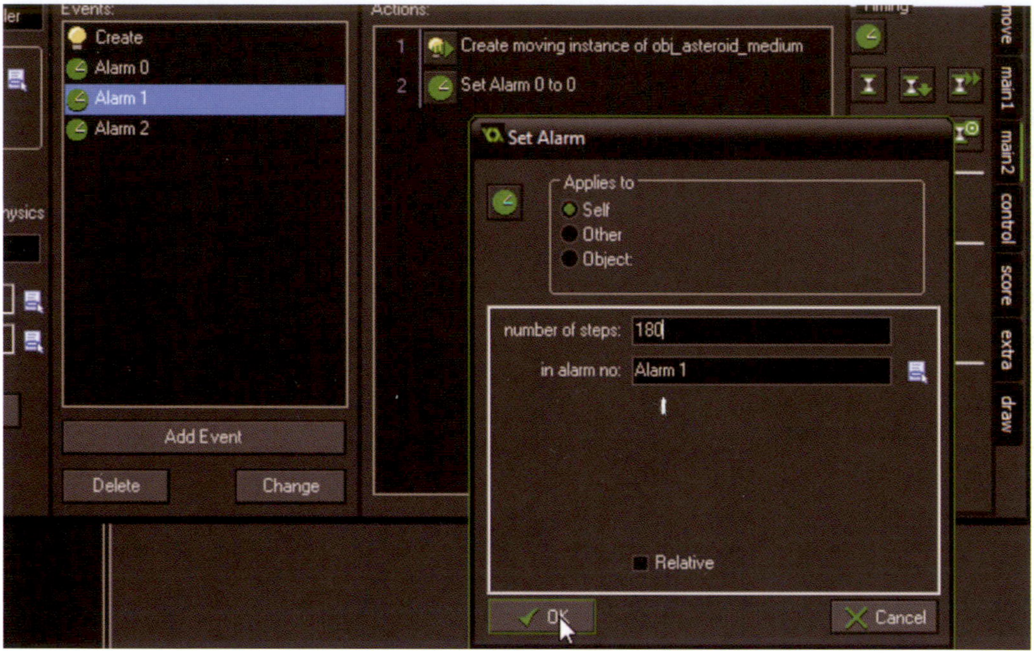

FIGURE 2.24

Step 17: Drag the **Set Alarm** Action into the Actions window and set the following in the Properties window:

Number of steps: 180
In alarm no: Alarm 1

Step 18: Click **OK** to close the box.

Step 19: Drag a second **Set Alarm** into the Actions window and set the following in the Properties window:

Number of steps: 360
In alarm no: Alarm 2

Step 20: Select **OK** to close the Properties window and select **OK** to close the Object Properties window.

Test your game. You should now see all three types of asteroids moving at different speeds. Although the asteroids are now spawning randomly, rotating, traveling at different speeds, and heading toward the hero ship, they are still not much of an obstacle seeing as our ship can fly straight through them without harm. We will create a challenge by adding a Collision Event that will destroy our ship if it comes in contact with an asteroid.

Adding Asteroid Collision Event

Step 1: Right-click Object, select **Create Object,** and name it: **obj_asteroid_controller**.

Step 2: Select **Add Event** and choose **Collision** and pick **obj_scout**.

Step 3: Select the **Main2** tab and beneath the **Info** submenu, drag the **Display Message** icon, which looks like a text balloon, into the Actions window.

Step 4: Type in the following message: **Game Over!**

Step 5: Click the **Main2** tab and under the **Game** submenu, drag the **End Game** icon into the Actions area. This icon looks like a little green square with a white circle and line inside.

Step 6: Select **OK** to close the Object Properties window.

Step 7: Under the Objects folder, open the **small asteroid** object.

Step 8: In the Object Properties window, next to **Parent** it is currently listed as: **<no parent>**. We need to click the icon next to **<no parent>** and change this to: **obj_asteroid_controller**.

Step 9: Repeat Steps 6 and 7 for the medium and large asteroid objects.

FIGURE 2.25

FIGURE 2.26

When you preview your game now, you should find that when the player ship comes in contact with an asteroid, a textbox pops up that reads, "Game Over!" Although this gets the basic point across to the player that the game is over, it looks a bit generic. Next, we will add a professional title screen and game over screen.

Creating the Title and End Game Screens

Step 1: Right-click on the **Rooms** folder and create two new rooms.

Step 2: Under the **Settings** tab in the Room Properties editor, name one room **room_title** and the other **room_defeat**.

Step 3: For each room, set the Width as **1024** and the Height as **576**.

Step 4: For each room, click the **Backgrounds** tab and set the background image. Use **bg_end** for the defeat room background and **bg_title** for the title screen background.

Step 5: For each room, click the **green check** button to save properties changes and close the Room Properties window.

Step 6: In the list on the left side of your screen, under the Rooms folder, make sure that the rooms are listed in the order you want them to appear in the game. To change the order of the rooms, click on the room in the Rooms folder that you want to move and drag it up or down to the appropriate location. For this project, make sure that **room_title** is first, **room0** is second, and **room_defeat** is listed last.

Step 7: Right-click on **Room0** and rename it: **room_game**.

Now we need to add buttons for the player to click which will either run the game or quit the game.

Creating the Start and Quit Buttons

Step 1: Create two objects and name them **obj_button_play** and **obj_button_quit**.

Step 2: Open **obj_button_play** and set the Sprite to **spr_button,** uncheck the **Visible** checkbox that is found below the select sprite section. This will make the object invisible to the player.

Step 3: Click the **Add Event** button and choose **Mouse>Left Button**. Select the **Main1** tab and drag a **Different Room** Action to the Action window. This icon is in the shape of a square with a green arrow pointing down.

Step 4: The setting for the different room is: **new room: room_game.**

Step 5: Open the **obj_button_quit** object and set the Sprite to **spr_button,** then uncheck the **Visible** checkbox.

Step 6: Click **Add Event** and choose **Mouse>Left Button**. Click the **Main2** tab and under the **Game** submenu, click and drag the icon for **End Game** into the **Actions** area. The icon looks like a green square with a white circle and line inside.

Step 7: Open the room: **Room_title**.

Step 8: Under the **Object** tab, pick the object: **obj_button_play**. You will find the drop down menu next to the text rectangle that reads **Object to add with left mouse:**

Step 9: This allows you to place the **Play** and **Quit** buttons over the appropriate spot. Place the **obj_button_play** object over the **Play Button** text in the room. Click and drag the bottom right square until the **obj_button_play** has been scaled big enough to cover the play button entirely. You may have to click and drag the button to position it correctly. To move or scale an object without it locking to the grid simply hold down the **Alt** key.

Step 10: Do the same with the Quit button so that it looks similar to **Figure 2.28**.

Step 11: Open the room: **Room_Defeat** and add the **Play** and **Quit** buttons to that room.

Step 12: Open the **obj_asteroid_controller** object and **delete** the existing **Actions** in the **Collision** Event by **right-clicking** and selecting **delete**. Replace them with

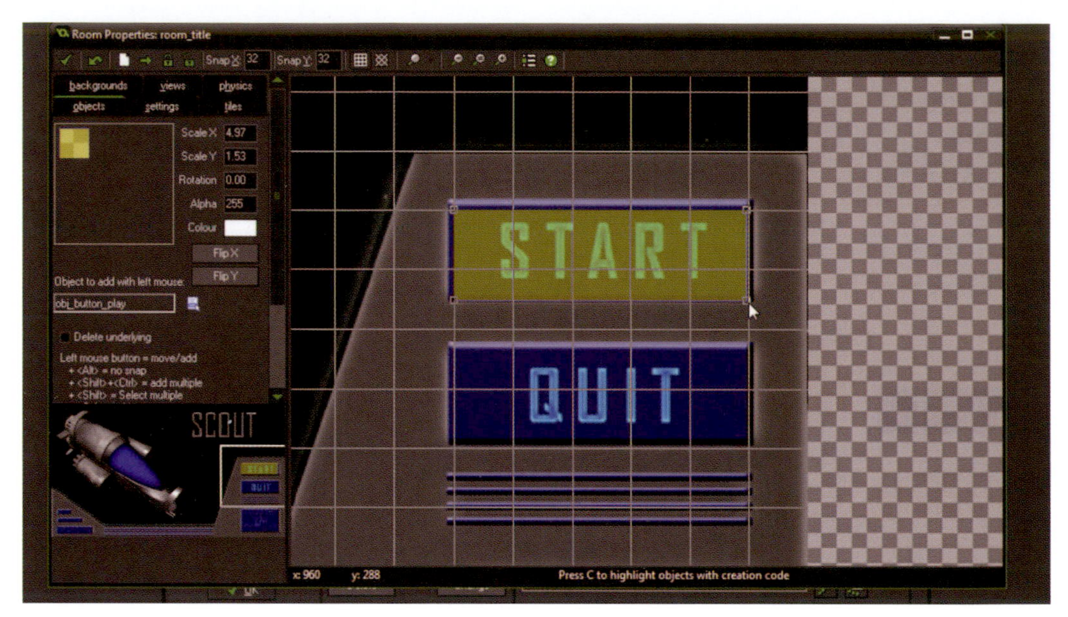

FIGURE 2.27

a **Different Room** Action. You can do this by clicking the **Main1** tab and choosing **Different Room** under the **Rooms** submenu.

Step 13: In the **Different Room** dialogue box, set the **New Room** to **Room_Defeat**.

Now when you test your game, the game should start by showing the game menu. The player then must select either Start (to play the game) or Quit (to exit the game). When the ship makes contact with an asteroid, the defeat screen should appear, allowing the player to play again or exit the game.

Setting Player's Lives

Step 1: Open the object Game Controller.

Step 2: With **Create** selected under Events, click the **Score** tab and drag the **Set Lives** icon to the Actions window. It is under the **Lives** submenu and looks like a list with a green X marking out the list.

Step 3: Set new lives to **3** and click **OK** to close the window.

Step 4: Click **Add Event**, choose **Step,** and then **Step** once more. With the **Score** tab still selected, drag the **Test Lives** Action to the Action window. This icon is a black square with a green heart inside.

FIGURE 2.28

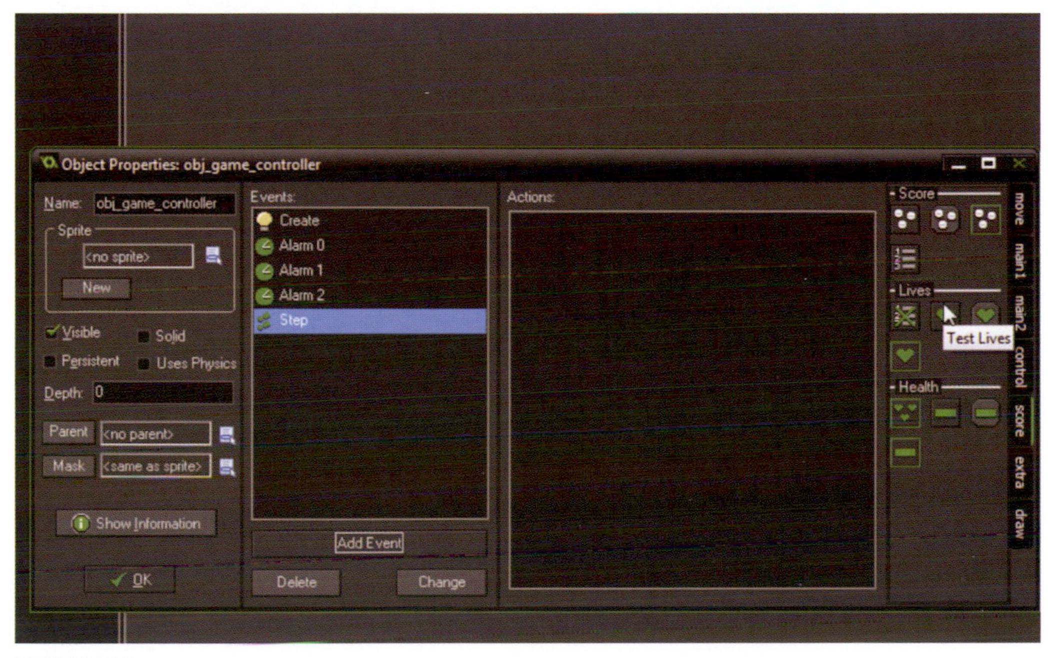

FIGURE 2.29

Step 5: Set the following in the Properties box:

Value: **1**
Operation: **smaller than**

Step 6: Select **OK**.

Step 7: Click on the **Main1** tab and then drag the **Different Room** icon to the Actions window.

Step 8: Set new room to **room_defeat** and click **OK**.

Step 9: In the left side of the window, change the Sprite to **spr_lives_strip3**.

Step 10: With **Create** selected under **Events**, choose the **Main1** tab and drag the **Change Sprite** icon above the **Set Alarm 0 to 1** Action.

Step 11: Make the following changes to the Change Sprite Properties window:

Sprite: spr_lives_strip3
Subimage: 2
Speed: 0

Step 12: Select **OK** to close the window.

Step 13: Open the object: **obj_asteroid_controller**.

FIGURE 2.30

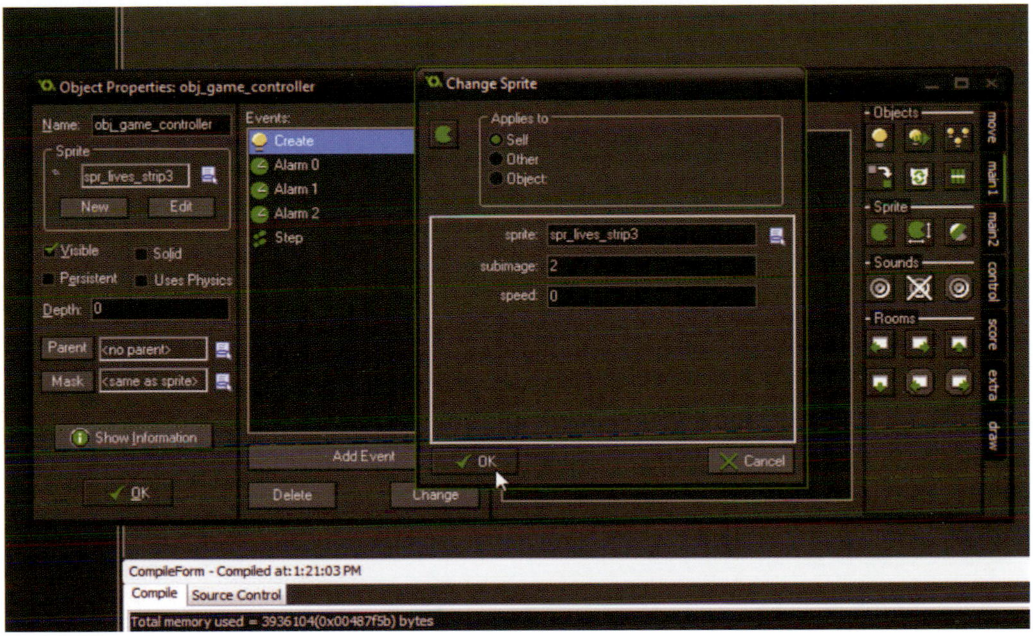

FIGURE 2.31

Step 14: Select the **Score** tab and then drag the **Set Lives** icon into the Actions window. Make the following changes to the Set Lives Properties box:

New lives: –1
Relative: checked

Step 15: Click **OK** to close the window.

Step 16: Next select the **Main1** tab and drag a **Change Sprite** Action into the Actions window. Make the following changes to the Change Sprite Properties window:

Applies to: Select Object and then choose obj_game_controller
Sprite: spr_lives_strip3
Subimage: lives—1
Speed: 0

Step 17: Click **OK** to close out of the window and select **OK** again to close out of the Object Properties window.

Step 18: You should notice that the **Obj_game_controller** now looks like a single tiny ship. This is the life counter. Open **room_game** and move the tiny ship to the top left of the screen.

Step 19: Open the Asteroid controller object **obj_asteroid_controller**. Select the **Main1** tab. Drag in a **Destroy Instance** Action into the Action window. The **Destroy Instance** icon looks like a recycling bin.

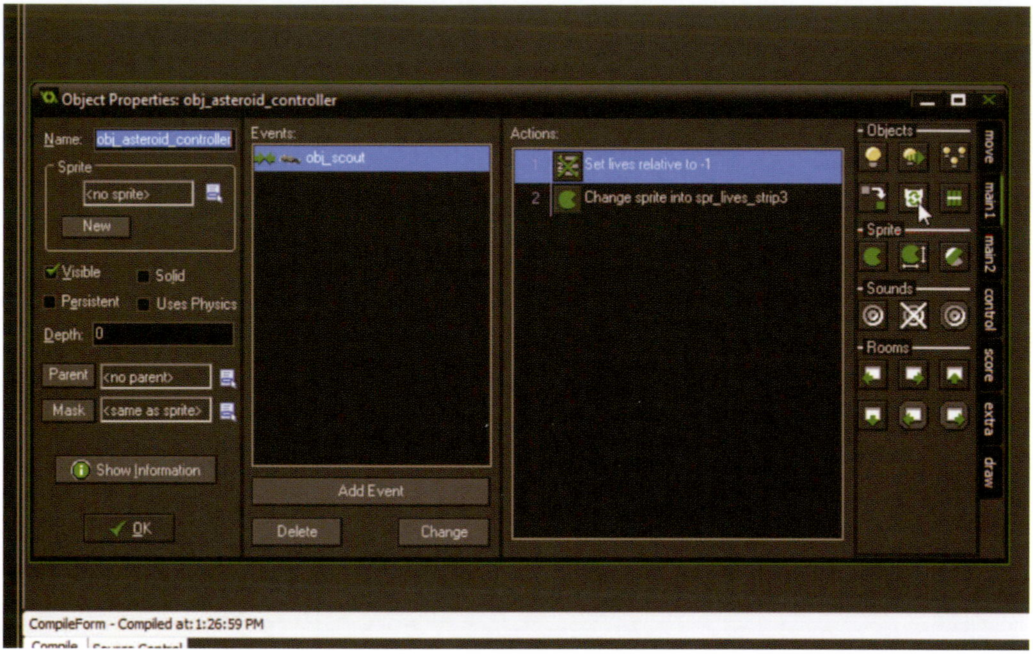

FIGURE 2.32

Step 20: Select **Self** and click **OK** to close the dialogue window. This will make the asteroid destroy itself when colliding with the ship.

Step 21: Delete the Action for **Go to Room_Defeat**. Click **OK** to save Object Properties.

Test your game. You should see three small ship images in the top left corner that represent the player's lives. Each time the player's ship collides with an asteroid one of the lives should disappear and the asteroid that is being collided with should also disappear. When all three of the player's lives are gone, the game should go to the "Game Over" screen.

Exploding Asteroids When They Collide with Ship

Step 1: Select **Object>Create Object**.

Step 2: Name the object: **obj_explosion**.

Step 3: Change the Sprite to: **spr_explosion_one_strip29**.

Step 4: Click **OK**.

Step 5: Open the **Asteroid Controller** object.

Step 6: Click on the **Destroy Instance** Action icon and **delete** it.

Step 7: Click on the **Main1** tab and drag a **Change Instance** Action to the Action window. This icon looks like a gray square with a white arrow pointing to a green square.

Step 8: In the Properties window make the following changes:

> Change into: obj_explosion
> Perform events: yes

Step 9: Click **OK**.

Step 10: Open **obj_explosion**. Select **Add Event>Other>Animation End**.

Step 11: Select the **Main1** tab, look under the **Objects** submenu, and drag and drop the **Destroy Instance** icon to the Actions window. Make sure the instance is set for **Self** and click **OK**.

Step 12: Select **Add Event>Create** and select the **Move** tab. Drag the **Moved Fixed** icon to the Actions window and select the **center block** in the directions options.

Step 13: Click **OK** to close out of the window and click **OK** again to close out of the object.

Step 14: Under the Sprites folder, open **spr_explosion_one_strip29.**

FIGURE 2.33

FIGURE 2.34

Step 15: Click to Edit the Sprite. Click **Center** and then **OK**. Click **OK** to save the Object Properties.

When you test your game, each of the asteroids should now explode when they collide with the player's ship.

Exploding Player Ship

Step 1: Select **Object>Create Object** and name the object: **obj_player_explosion**.

Step 2: Choose the Sprite: **spr_explosion_ship_strip23** and select **OK**.

Step 3: Open the **Game Controller** Object and click **Step** in the Events window.

Step 4: Select **Go to Room—Room Defeat** and **delete** it.

Step 5: Select the **Main** tab and drag a **Change Instance** Action and drop it in the Actions window.

Make the following changes:

Applies to: should be set to Object: obj_scout
Change into: obj_player_explosion
Perform events: yes

Step 6: Click **OK** to close the window and **OK** to close the Game Controller window.

FIGURE 2.35

FIGURE 2.36

Step 7: Open the **Player Explosion** object, select **Add Event>Create** and select the **Move** tab.

Step 8: Drag and drop a **Fixed Movement** Action to the Action window. Select the **center** direction option and close the **Move Fixed** Properties window by clicking **OK**.

Step 9: Click **Add Event** and select **Other>Animation End**.

Step 10: Select the **Main1** tab.

Step 11: Under the Rooms heading drag and drop the **Different Room** Action into the Action pane.

Step 12: Change the new room option to: **room_defeat**.

Step 13: Click **OK** to close the box and **OK** again to close the Object Properties.

Step 14: Under the Sprites folder open the sprite **spr_explosion_ship_strip23**. Select **Center** in the origin section then click **OK**.

Step 15: Open up the **Player Explosion** object. With the **Create** Event selected, select the **Main1** tab and then drag and drop a **Change Sprite** Action to the Action pane. Change the Sprite to **spr_explosion_ship_strip23** and select **OK** to close the box and **OK** again to close the Object Properties.

When you test your game now, you should see the player's ship explode after all lives have been lost. Immediately after the player's ship explodes, the game will automatically go to the **Game Over** Screen.

Now it is time to install some weaponry to our ship so that we can destroy the asteroids before they slam into our ship.

Adding Bullets to Player Object

Step 1: Go to **Object>Create Object** and name the object: **obj_laser**. Then set the Sprite to: **spr_laser**. Click **OK** to close the Object Properties window.

Step 2: Select the **Scout** object and select **Add Event>Key Press>Space**. We will use the Space bar because it is the largest button on the keyboard. Some keys are not ideal to use for game controls because hitting them multiple times may trigger a specific keyboard function. For example, the Shift key, if hit five times in a row, will trigger "Sticky Keys" which, as you can imagine, would cause problems with our game.

Step 3: Select the **Main1** tab and under the Objects heading, drag and drop a **Moving Instance** of action into the Action pane.

Make the following changes:

Applies to: Self
Object: obj_laser
x: +30
y: +6

Speed: 25
Direction: 0
Relative: checked

Step 4: Select **OK** to close out of the window.

Step 5: Select the **Control** tab and drag and drop a **Test Instance Count** Action into the Action pane above the **Create Moving** Action. The test instance icon looks like a green circle with the numbers 1, 2, and 3 beneath it.

Adjust the following options:

Object: obj_laser
Number: 1
Operation: smaller than

Step 6: Choose **OK** to exit out of the window and **OK** again to exit out of the Object Properties.

Step 7: Under the Objects folder choose**: obj_laser**.

Step 8: Choose **Add Event>Other>Outside Room.**

Step 9: Select the **Main1** tab and drag and drop a **Destroy Instance** Action into the Action pane. The instance should be applied to **Self**.

Step 10: Select **Add Event** again and choose **Collision>obj_asteroid_controller.**

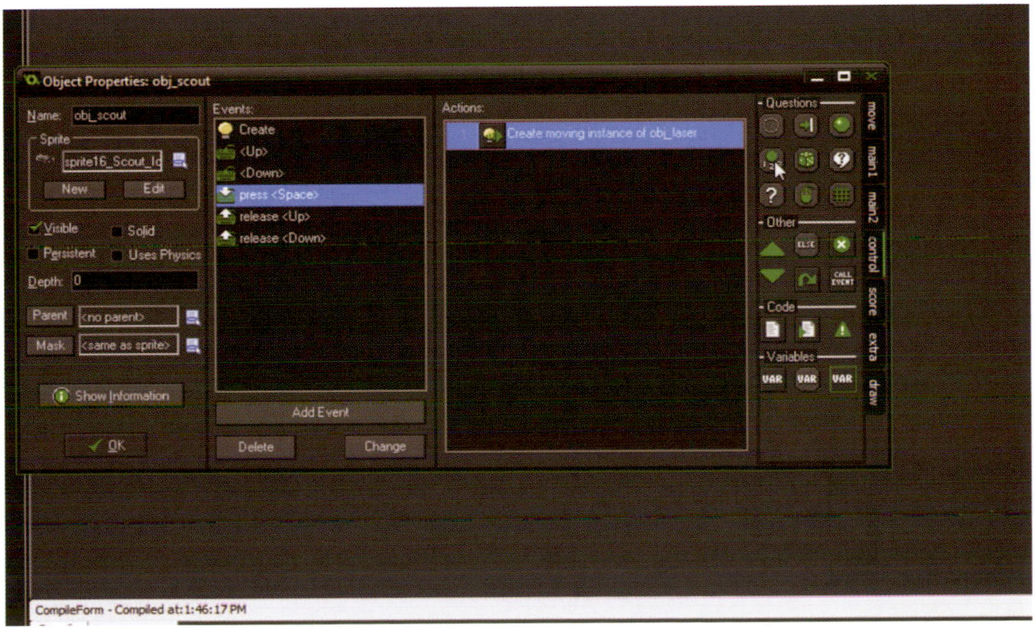

FIGURE 2.37

Step 11: Select the **Main1** tab and drag and drop a **Destroy Instance** Action into the Action pane. Make sure the instance is set for **Self** and click **OK**.

Step 12: Under the **Sprite** folder open the laser sprite. **Center** the origin, then select **Modify Mask,** and set the shape to **precise**.

Step 13: Select **OK** twice to close out of the windows.

Step 14: Under the Objects folder open the **Small asteroid** object.

Step 15: Select **Add Event>Create.**

Step 16: Select the **Control** tab then drag a **Set Variable** Action into the Action pane.

Set the following:

Variable: hp
Value: 2

Step 17: Select **OK.**

Step 18: Go to **Add Event>Collision>Obj_laser.**

Step 19: Select the Control tab and drag and drop the **Set Variable** Action into the Action pane.

Set the following:

Variable: hp
Value: –1
Relative: checked

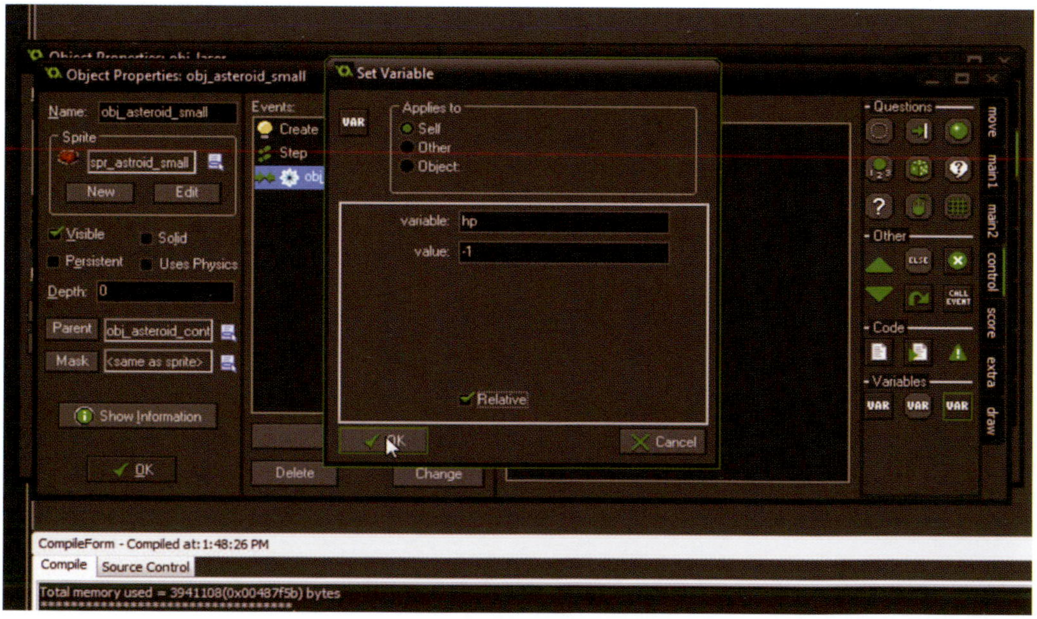

FIGURE 2.38

Step 20: Click **OK**.

Step 21: Drag and drop a **Test Variable** Action into the Action pane.

Set the following:

Variable: hp
Value: 0
Operation: equal to

Step 22: Click **OK**.

Step 23: Select the **Control** tab. Under the **Other** heading, drag a **Start of a Block** Action into the Action pane beneath the two variables.

Step 24: Select the **Main1** tab.

Step 25: Under the **Objects** heading, drag and drop a **Change Instance** Action into the Action pane.

Step 26: Set the following:

Change into: obj_explosion
Perform events: yes

Step 27: Click **OK**.

Step 28: Select the **Control** tab and drag and drop an **End of a Block** Action into the Action pane.

Step 29: Select actions two through five by holding down the **shift** button and clicking on the first action you want to select, then the last item you want. **Right-click** and copy them.

Step 30: Click **OK** to close out the window.

Step 31: Under the Objects folder open up the **Medium Asteroid** object.

Step 32: Select **Add Event>Create.**

Step 33: Select the **Control** tab and drag and drop a **Set Variable** Action into the Action pane. Set the variable to **hp** and the value to **4.**

Step 34: Click **OK** to close the window.

Step 35: Select **Add>Event>Collision>Obj_laser.**

Step 36: Select the **Control** tab and drag and drop a **Set Variable** Action into the Action pane.

Variable: hp
Value: –1
Relative: checked

Step 37: Underneath the Variable in the Action pane, use the keyboard shortcut **CTRL+V** to paste the actions we recently copied. Click **OK** to close out of the window.

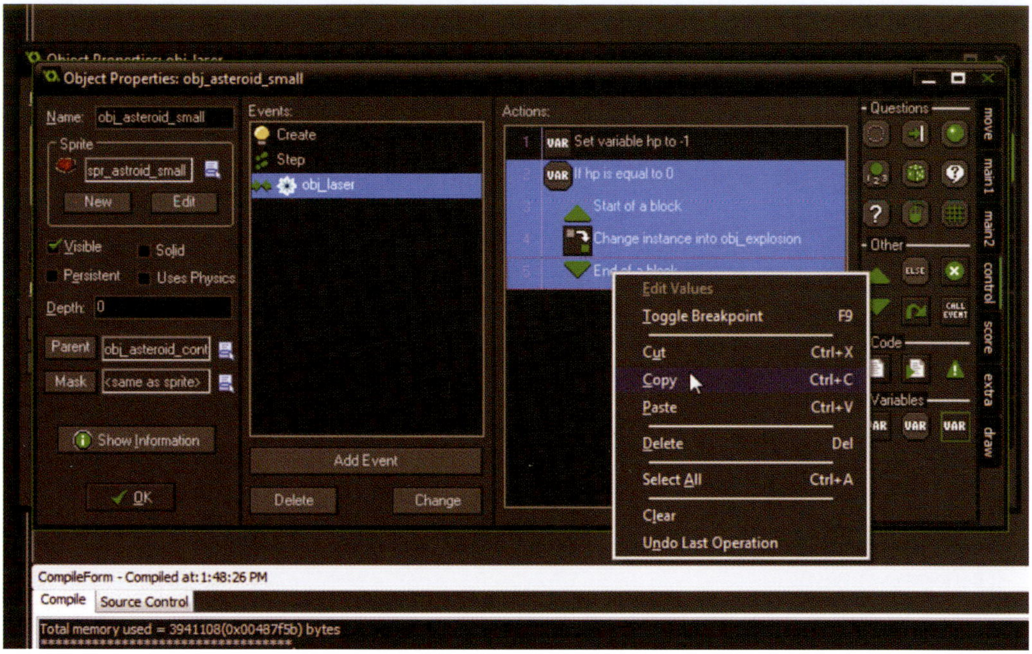

FIGURE 2.39

Step 38: Under the Objects folder open the **Large Asteroid** object.

Step 39: Select **Add Event>Create**.

Step 40: Select the **Control** tab. Drag and drop a **Set Variable** Action into the Action pane. Set variable to **hp** and the value to **6**.

Step 41: Click **OK**.

Step 42: Select **Add Event>Collision>obj_laser.**

Step 43: Select the **Control** tab. Under the **Variables** heading drag and drop a **Set Variable** Action into the Action pane.

Variable: hp
Value: −1
Relative: checked

Step 44: Use the keyboard shortcut **CTRL+V** to paste the actions we copied earlier.

Step 45: Click **OK**.

Now our game is really taking form. Test the game.

Let's add an extra incentive to motivate the player to destroy the asteroids, in addition to seeing fun explosions and avoiding being hit by them. Now we will create a scoring system which awards the player with points for destroying each asteroid.

Create Score Counter

Step 1: Open up the **Laser** object.

Step 2: Right-click on the **obj_asteroid_controller** Collision Event located in the Events window.

Step 3: Select: **Delete Event**. If a dialog box appears asking, "Are you sure you want to remove the event with all its actions?", select **Yes**. This will remove the **obj_asteroid_controller** Event from the Events window.

Step 4: Select **OK** to close the Object Properties window.

Step 5: Open the **Small Asteroid**.

Step 6: Select the **Laser** object in the Events window.

Step 7: Choose the **Main1** tab and under the Objects heading drag and drop the **Destroy Instance** Action to the top of the list of actions in the Actions panel.

Step 8: In the **Destroy Instance** option window that appears select **Other,** then click **OK** to close the window. Select **OK** again to close the Object Properties window.

Step 9: Open the **obj_game_controller** and under the **Score** tab, add a **Set Score** Action and set to **0**.

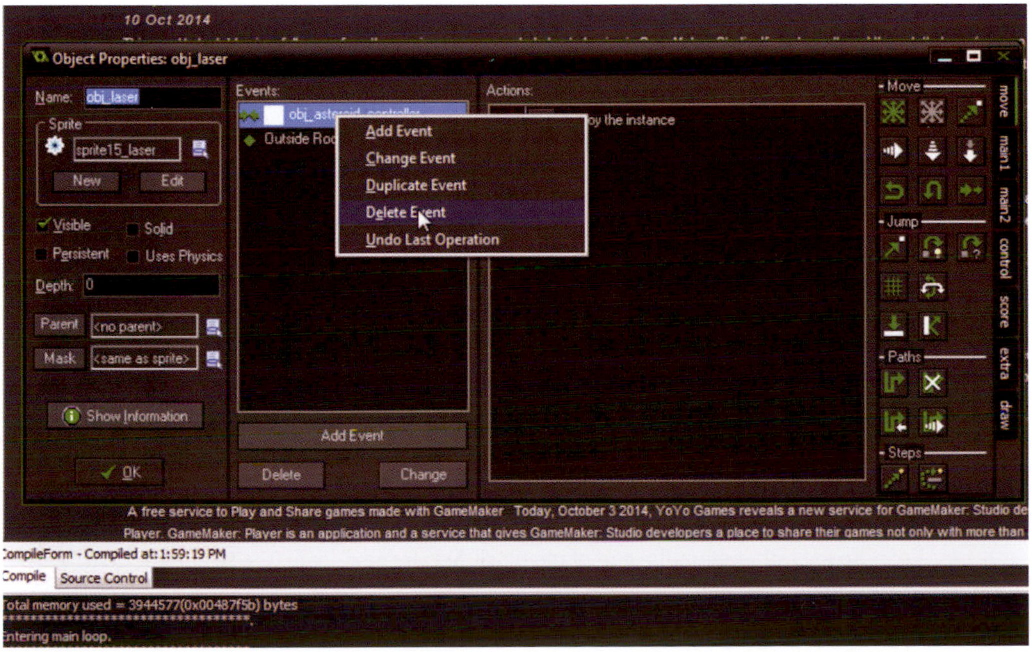

FIGURE 2.40

FIGURE 2.41

Step 10: While still in the **obj_game_controller**, add a **Draw GUI** Event. Drag in a **Set Color** Action under the Draw tab and set the color to lime green and select **OK** to close the Set Color window.

Step 11: Drag in a **Draw Score** Action from under the **Score** tab on the right and set the **x** value to **900** and the **y** value to **12**. Select **OK** to close the box. Click **OK** on the **obj_game_controller** to close the object.

Step 12: Open **obj_asteroid_small** and click on the **obj_laser** Event.

Step 13: Under the **Score** tab, drag in a **Set Score** Action right before the end of the block. Set the new score to **+10** and check the **Relative** box. Click **OK** to close the Set Score window. Click **OK** again to close the **Obj_asteroid_small**.

Step 14: Open **obj_asteroid_medium** and click on the **obj_laser** Event.

Step 15: Just like before, drag in a **Set Score** Action right before the end of the block, only this time set the new score to **+20**. Check the **Relative** box. Click **OK** to close out of the Object Properties window.

Step 16: Open **obj_asteroid_large** and click on the **obj_laser**. Drag in a **Set Score** Action right before the end of the block. Set the new score to **+50** and click **OK**. Make sure the **Relative** box is checked.

Test the game again to make sure all of the asteroids are producing points in the score area when destroyed.

FIGURE 2.42

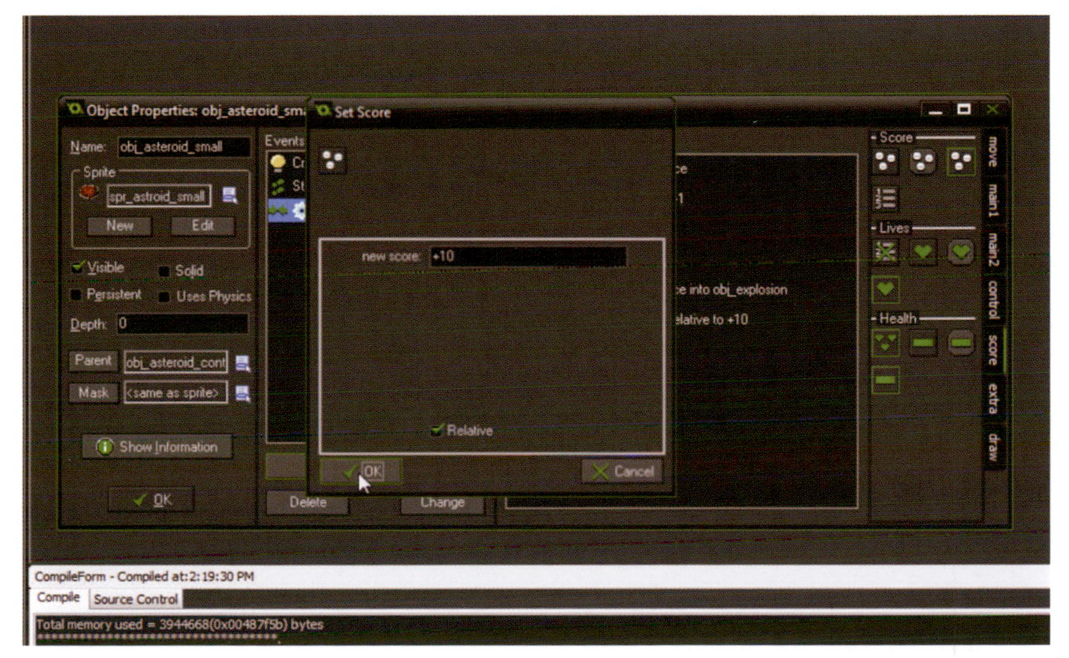

FIGURE 2.43

Another incentive to destroy the asteroids is that some have surprises inside them. These surprises are power-ups that temporarily give the player's ship special abilities. For this game, we will add two different power-ups, a shield for our ship and a multishot weapon.

Adding Shield Power-Up

Step 1: Right-click obj_scout and **Duplicate** the object. Name the new object **obj_scout_shielded** and click **OK**.

Step 2: Duplicate the **obj_scout** object again and rename this third copy **obj_scout_multishot**.

Step 3: Open the Sprites folder and duplicate **spr_scout_ship3** and name the copy **spr_scout_shielded**.

Step 4: Select **Edit Sprite>Transform>Resize Canvas** and change the width to **150**. Have the **Keep Aspect Ratio** box **checked** so the other values will change accordingly.

Step 5: Select **OK**.

Step 6: Under the **Images** tab at the top, Select **Glow**.

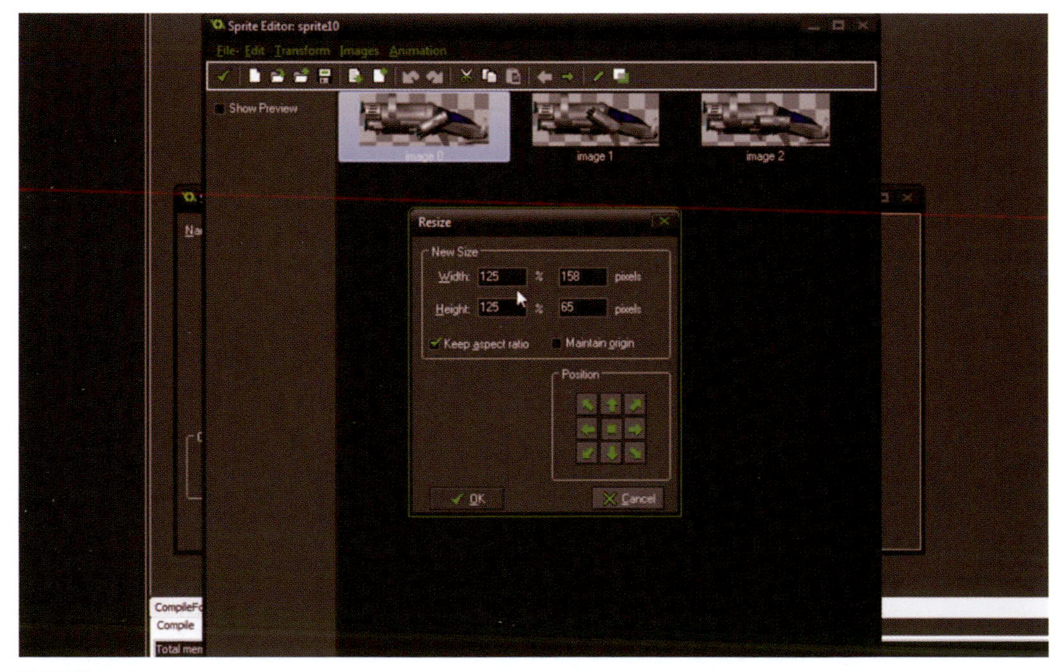

FIGURE 2.44

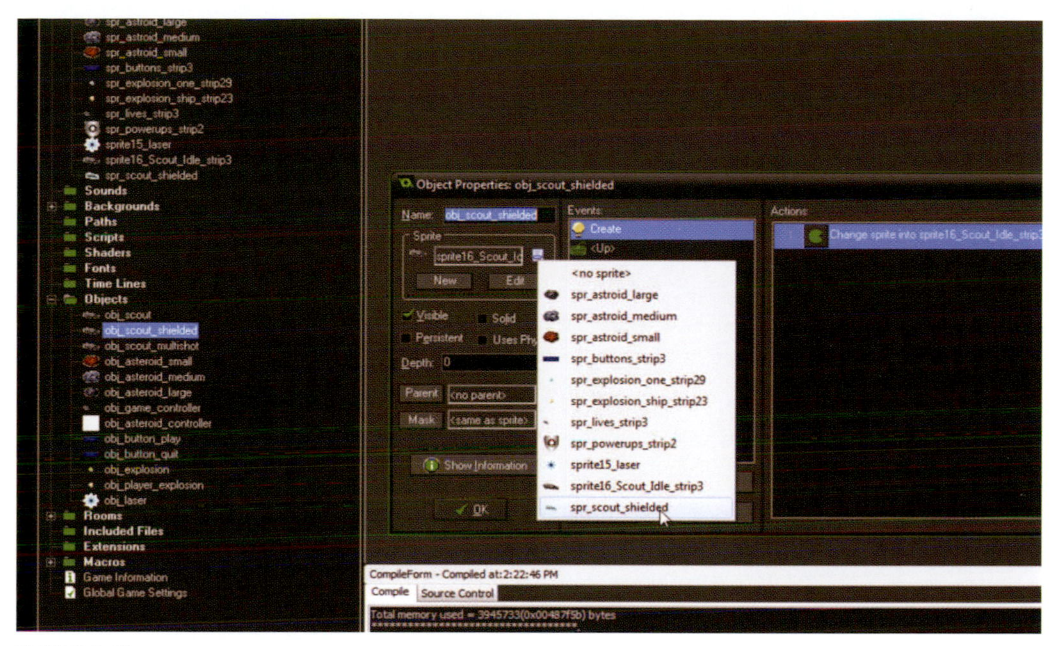

FIGURE 2.45

Step 7: Change the color to a light blue (cyan) and select **OK**. This will add a glowing shield around our ship.

Step 8: Change the Opacity (alpha) value to **77** and the Thickness value to **10**. Select **OK** to close the window and **OK** again to return to the Sprite Properties window.

Step 9: Click the **Center** button and then select **OK** to close out of the Sprite.

Step 10: Open the **obj_scout_shielded** and click the tab beside the Sprite in the image, and select **spr_scout_shielded**.

Step 11: In the **Create** Event open the action **Change Sprite Into** that is already in the object. Change the Sprite to **spr_scout_shielded**. Select **OK**.

Step 12: In the **Up** Event, select the **Change Sprite Into** Action and change it to the **spr_scout_shielded** as well. Continue to do this step for each event in the object so the shield will remain visible while the ship is moving up and down. Once this is done, select **OK** to close out of the object.

Adding Multishot Power-Up

Step 1: Open the **Object obj_scout_multishot**. Click on the **Press<Space>** Event and **right-click** the **Create Moving Instance of obj_laser** Action. **Copy** this action and **paste it twice**.

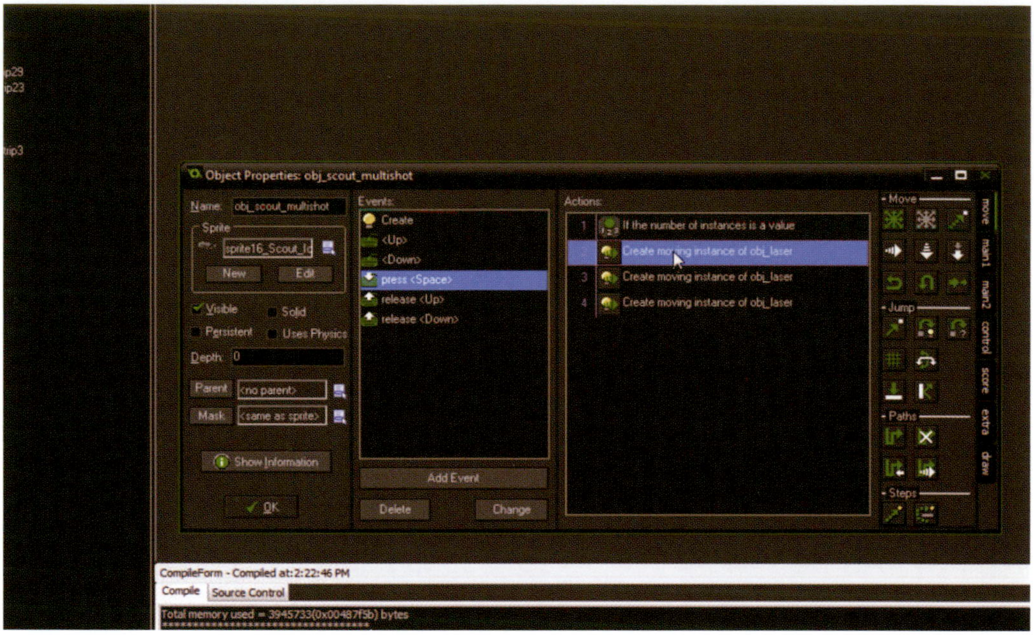

FIGURE 2.46

Step 2: Open the first **Create Moving** instance and change the direction value to **25**. Click **OK**. Open the **third** instance, and change the value to **–25**. Select **OK**.

Step 3: Right-click on the **If the number of instances is a value** Action and **delete** it. Click **OK** to close the Object Properties window.

Step 4: Open the **obj_asteroid_controller** and add a **Collision** Event involving the **obj_scout_multishot**.

Step 5: Click on the **Collision** Event with **obj_scout** Event and select **each of the three actions** under it. **Copy** them and **paste** them into the **obj_scout_multishot** Event. Select **OK** to close the object.

Step 6: Open the **obj_game_controller** and click on the **Step** Event.

Step 7: Under the **Control** tab, drag in a **Start of a Block** arrow in between the two existing actions.

Step 8: Drag in a **Test Instance Count** Action right after the **Start of a Block** arrow.

Step 9: Select **obj_Scout** and change the number to **1** and click **OK**.

Step 10: Add an **Else** Action at the end.

Step 11: Add a **Change Instance** Action after the **Else** Action.

Step 12: Click the **Applies to: Object** radio button and select **obj_scout_multishot**. Change it into **obj_player_explosion**.

Step 13: The **Perform** Events box should be set to **yes**. Click **OK**.

FIGURE 2.47

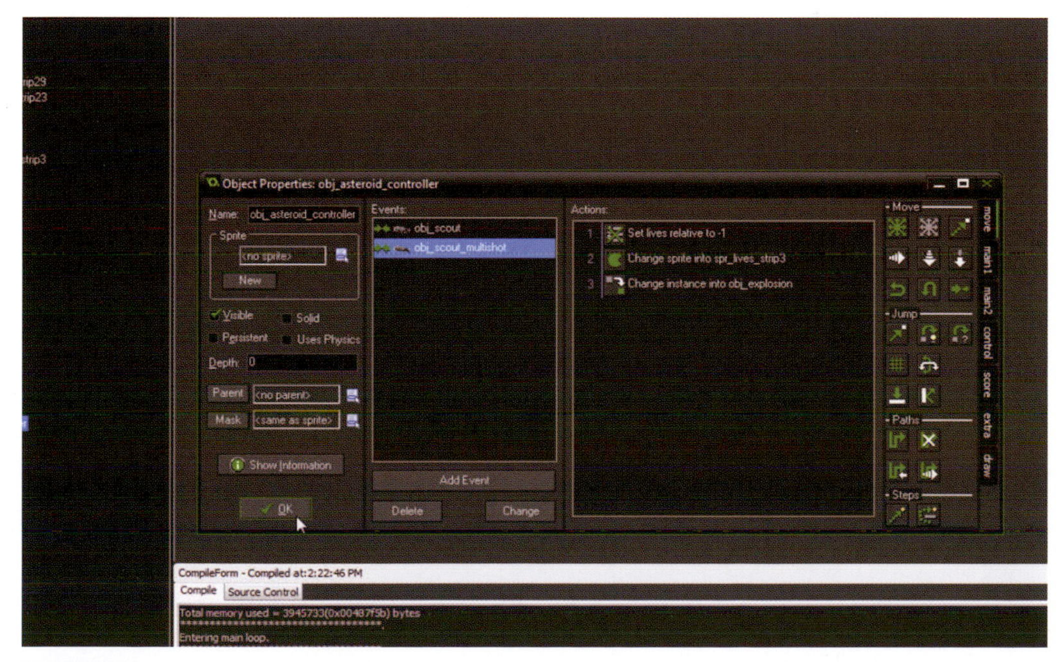

FIGURE 2.48

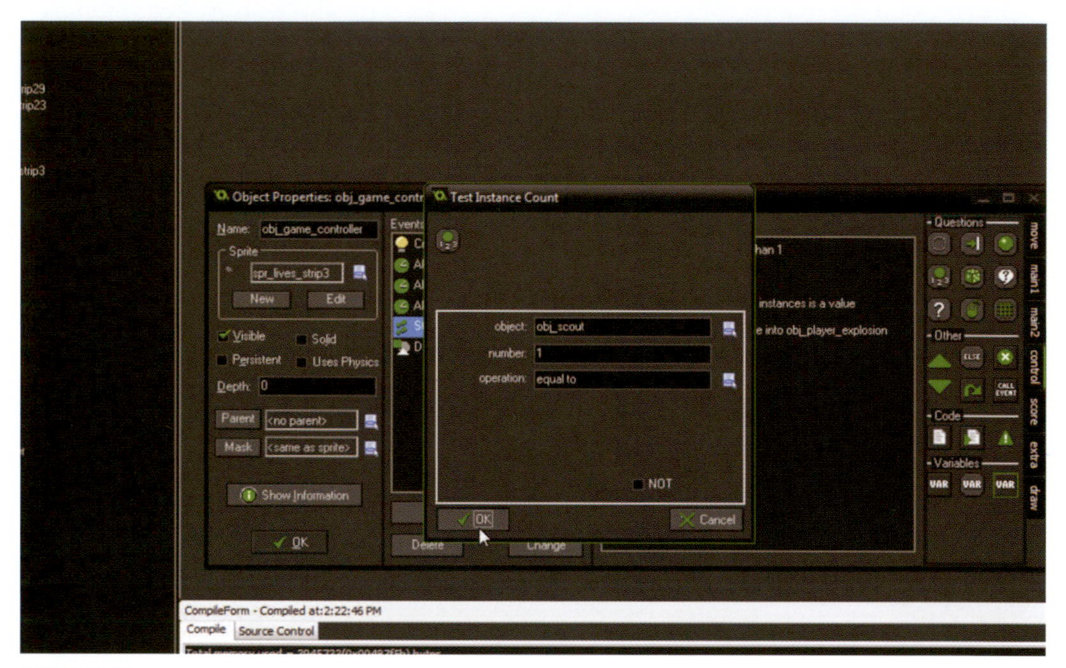

FIGURE 2.49

FIGURE 2.50

Step 14: Add the **End of a Block** Action to the very bottom and select **OK** to close out of the object.

Step 15: Create a new object and name it **obj_shield**.

Step 16: Set the Sprite to **spr_powerups_strip2**.

Step 17: Add a **Create** Event and drag in a **Change Sprite** Action. Change the speed to **0** and change the Sprite to **spr_powerups_strip2**. Select **OK**.

Step 18: Duplicate **obj_shield** and name it **obj_multishot**.

Step 19: Open the **Change Sprite** Action and change the subimage to **1**. Select **OK** twice to close out of both windows.

Step 20: In **obj_scout** add a **Collision** Event with **obj_shield** and **obj_multishot**.

Step 21: In the **obj_shield** Collision Event, drag in a **Destroy Instance** Action that applies to **Other** and click **OK**.

Step 22: Drag in a **Change Instance** Action and change into **obj_scout_shielded**.

Step 23: Set the Perform Events box to **Yes** and select **OK**.

Step 24: In the **obj_multishots** Collision Event, drag in the same **Destroy Instance** with the same settings, followed by a **Change Instance**. However, this time change it into the **obj_scout_multishot**. Make sure you change the Perform Events box to **Yes** then select **OK**.

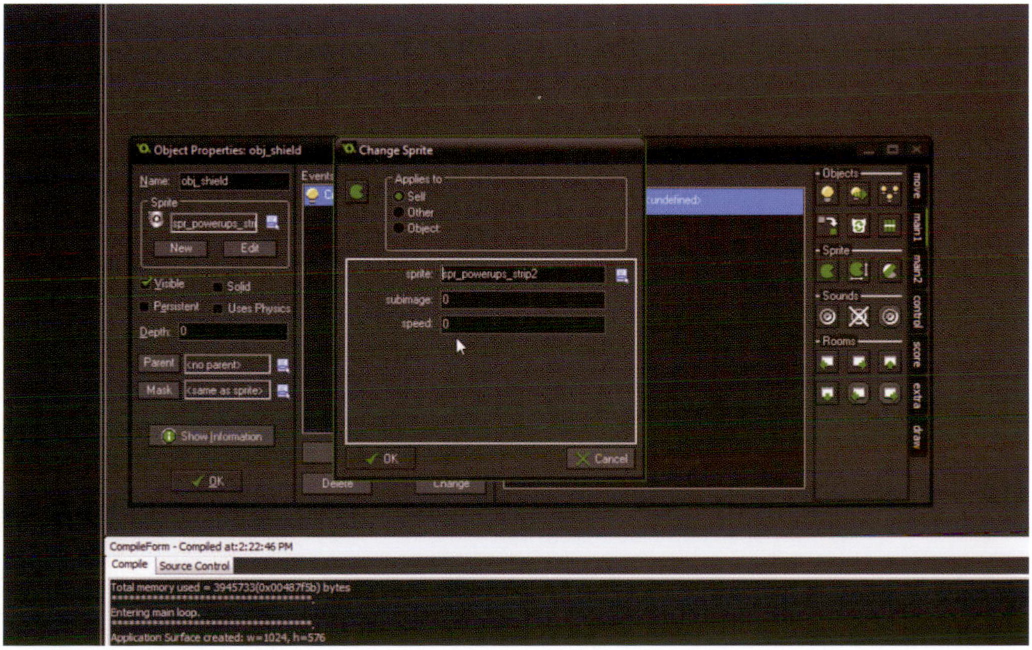

FIGURE 2.51

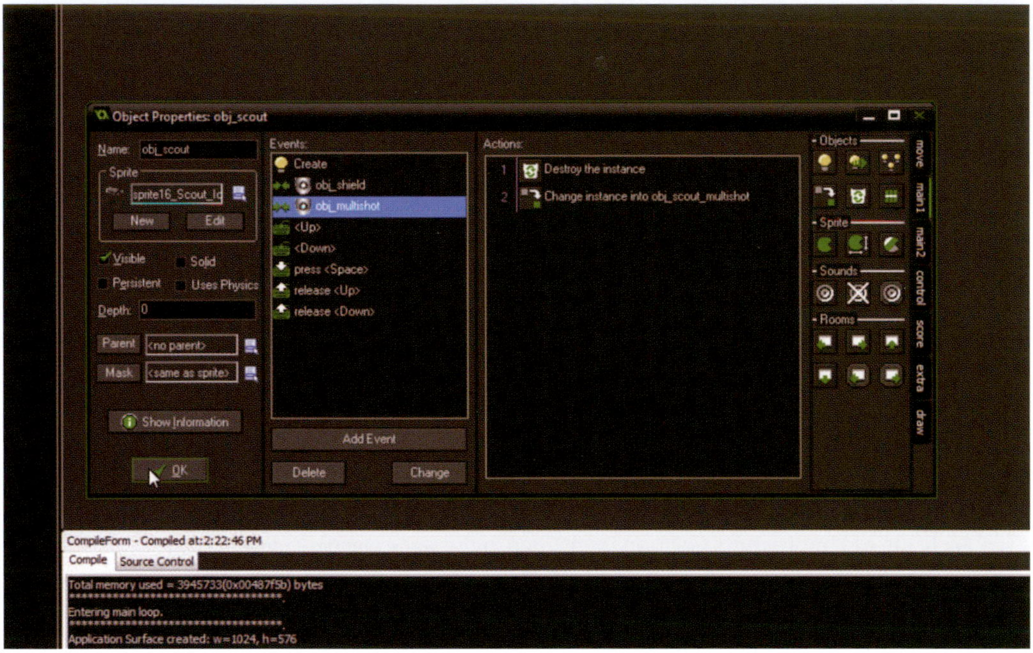

FIGURE 2.52

Step 25: Open the **obj_scout_shielded** and create a **Collision** Event with **obj_multishot**.

Step 26: Drag in a **Change Instance** Action.

Step 27: Change into **obj_scout_multishot** and set the Perform Events to **Yes**.

Step 28: Drag in a **Destroy Instance** above it and set it to apply to **Other**. Click **OK**.

Step 29: Open the **obj_scout_multishot** and add a **Collision** Event with **obj_shield**.

Step 30: Drag in a **Destroy Instance** Action with **Other** and click **OK**. Then drag in a **Change Instance** Action into **obj_scout_shielded** and set Perform Events to **Yes**.

Step 31: Open **obj_scout_shielded** and add an **Alarm** Event (Alarm 0).

Step 32: Drag in a **Change Instance** Action changing into **obj_scout** and set Perform Events to **Yes**. Select **OK**.

Step 33: In the **Create** Event box drag in a **Set Alarm** Action and set the number of steps to **390 in Alarm: Alarm 0**. Click **OK**.

Step 34: Open **obj_scout_multishot** and add an **Alarm** Event (Alarm 0). Follow the same steps as above, only change the steps to **90** this time rather than **390** in Alarm 0. Click **OK**.

Step 35: Open the **room_game** and drag the **obj_shield** Sprite into the map over the ship.

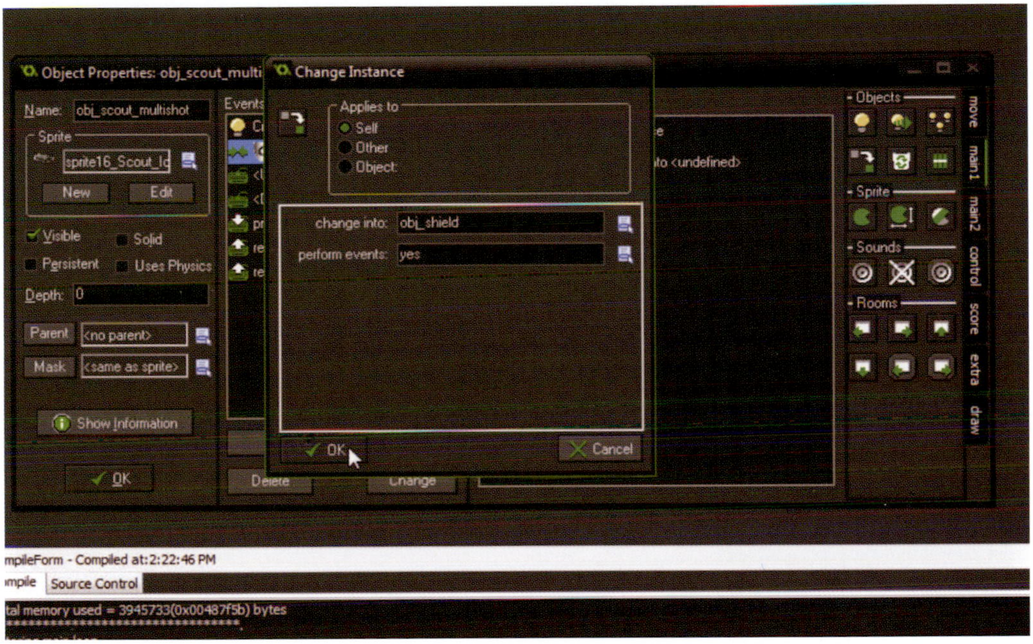

FIGURE 2.53

Step 36: Drag in the **obj_multishot** Sprite below the ship. Select **OK**.

Test the game and collide with each power-up to make sure they are working properly.

Now that the shield and multishot power-ups are ready, we need to place them so that they randomly spawn when the asteroids explode.

Embed Randomly Spawning Power-Ups

Step 1: Open **obj_asteroid** controller and add a Collision Event with **obj_scout_shielded**.

Step 2: Add a **Change Instance** Action into **obj_explosion**.

Step 3: Set Perform Events to **Yes** and select **OK**.

Step 4: Add a **Destroy** Event and drag in a **Set Variable** Action with the variable set to **i** and the value to **irandom(100),** then select **OK**.

Step 5: Drag in a **Test Variable** Action. Set the variable to **i** and the value to **10**. The operations should be **less than or equal to**. Click **OK**.

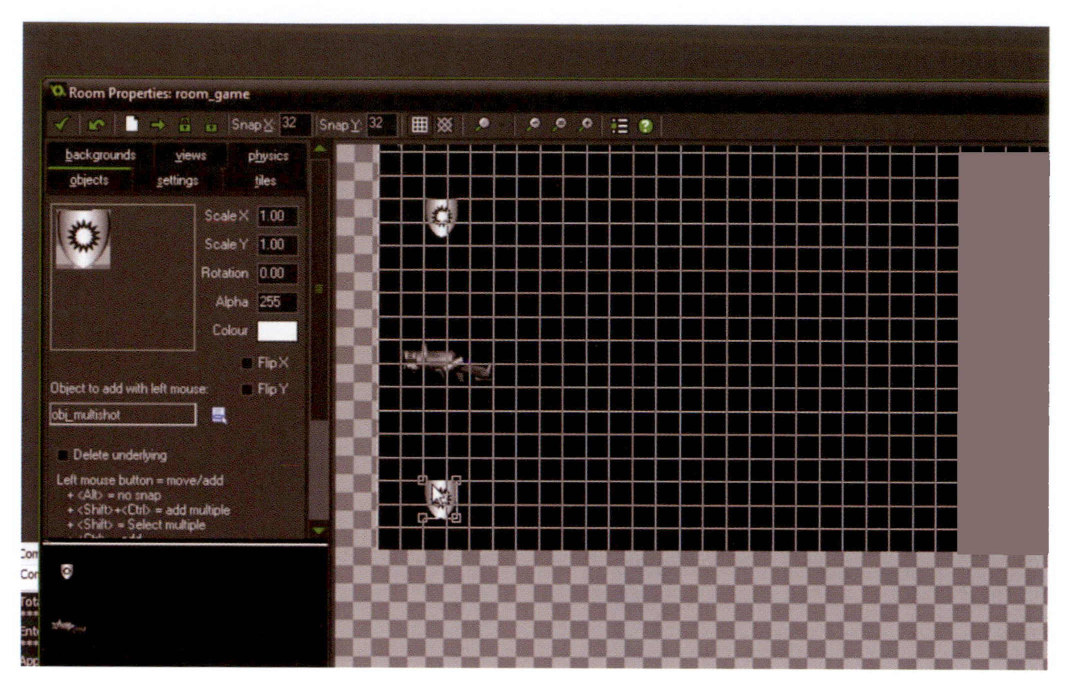

FIGURE 2.54

Step 6: Drag in the **Start of a Block**, followed by a **Create Moving** Action. Set the object to **obj_shield**, speed to **6**, and direction to **180**. Leave x and y at **0**. Check the Relative box and click **OK**.

Step 7: Drag in an **Exit This Event** Action, followed by the **End of a Block**.

Step 8: Drag in a **Set Variable** Action. Set the variable to **i** and the value to **irandom(100),** then click **OK**.

Step 9: Drag in a **Test Variable** Action with the variable set to **i**, the value set to **10**. Set the operation to **less than or equal to,** then select **OK**.

Step 10: Drag in a **Start of a Block** and then drag in a **Create Moving** Action.

Step 11: Set the object to **obj_multishot**. Set the speed to **6** and the direction to **180**. Check the **Relative** box then click **OK**.

Step 12: Drag in an **End of a Block** and click **OK** to close out of the Object Properties.

Step 13: Go into your **room_game** and delete the **shield powerup** and **multishot powerup,** which were placed above and below your ship, respectively.

Now it is time to test your game, which is nearly complete. Your title screen start button should run the game and your ship should move up and down and shoot. The background and asteroids should all be moving as intended, and as you destroy the asteroids you should see explosions, receive points, and gather power-ups to give the

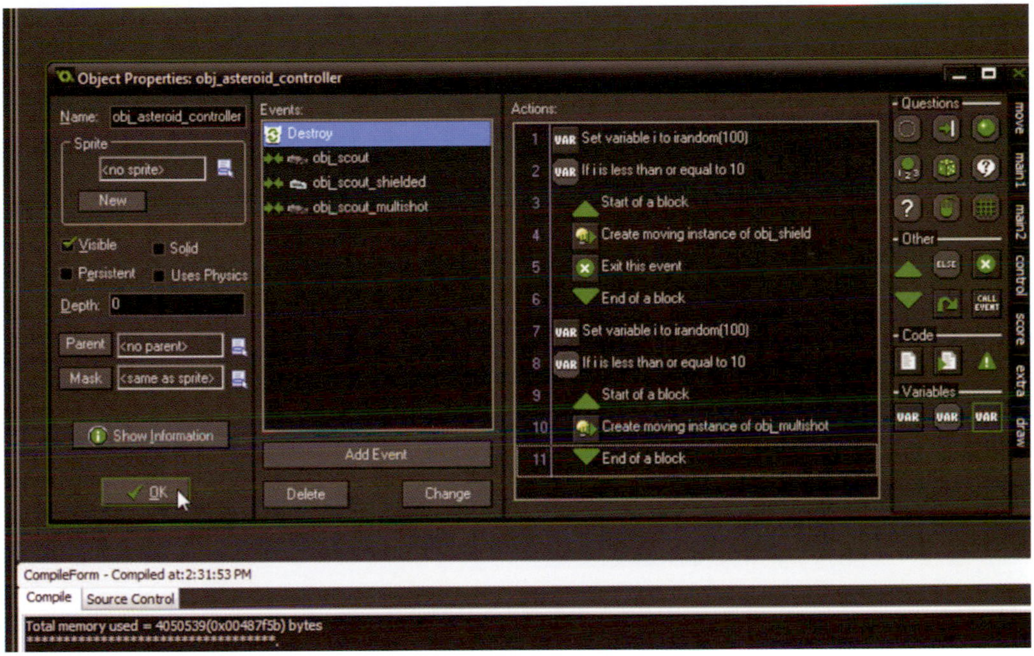

FIGURE 2.55

ship special abilities. We have just one last addition and then our game will be complete; it is time to add music and sound effects.

Adding Music and Sound Effects

Step 1: If you have not already, add in the sounds: **laser_1**, **laser_2**, **Scout_Theme**, **Shield**, **Ship_explosion**, and the **three asteroid sounds**.

Step 2: Open **obj_scout** and click on the **Press<Space>** Event.

Step 3: Drag in a **Start of a Block** Action between the two pre-existing actions.

Step 4: Add a **Play Sound** Event for **laser_1**. Drag in the **End of a Block** arrow and close the object.

Step 5: Open **obj_scout_shielded** and on the **Press<Space>** Event, add a **Start of a Block** between the two pre-existing actions.

Step 6: Add a **Play Sound** Event for **laser_1**. Drag in the **End of a Block** and select **OK**.

Step 7: Open **obj_scout** again and on the **obj_shields** Event, add a **Play Sound** Event for **sound_shield**. Click **OK**.

Step 8: Open **obj_scout_multishot** and add a **Play Sound** Action with the sound for **sound shield**. Click **OK**.

Step 9: On the **Press<Space>** Event, add in a play sound for **laser_2,** then click **OK**.

Step 10: On **obj_scout**, on the **Create** Event, add a Play Sound Action for **sound_scout_theme**.

Step 11: Set the loop to **TRUE** and click **OK**.

Step 12: Open **obj_player_explosion** and on **Animation End** add in a **STOP** sound for **sound_scout_theme,** then click **OK**.

Step 13: On the **Create** Event, add a **Play Sound** for **sound_ship_explosion,** then select **OK**.

Step 14: Open the **obj_asteroid_small** and on the **obj_laser** Event, add a **Play Sound** for **sound_explosion_small**.

Step 15: Repeat Step 14 for **obj_asteroid_medium** and **obj_asteroid_large** with their corresponding sounds.

FINAL STEP: Open the **room_game** and under **Settings**, change the speed to **60**. **Save and play the game**.

Congratulations! You've just created your first video game using GameMaker: Studio. Included in the Game Assets folder is a subfolder titled "Modifications." This folder includes additional game assets which you can use to experiment with modifying your game.

Resource

"GameMaker: Coordinate System and Sprite Origins." YouTube. Accessed March 15, 2015. https://www.youtube.com/watch?v=HbJV5W9wYSg.

Multi-Level Games

Learning Objectives—Upon completion of Chapter 3 readers will be able to:

- Incorporate transporters that navigate to additional levels
- Create additional levels
- Incorporate puzzle design elements to their game
- Program Artificial Intelligence (AI) behavior
- Use tile sets to add objects to their game
- Show the player how to play the game without using text directions
- Modify their game using game objects, sound files, and graphics provided

Project Overview: *Lost Dog*

There is nothing worse than being lost, especially when you are a little puppy that has wandered too far from home. In the game *Lost Dog* which we are about to create, the player is a small dog trying to find its way home. The dog will journey through a haunted graveyard as well as a mysterious underground cavern before finding its way home. Although we will only be creating two levels for this game, the concept could allow designers to create many different types of strange levels that the dog must navigate through before making it home.

Through creation of this game, readers will learn how to create multi-level games and incorporate simple puzzle elements into their game to make it more challenging. This chapter will also introduce artificial intelligence programming as we add ghosts to the graveyard and have them patrol certain areas. The player must recognize the patrol patterns in order to avoid touching the ghost—which would spell certain doom for our little dog. While working through the previous chapter, each step was listed out in full detail, however, now that we are starting to understand the GameMaker interface, the instructions will be slightly less detailed in order for readers to gain confidence in their developing game-building skills and allowing for a little creative freedom in the design process. Download the Lost Dog assets from the GameMaker Standard website at www.thegamemakerstandard.com/lostdog. After downloading the assets folder read over the updates.pdf document which contains any changes since the publication of this book. We will start making our game by creating a new project, just as we did for our previous game.

Creating a New Project and Importing Assets

Step 1: Click the **New** tab to create a new project and name it: **Lost_Dog.**

Step 2: Click the **Create** button and drag the images from the downloaded Lost Dog Sprite folder into the GameMaker window.

Step 3: Select the **Sprite** option for all images.

Step 4: Rename the images accordingly so they appear similar to those found in **Figure 3.1**.

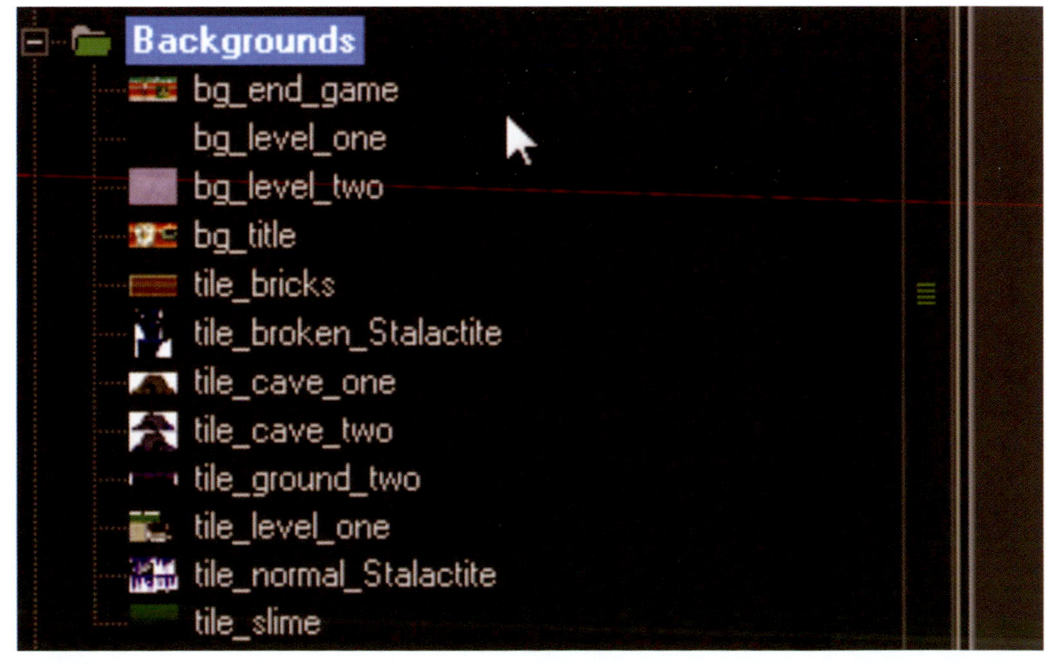

FIGURE 3.1

Our dog will appear differently depending on what the player is doing. When the dog is standing still the **idle** sprite of the dog will be visible. When the dog is running the **running** sprite animation will replace the idle sprite. The same type of state switch will occur when the dog is jumping and when the dog dies.

Setting up the Player Character Animations

Step 1: Double click on **spr_dog_idle, spr_dead, spr_dog_jumping**, and **spr_dog_running**.

Step 2: Click the **Modify Mask** option.

Step 3: Make sure all the sprites have the **Shape** set to **Rectangle** and the **Bounding Box** set to **Manual**. Then set the following.

Left: 9
Right: 73
Top: 4
Bottom: 55

Step 4: Click the **Center** button on each sprite then click **OK**.

FIGURE 3.2

FIGURE 3.3

As we found out when creating our previous game, sprites are simply graphics that do not do anything. In order for our dog to do anything other than stand still we need to create an object that we can add our sprites to. Objects tell the sprites how they should appear and act.

Create the Dog Object

Step 1: Right click on the **Objects** folder and select **Create Object**.

Step 2: Name the object: **obj_collider** and set its sprite to **spr_collider**. Check the **Solid** box then click **OK**.

Step 3: Create a new object and name it **obj_dog.**

Step 4: Set its sprite to **spr_dog_idle**.

We will now create an event that will allow our dog to move left and right on the screen. While the dog will appear to be moving, GameMaker will be checking to see if there are any objects our player would collide with. If there is a solid object immediately in front of where the dog is moving, the dog will collide with the object and will not be able to continue moving in that particular direction.

Moving the Dog Left and Right

Step 1: With **obj_dog** open, click **Add Event** and choose **Keyboard <Left>.**

Step 2: Click the **Control** tab and drag a **Check Object** Action into the **Actions** panel. Set the following:

Object: obj_collider
x: −4
y: 0
Check both the **Relative** box and the **NOT** box.

This makes sure the **obj_collider** object is not four spaces to the left of the player.

Step 3: Click the **Move** tab and drag a **Jump to Position** Action under the **Check Object** Action we just created. Set the following

x: −4
y: 0
Relative: checked

Step 4: Click **Add Event** and choose **Keyboard <Right>**

Step 5: Repeat the previous four steps except make the **x: 4** instead of **−4** for both actions. Your Events will look similar to **Figure 3.4**.

Step 6: Click **OK** to exit the **obj_dog**.

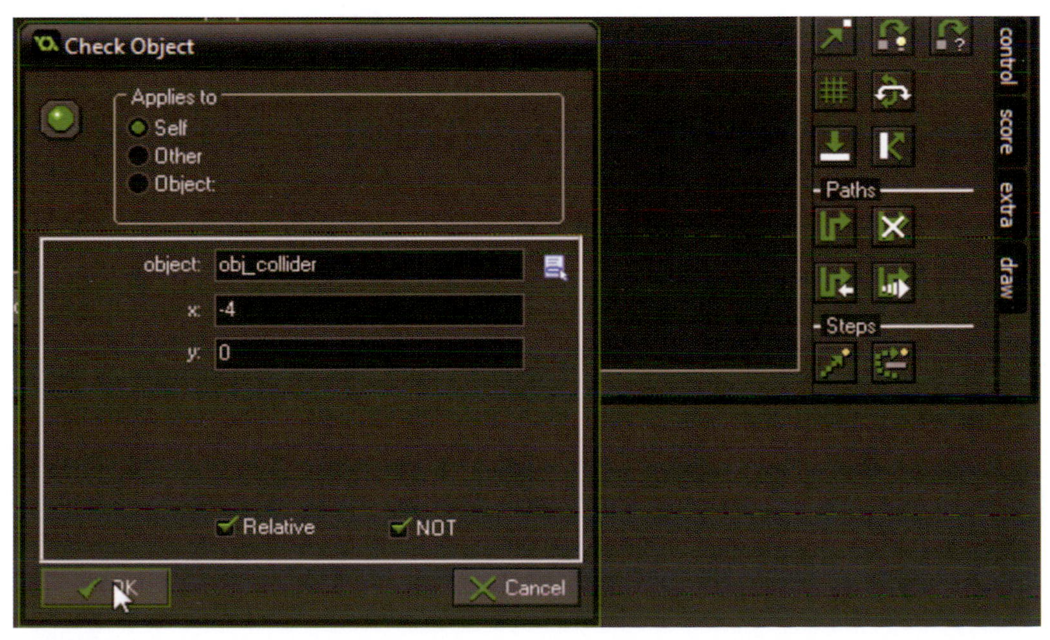

FIGURE 3.4

Creating the First Level

Step 1: Create a new room.

Step 2: Click the Settings tab.

Step 3: For this game we're going to use a Width of **1024**, and a Height of **544** and a Speed of **60**. To do this set the following:

Name: room_level_one
Width: 1024
Height: 544
Speed: 60

Adding the Dog to the Environment

Step 1: Click the **Objects** tab.

Step 2: Select the **obj_dog** as shown in **Figure 3.5**.

Step 3: Place the dog in the middle of the room.

Step 4: Select the **obj_collider**.

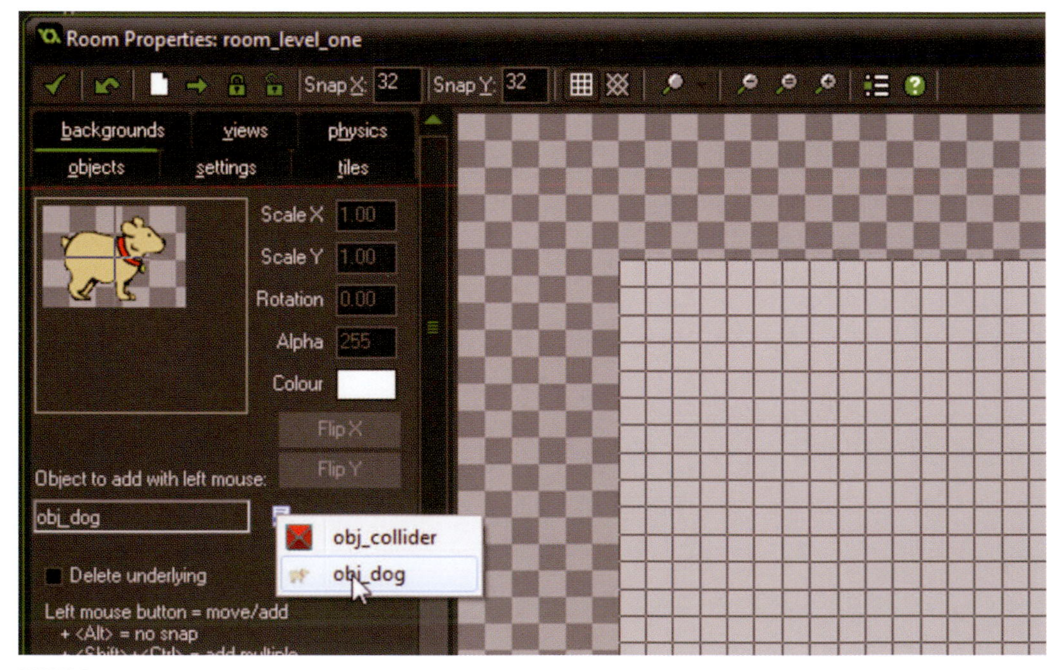

FIGURE 3.5

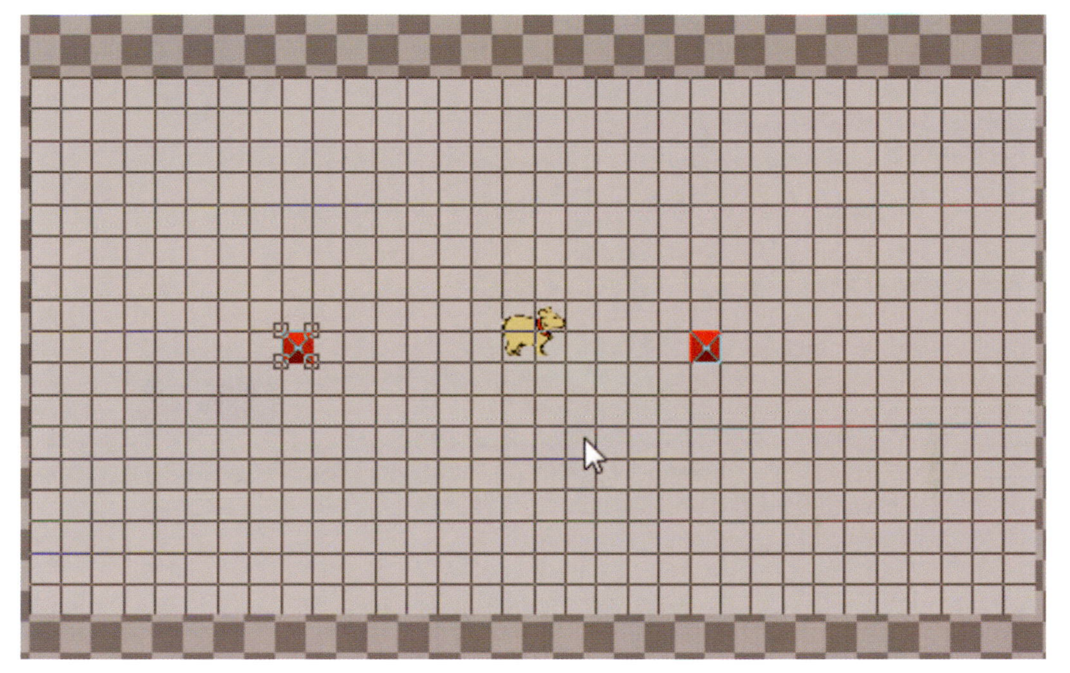

FIGURE 3.6

Step 5: Place one **obj_collider** a short distance in front of the dog and another behind the dog similar to those shown in **Figure 3.6**.

Step 6: Select the **green check** at the top left of the room window.

Testing Character Movement

Step 1: Click the **green** arrow at the top of the screen to run the game.

As you press the left and right keys the dog should slide left and right. With the object colliders in place the dog should stop when it touches the two red squares. We have not added the run animation yet so do not be surprised when your dog appears to be sliding back and forth as if it were wearing roller skates. We will be adding the run animation shortly.

Step 2: Close the window.

Thanks to gravity, what goes up must come down, at least that is our plan once we add gravity to the environment. By adding gravity to the level the dog will return to the ground in a natural way after jumping. Without gravity the dog would continue to float away when jumping. Although this would be fun to witness it would make for a very short game.

Adding Gravity to the Dog

Step 1: Open the obj_dog.

Step 2: Click **Add Event** and choose **Step** and then **Step** again.

Step 3: Select the control tab and drag a **Check Empty** Action into the Actions box. Set the following:

x: 0
y: 1
Objects: Only Solid
Relative: Checked

Step 4: Click **OK**.

Step 5: Select the Move tab and drag a **Set Gravity** Action into the Actions window. Set the following:

Direction: 270
Gravity: 0.5

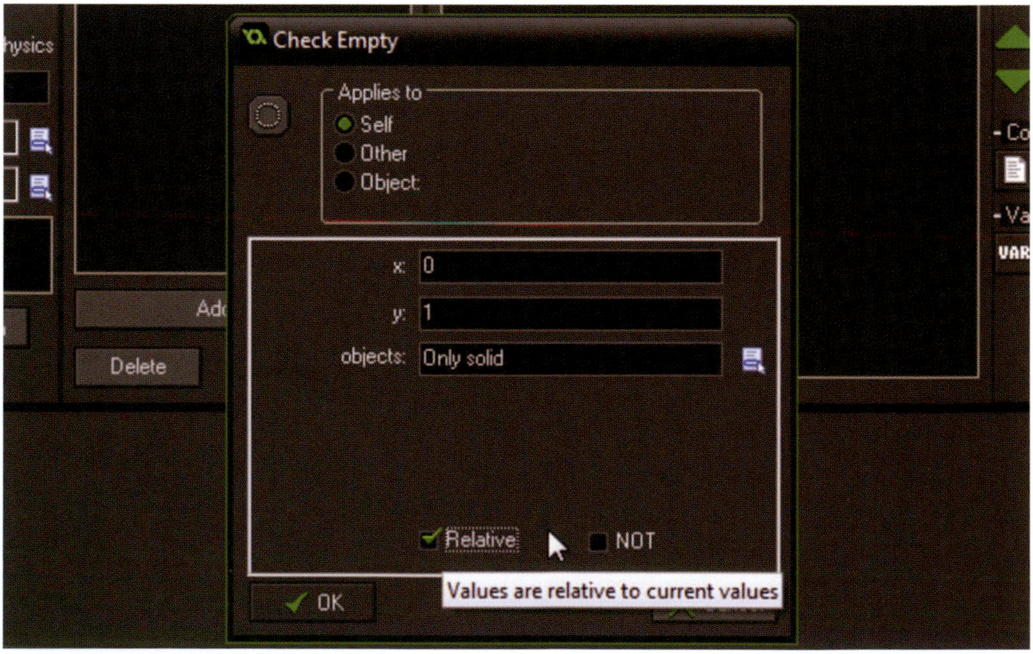

FIGURE 3.7

FIGURE 3.8

Step 6: Click back on the Control tab and drag an **Else** Action into the Actions window beneath the **Set Gravity** Action we just added.

Step 7: Click back to the **Move** tab and add another **Set Gravity** Action below the **Else** Action and set the following:

Direction: 270
Gravity: 0

Making the Dog Fall

Step 1: Select **Add Event** and choose **Collision** and select **obj_colider**.

Step 2: Under the **Move** tab in the **Jump** section drag a **Move to Contact** Action into the Actions window. Set the following:

Direction: direction
Maximum: sprite_height
Against: solid objects

FIGURE 3.9

Step 3: Under the same Move tab drag a **Speed Vertical** Action under the **Move to Contact** Action we had just added. Set the following:

Vert. Speed: 0

Step 4: Click **OK** on the dog object.

Step 5: Open the room_level_one.

Step 6: Click the **Objects** tab and choose the **obj_collider.**

Step 7: Place an obj_collider under the dog and another a short distance in front as depicted in **Figure 3.10**.

Step 8: Click the **green check** on the room to run the game.

Using your arrow keys move the dog to the right. As the dog moves to the right of the screen it should move along the colliders and fall down. Do not feel bad when the dog falls down; we have not added any damage to the game so the dog cannot feel anything. Now it is time to make the dog jump so that it can avoid obstacles we place in front of it.

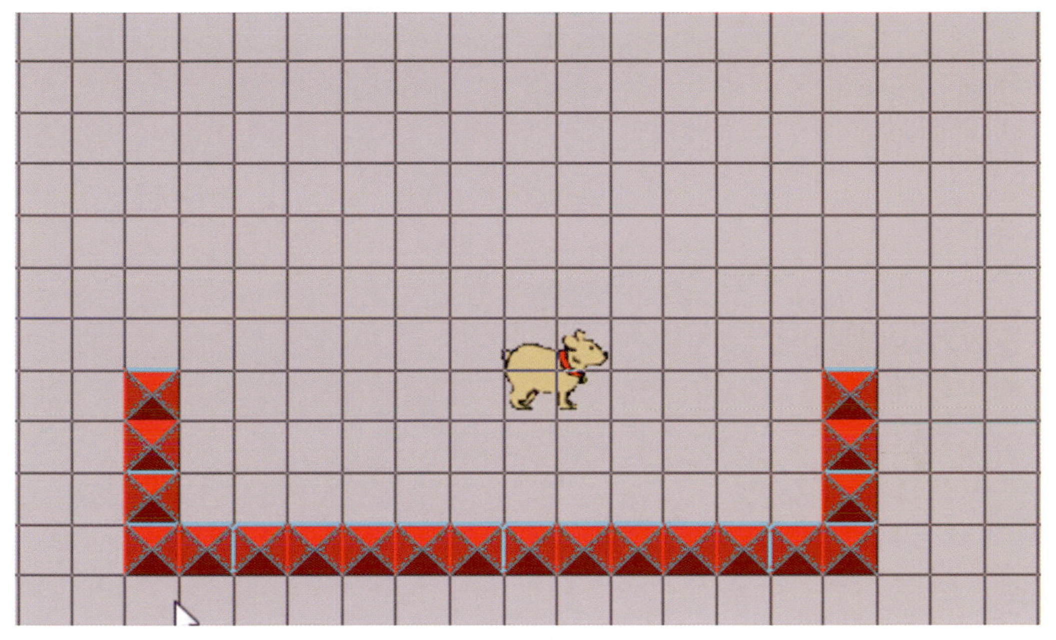

FIGURE 3.10

Making the Dog Jump

Step 1: Reopen **obj_dog.**

Step 2: Click **Add Event** and select **Key Press <Up>**

Step 3: Choose the **Control** tab and drag a **Check Empty** Action into the Actions window. Set the following:

x: 0
y: 1
Objects: only solid
Relative: checked NOT: checked

This will check to make sure one space under the dog has a solid object.

Step 4: Click the **Move** tab and drag a **Speed Vertical** Action under the **Check Empty** Action we just added. Set the following:

Vert. speed: −12

Step 5: Click **OK** on the **obj_dog**.

Step 6: Open room_level_one and arrange a series of obj_colliders like those shown in **Figure 3.12**.

Step 7: Run the game.

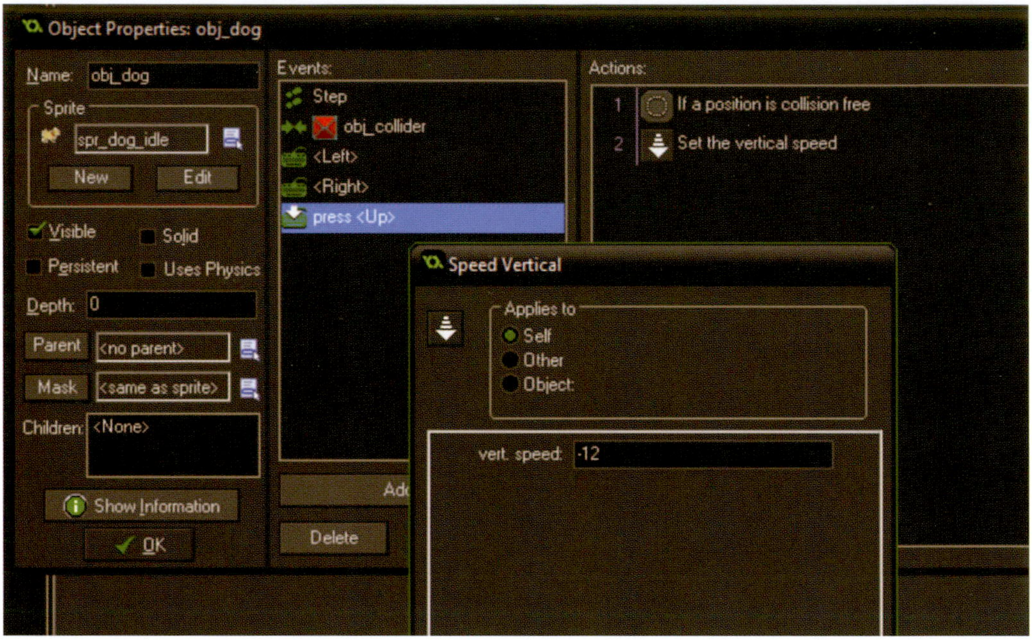

FIGURE 3.11

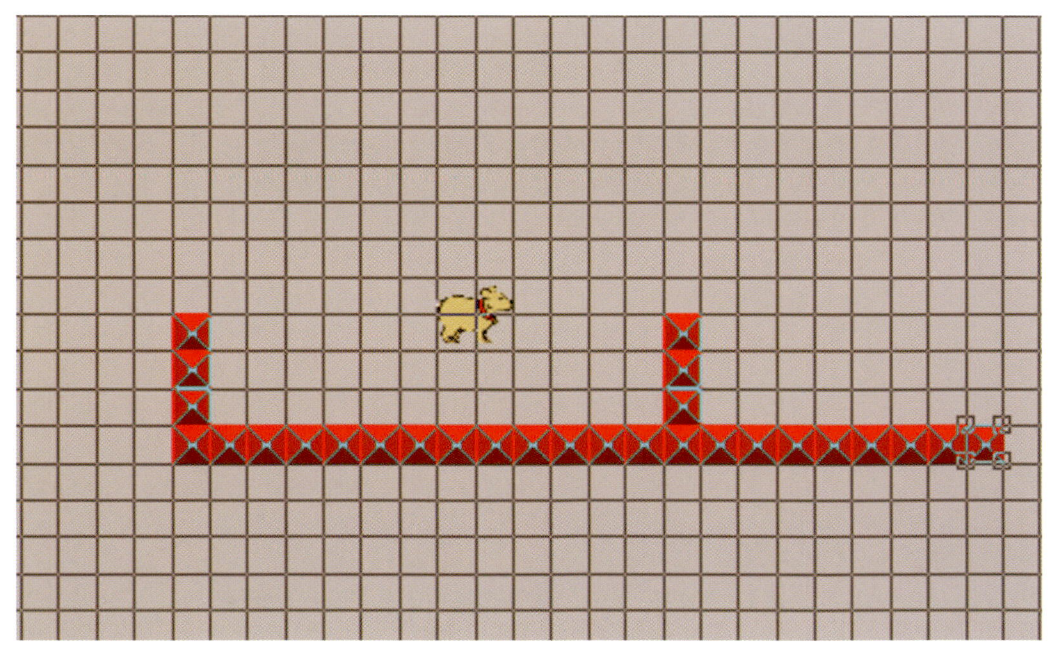

FIGURE 3.12

Press the up key while moving to test the new jump mechanic. The dog should not move up vertically. Our dog looks a bit silly sliding around and hopping without moving its legs. It is time to add running and jumping animations.

Adding a Running Animation to the Dog

Step 1: Open the **obj_dog.**

Step 2: Click the **<Left>** Event.

Step 3: Under the **Control** tab in the **Variables** section, drag a **Test Variable** Action under the **Jump to Position** Action. Set the following for the **Test Variable** Action:

Variable: sprite_index
Value: spr_dog_running
Operation: equal to
NOT = checked

This will test to see if the dog is currently using the running sprite, if the dog is not, then the next action will execute.

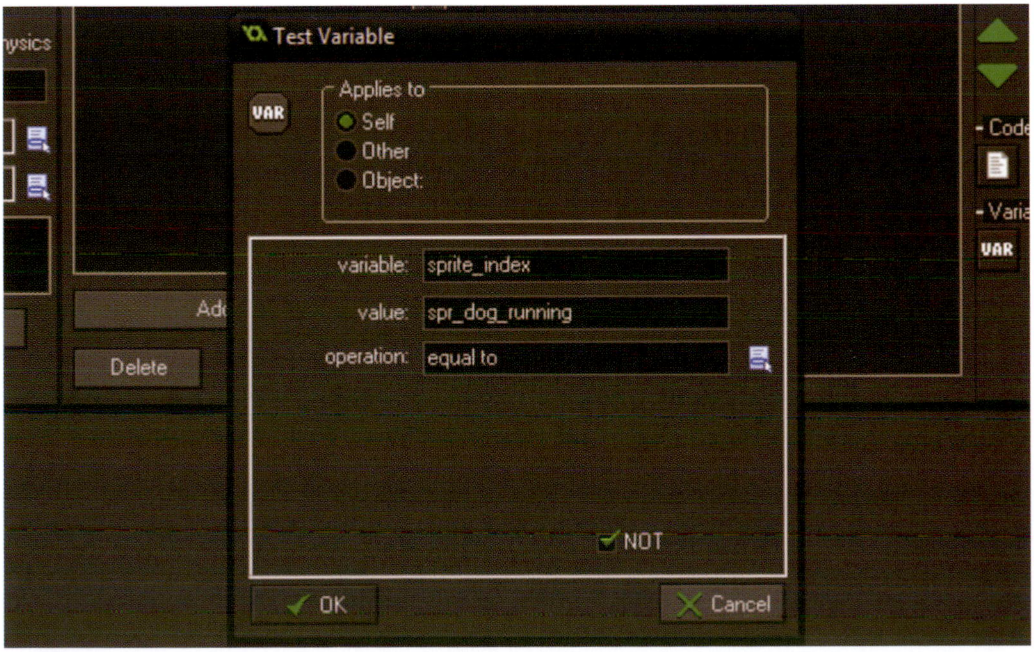

FIGURE 3.13

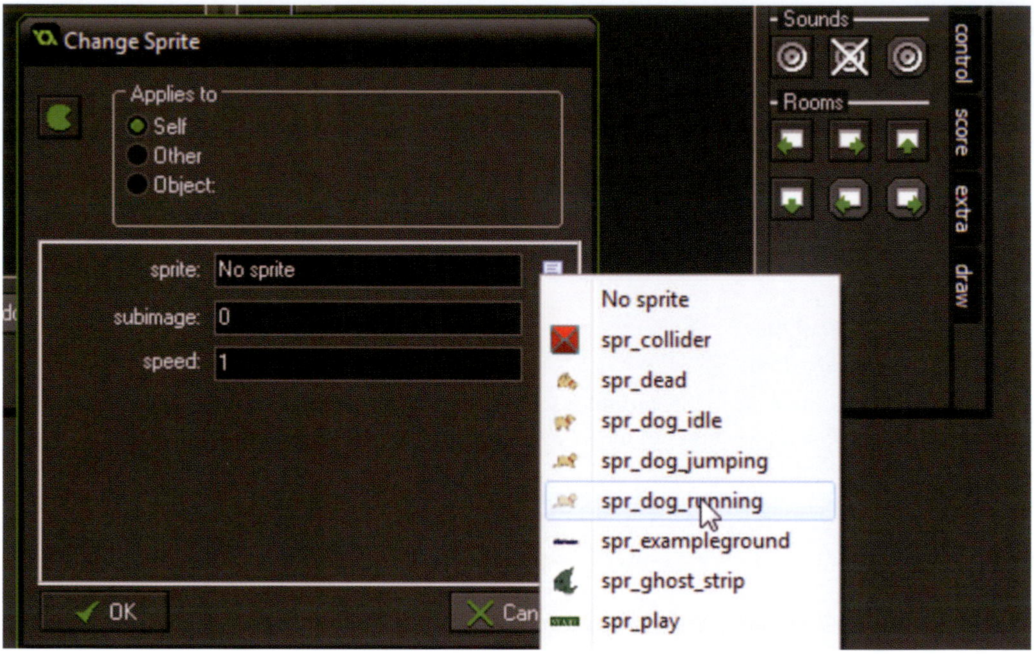

FIGURE 3.14

Step 4: Under the **Main1** tab in the **Sprite** section, drag a **Change Sprite** Action below the **Test Variable** Action we just created. Set the following for the **Change Sprite** Action:

Sprite: spr_dog_running
Subimage: 0
Speed: 1

Now GameMaker will check to see if the dog is not currently using the sprite **spr_dog_running** animation while the left key is pressed. If the dog is not using the **spr_dog_running** animation, GameMaker will tell it to.

Step 5: Repeat the previous steps in the **<Right>** Event.

Oh dear, now the dog won't stop running. This is probably how the dog got lost in the first place. We need to fix this.

Stopping the Dog from Running

Step 1: Open the **obj_dog** if it's not already open.

Step 2: Click the **Add Event** and choose **Key Release <Left>**

Step 3: Drag a **Change Sprite** Action into the Actions window and set the following:

Sprite: spr_dog_idle
Subimage: 0
Speed: 0

This will change the dog sprite back into **spr_dog_idle** when the left key is released.

Step 4: Click **Add Event** and select **Key Release <Right>**

Step 5: Drag a **Change Sprite** Action into the Actions window and set the following:

Settings for the change sprite:

Sprite: spr_dog_idle
Subimage: 0
Speed: 0

Now when the right key is released it will also change the dog back to idle. Although our dog can now run and stop, the poor thing still cannot turn around. It is time to allow our dog to run facing the right direction in addition to the left.

Turning the Dog Around

Step 1: Open **obj_dog** if it is not already open.

Step 2: Click the **<Left>** Event.

Step 3: In the **Control** tab drag a **Test Variable** Action under the other four actions already there. Set the following:

Variable: image_xscale
Value: 1
Operation: equal to

Step 4: In the **Main1** tab drag a **Transform Sprite** Action under the **Check Variable** and set the following for the **Transform Sprite**:

xscale: −1
yscale: 1
Angel: 0
Mirroring: no mirroring

Step 5: Click the **<Right>** Event.

Step 6: Under the **Control** tab drag a **Check Variable** Action under the other four actions and set the following:

Variable: image_xscale
Value: −1
Operation: equal to

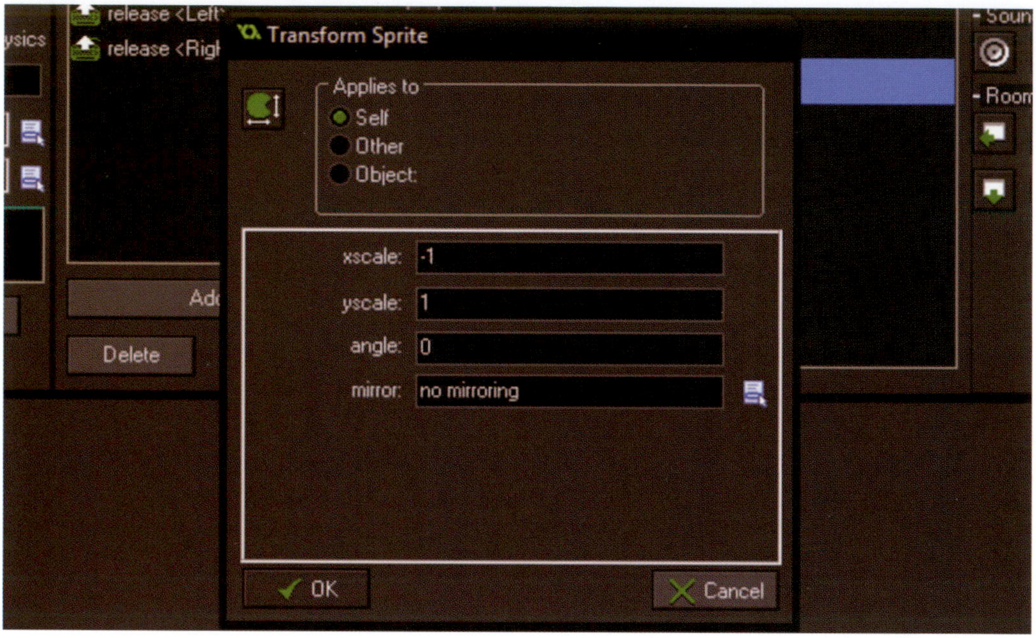

FIGURE 3.15

Step 7: In the **Main1** tab drag a **Transform Sprite** Action under the **Check Variable** and set the following for the **Transform Sprite**:

xscale: 1
yscale: 1
Angel: 0
Mirroring: no mirroring

This will flip the dog sprite horizontally so when the dog is moving toward the right the dog will be facing the right of the screen. Now we need to add a jump animation to the dog so that it does not appear that the dog is running through the air.

Adding a Jump Animation

Step 1: Open **obj_dog.**

Step 2: Click the **Step** Event and drag a **Change Sprite** Action in between the **Set the Gravity** and **Else** Actions. Set the following for the **Change Sprite** Action:

Sprite: spr_dog_jumping
Subimage: 0
Speed: 0

Step 3: Under the **Control** tab look for what looks like a green up arrow. This is a start block. Drag the **Start of a Block** Action between the **if position is collision free** and first **Set the Gravity** Actions.

Step 4: Look for what looks like a green arrow pointing downward. This is an end block. Drag the **End of a Block** between the **Change sprite into spr_dog_jumping** and the **Else** Actions. Your screen should now look similar to **Figure 3.16**.

Step 5: Click the **Collision** Event with **obj_collider.**

Step 6: In the **Control** tab drag a **Test Expression** below the **Set the Vertical Speed** and set the following:

Setting for the Test Expression:

> Expression: keyboard_check(vk_left) || keyboard_check(vk_right)
> NOT = checked
>
> This expression will check if the left or right keyboard keys are being pressed. The ||characters means **or** in programming language.

Step 7: Drag a **Change Sprite** below the **Test Expression** and set the following:

> Sprite: spr_dog_idle
> Subimage: 0
> Speed: 0

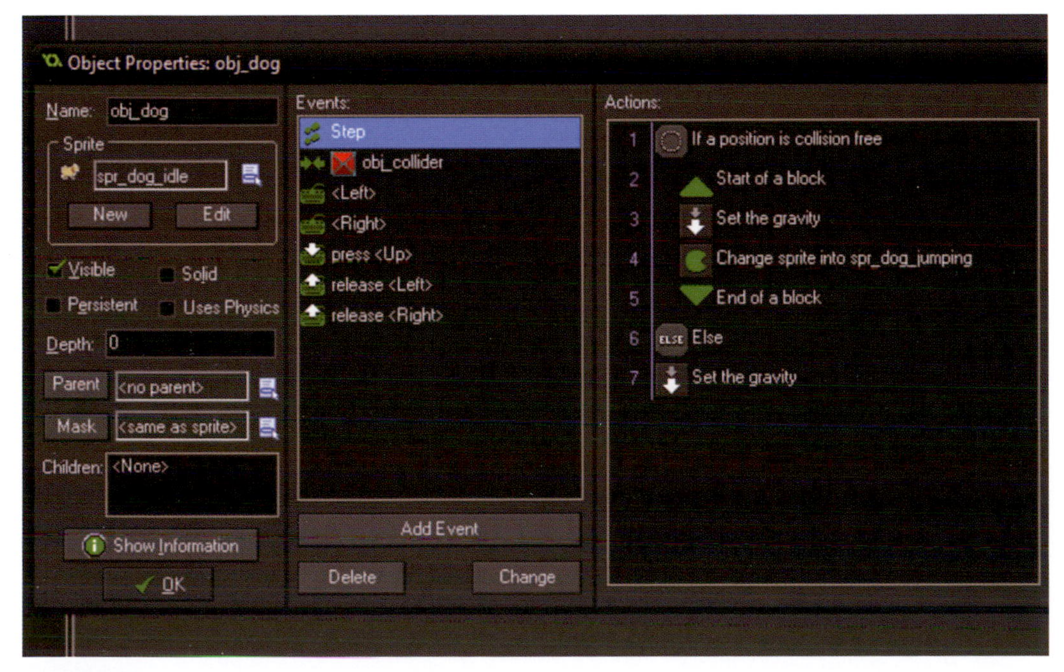

FIGURE 3.16

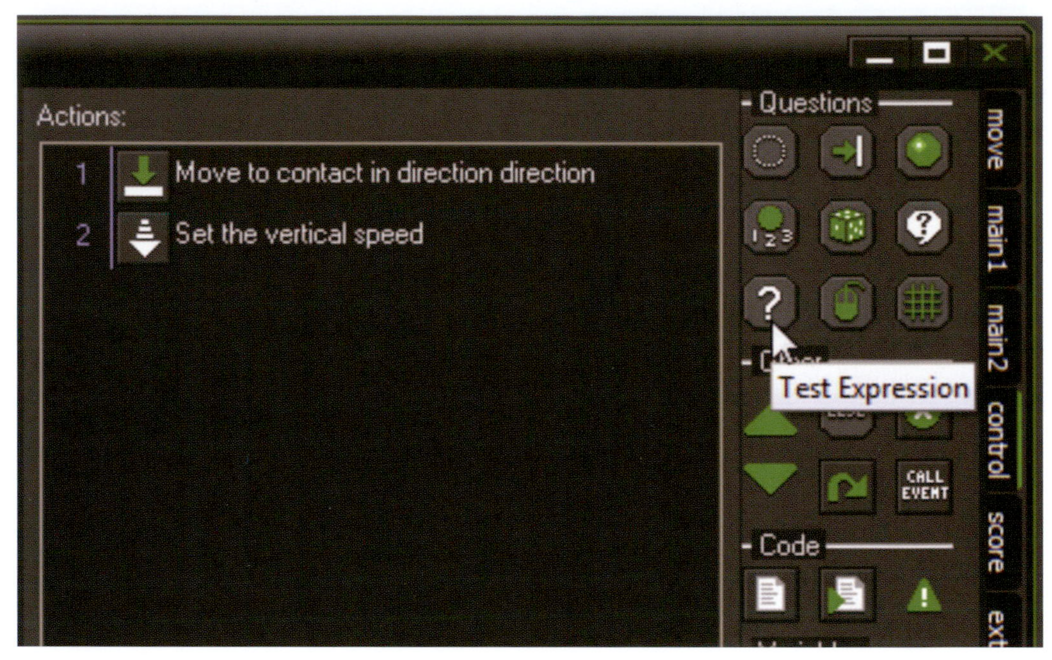

FIGURE 3.17

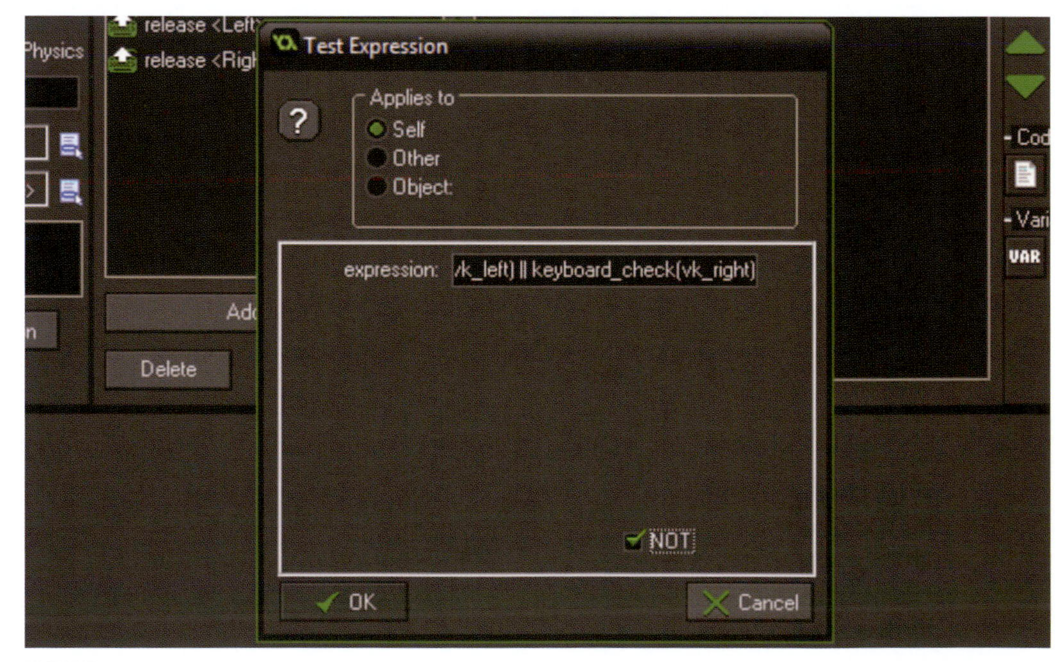

FIGURE 3.18

If we play the game now, the dog will run, jump, and sit idle as it should. The dog will be able to face both directions, run in both directions, and jump in both directions with the appropriate animations visible during each action. Our dog is now ready to begin its journey home, which means it is time for us to create the first level.

Adding Scenery to Level One

Step 1: Locate the *Lost Dog* assets folder you downloaded earlier and open the background folder. Just as we did with our sprites at the beginning of this chapter we need to drag all the images into the GameMaker window. Set all the images as backgrounds and name them so they appear similar to **Figure 3.19**.

Step 2: Open the **tile_level_one** background and click the block that reads **Use as tile set**.

Step 3: Click **OK**.

Step 4: Open **room_level_one**.

Step 5: Click the **Tiles** tab at the top and click the word that reads **<undefined>** and select **tile_level_one.**

Step 6: Click the top left corner of the grass section on the tile set, then hold down the Shift key on your keyboard and drag the mouse down to the bottom right corner of the grass section to select it.

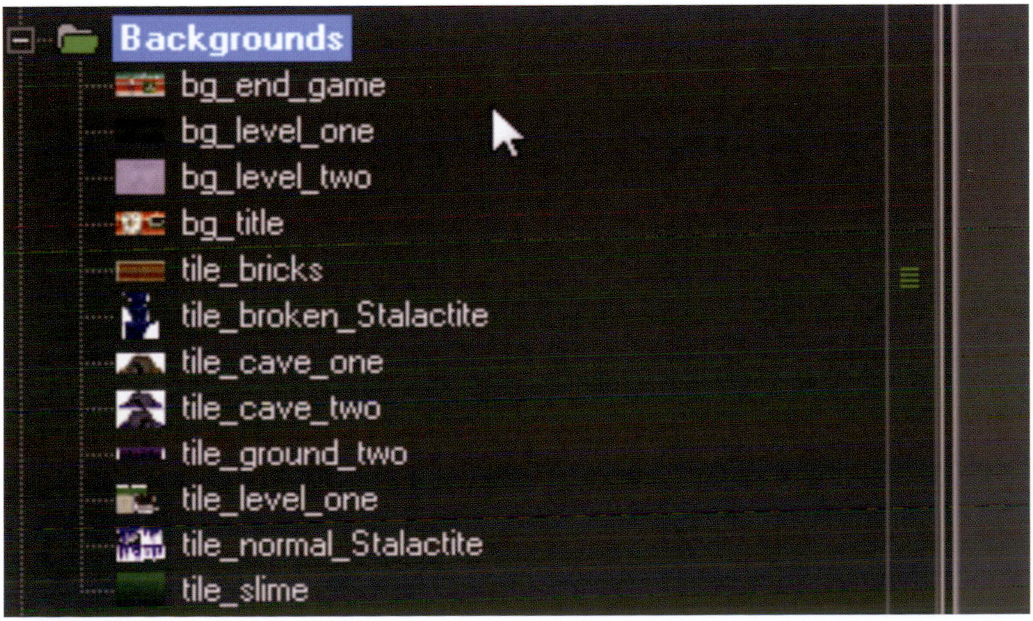

FIGURE 3.19

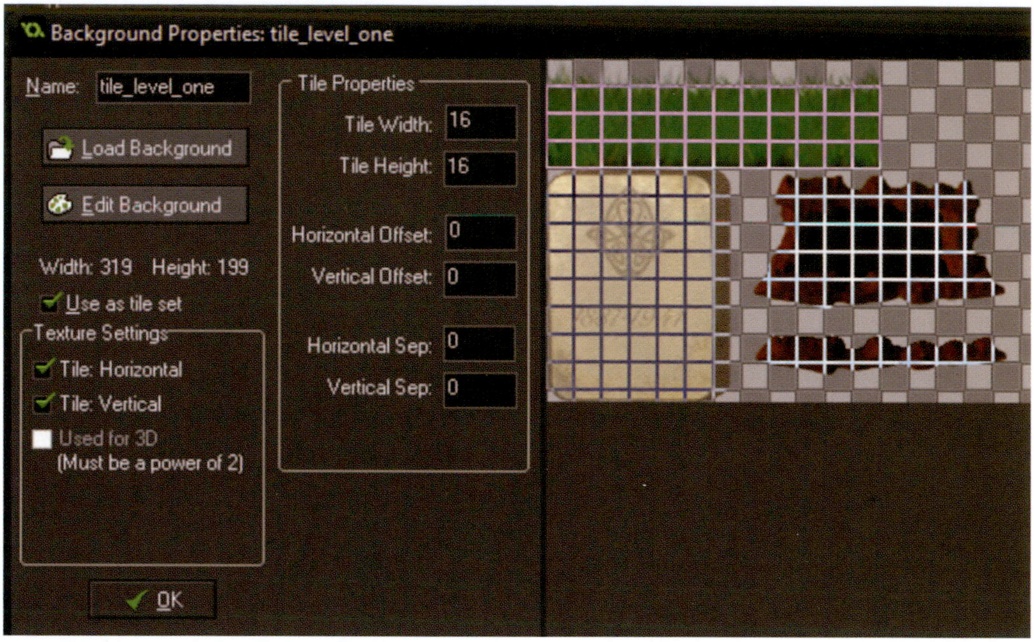

FIGURE 3.20

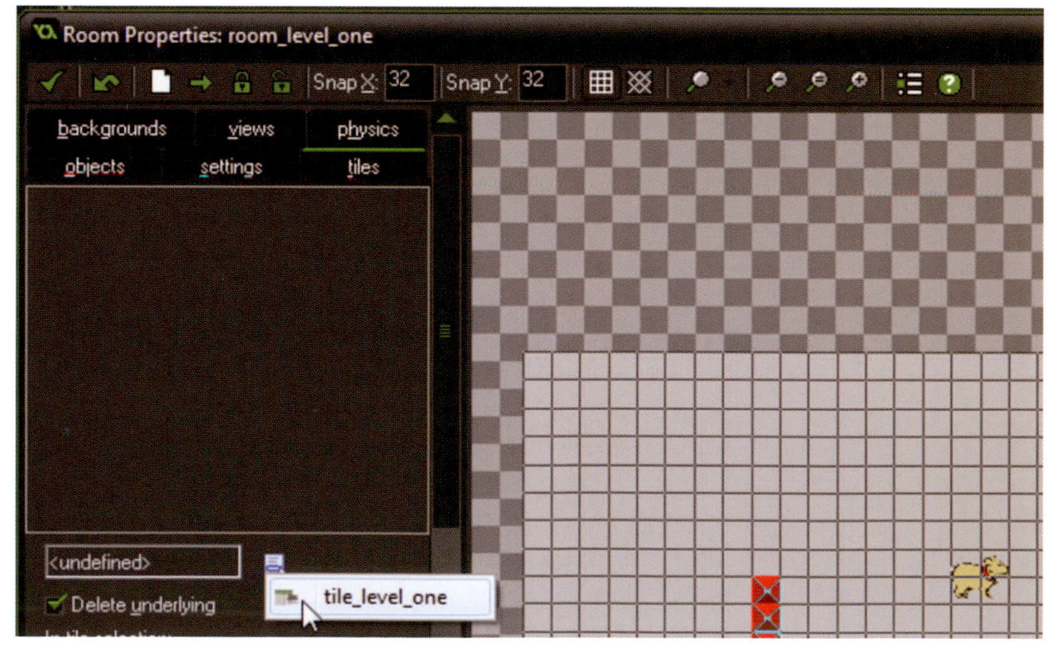

FIGURE 3.21

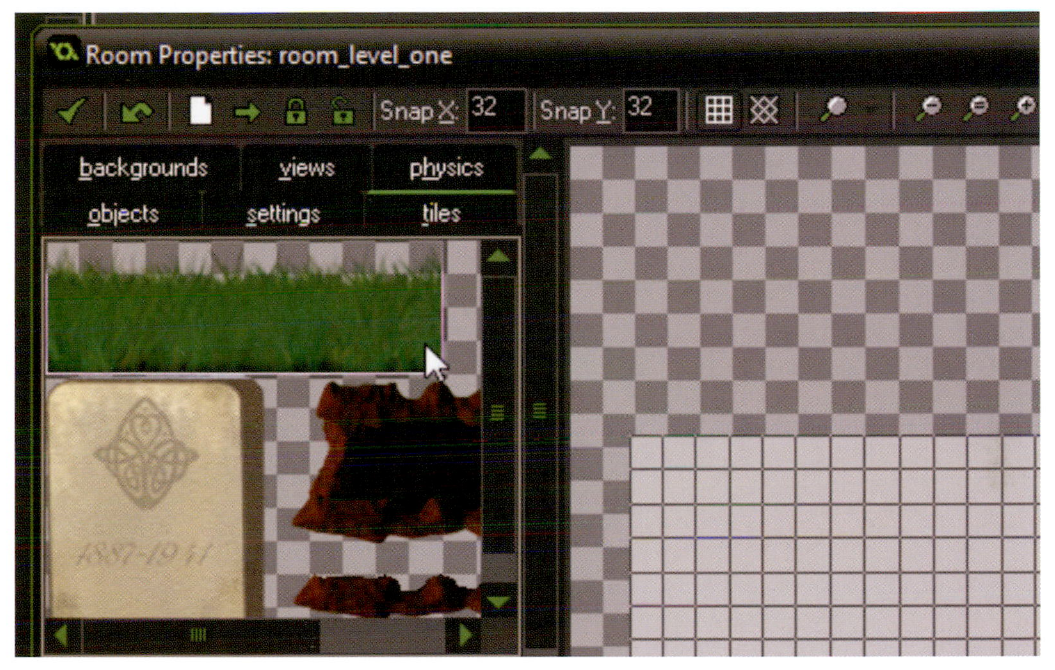

FIGURE 3.22

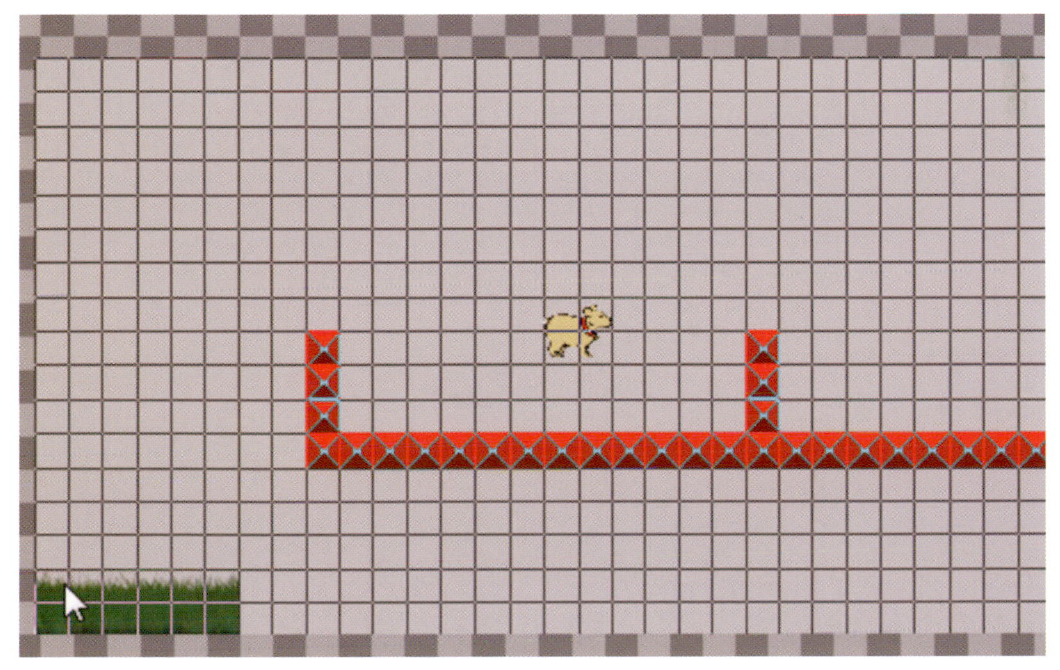

FIGURE 3.23

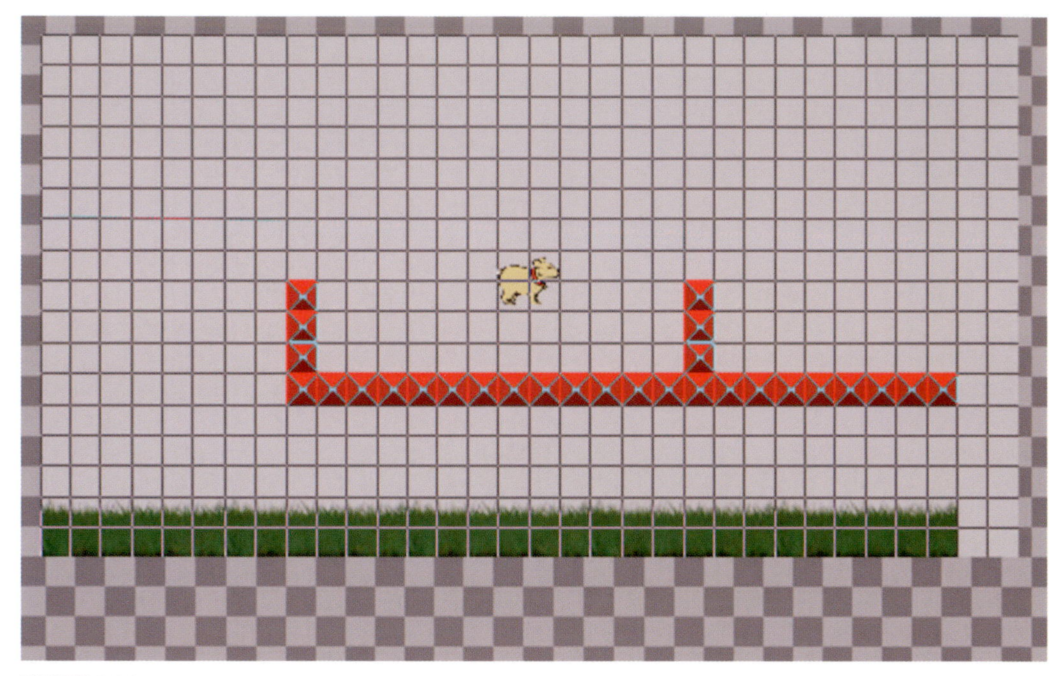

FIGURE 3.24

Step 7: Release the Shift key and click on the bottom left corner of the game room. This will place the grass tile into the level as shown in **Figure 3.23**.

Step 8: Continue placing grass tiles until the bottom of the screen looks similar to **Figure 3.24**.

Currently the grass tiles we placed in the game are not solid objects. We want our dog to be able to walk on the grass rather than in front of it or behind it. In order to make the grass solid we will need to place object colliders on the grass. The object colliders will appear as red boxes. This helps us to know where we have placed the colliders and where others are needed. We will eventually make these colliders invisible so they will not be seen during actual game play.

Making Image Tiles into Solid Objects

Step 1: Click the **Objects** tab and make sure **obj_collider** is selected.

Step 2: Place the object colliders along the grass similar to those shown in **Figure 3.25**. You can hold the Ctrl key and Shift while dragging to place multiple objects.

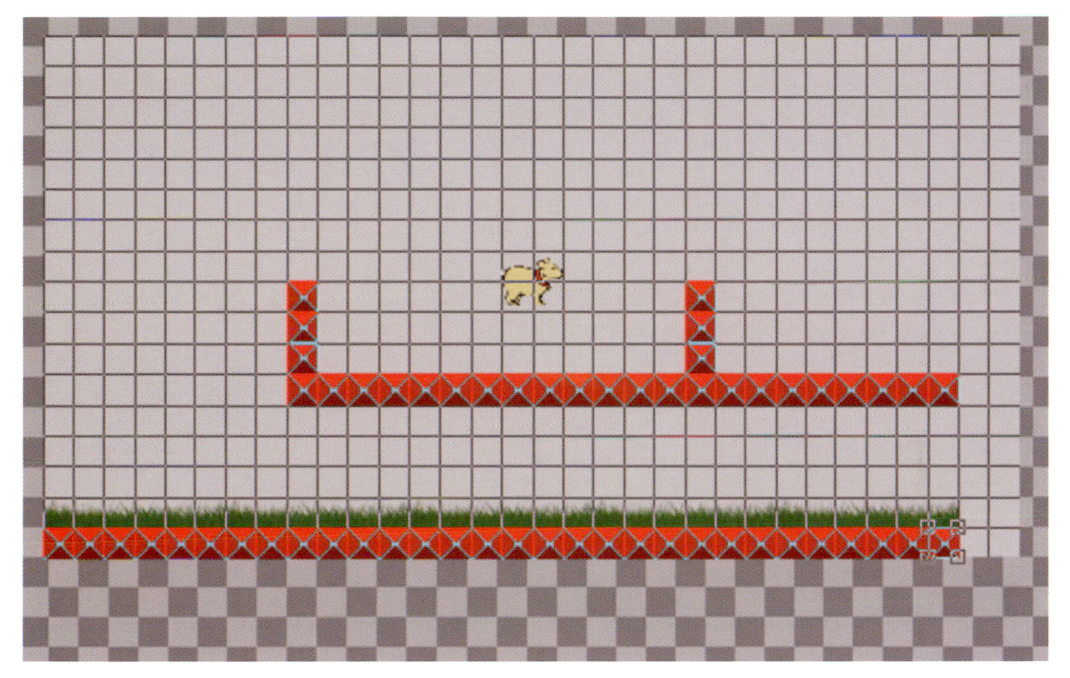

FIGURE 3.25

Step 3: Delete the **obj_colliders** that are floating in the air. You can hold the Shift key and use the right mouse button while dragging to delete objects faster.

If you play the game now you will notice that the red boxes are currently visible during game play. We will now make the object collider boxes invisible so that it appears that the dog is walking on top of the grass.

Step 4: Open **obj_collider.**

Step 5: Uncheck the checkbox labeled **Visible**.

Our dog is very happy to have a nice grassy path to run along, however, our level is not very long at the moment so the dog cannot go very far. We are going to increase the horizontal size of the level. If we were to play the game immediately after doing this, it would appear that the dog is very small in comparison to the level since we would see the entire level at once. We will later change the way the camera works so that the camera will follow the dog and the level will scroll to the right. This will allow us to create a large level while still allowing the dog to appear close up on the screen.

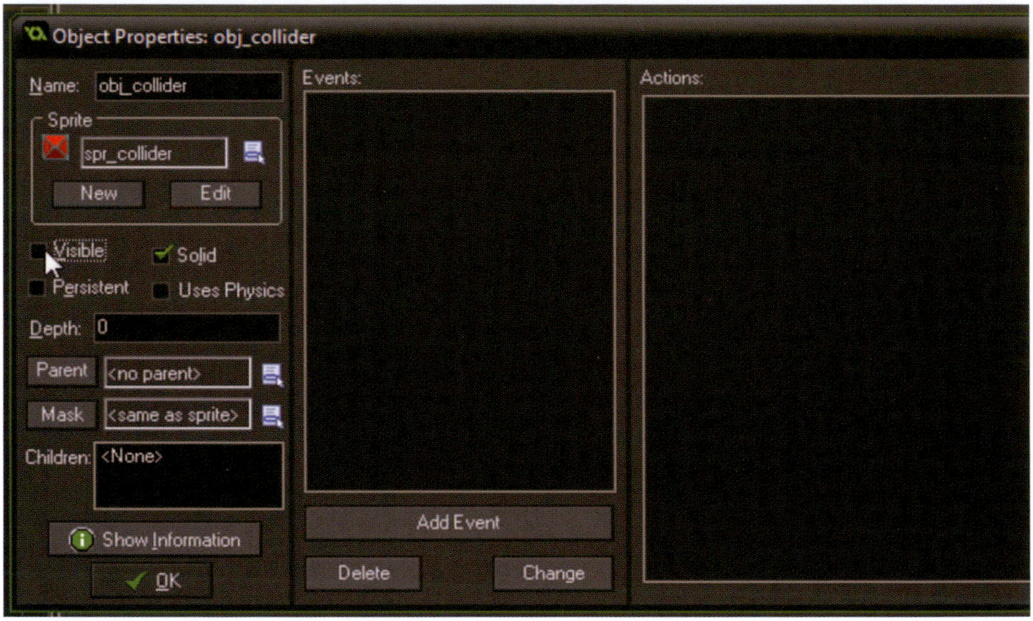

FIGURE 3.26

Adjusting Level Horizontal Dimensions

Step 1: Open room_level_one.

Step 2: Click the **Settings** tab.

Step 3: Change the width to **4800.**

Step 4: Select the **View** tab.

Step 5: Click **Enable the use of views** so it is checked. Set the view tab settings as follows:

Visible when room starts: checked
View in room:
x: 0 W: 1024
y: 0 H: 544
Port on screen:
x: 0 W: 1024
y: 0 H: 544
Object Following:
Obj_dog
Hbor: 512 Hsp: –1
Vbor: 32 Vsp: –1

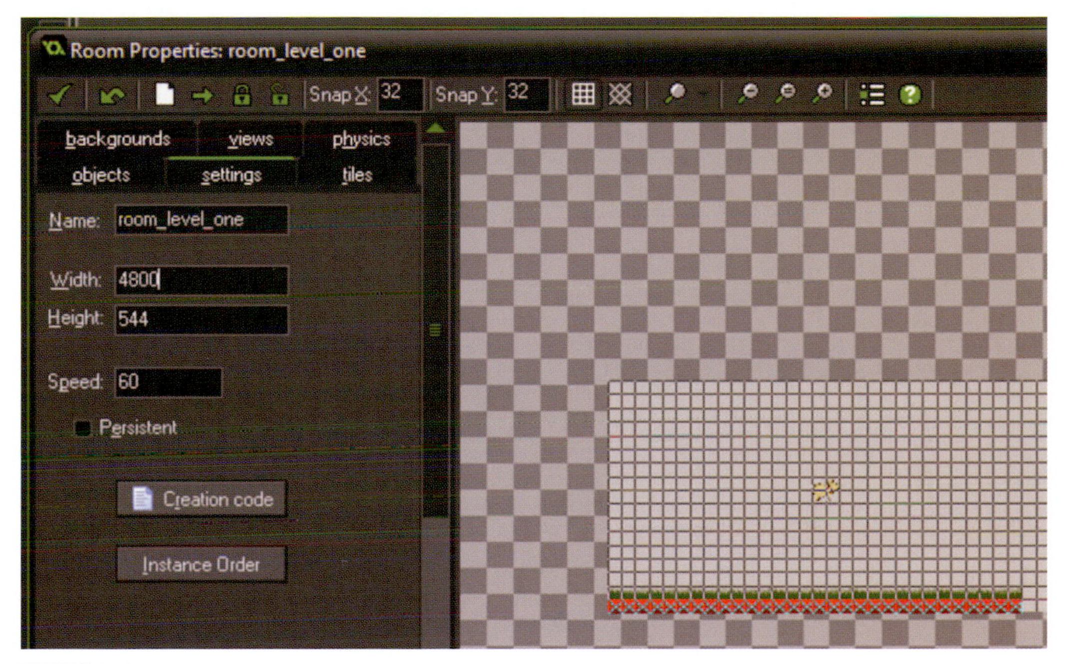

FIGURE 3.27

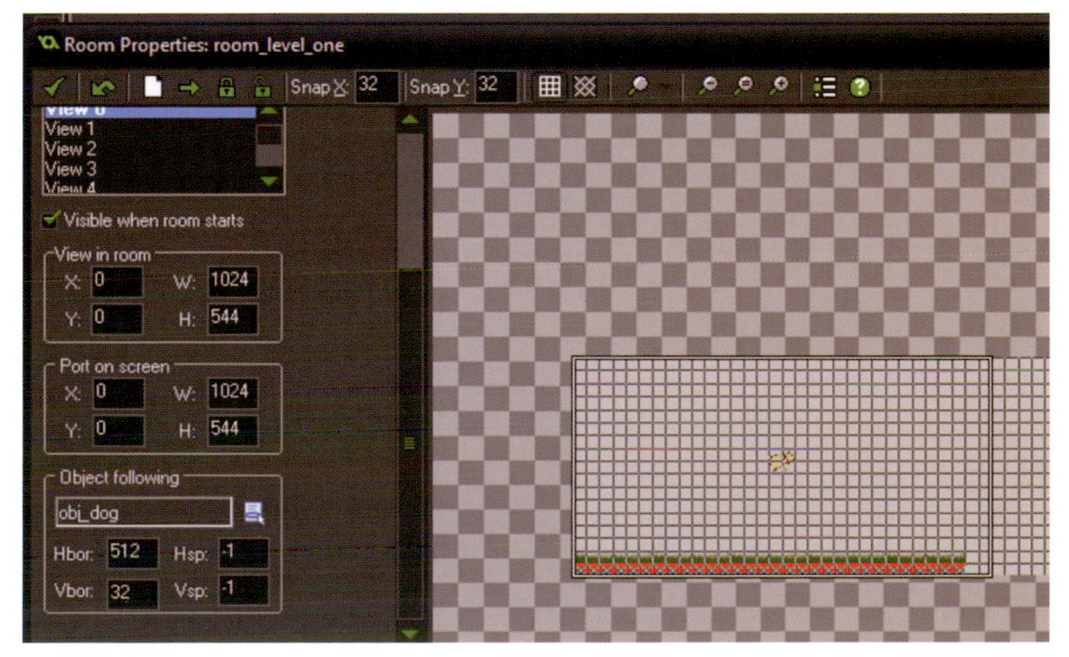

FIGURE 3.28

Now when we run the game we can see that as the dog reaches the center of the screen, the camera, or viewpoint of the player, will follow it. This allows the player to always see the playable character, in this case the dog, and the rest of the game objects scroll from right to left as the dog runs to the left. This is why this type of game is called a side-scroller. Now we need to populate our game with some obstacles for the dog to overcome.

Incorporating Obstacles

Step 1: Go back to the **Tiles** tab and fill out the rest of the level with grass.

Step 2: Now let's place some graves for the player to fall into. Under the **Tiles** tab, uncheck the **Delete Underlying** option.

Step 3: Select the **Add** button below the **Current tile layer:** box.

In order for the hole to show in front of the grass we will need to place it on a layer closer to the viewer. Items in GameMaker that have a higher number depth are located closer to the viewer and those with a lower number depth or a negative number depth are farther away. For example, if we wanted our dog to walk in front of a tree, we might have the tree set for a depth of zero and set the dog with the depth of five. If we reversed those numbers, the dog would appear to walk behind the tree.

Step 4: Type **1000** into the box labeled **Depth** and hit **OK**.

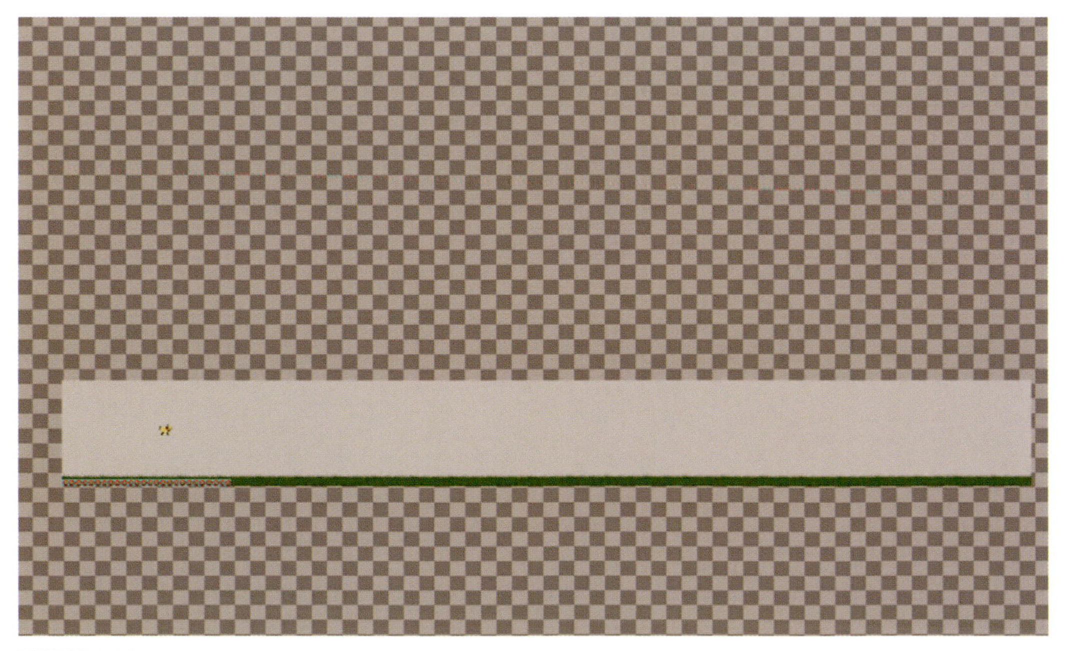

FIGURE 3.29

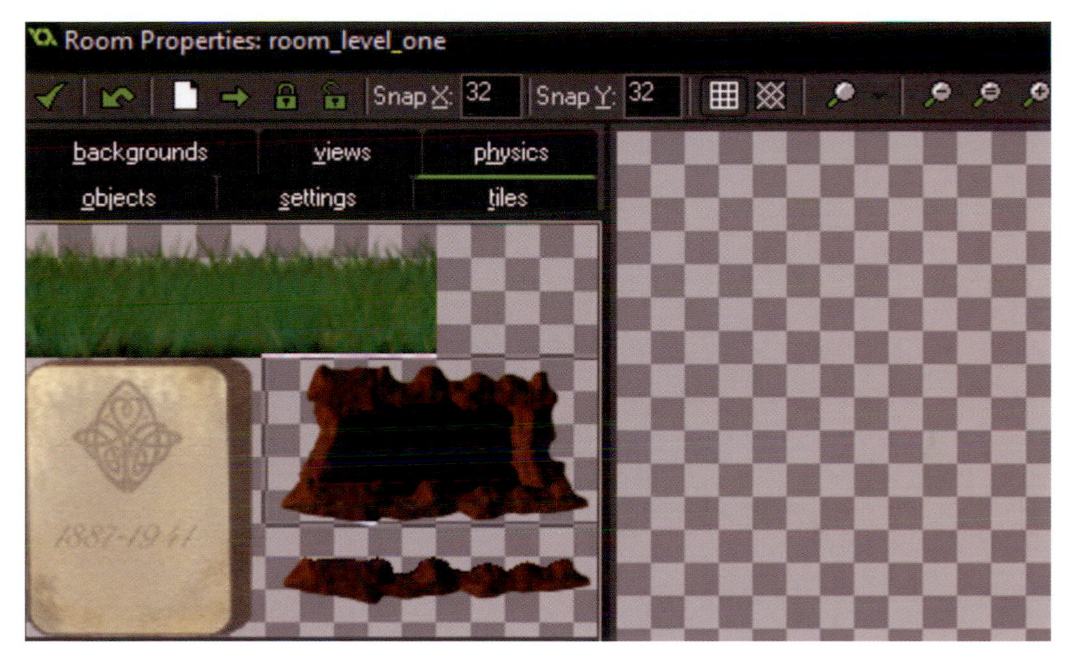

FIGURE 3.30

Step 5: Select the **Dirt Patch** tile in the same way we selected the grass tile earlier.

Step 6: Place the dirt title throughout the level on the grass tile so that your level looks similar to the one in **Figure 3.31**. The bottom of the dirt will be outside the room a little bit, which is fine.

In order to give the appearance that the dog has fallen into the hole, we will need to add some dirt in front of the hole which is also a bit closer to the viewer than the dog is. Using the patch of dirt that is just below the hole we can create this illusion.

Step 7: Add a new layer with a depth of −3.

Step 8: Select the patch of dirt as shown in **Figure 3.32**.

Step 9: Place the dirt patch in the room, hold down the Alt key to precisely line it up with the bottom section of dirt as shown in **Figures 3.33** and **3.34**.

Step 10: Repeat this for all of the holes you placed in the room.

Step 11: Before we can test the level we need to place colliders along the grass for the dog to run on. Click the **Objects** tab on **room_level_one**.

Step 12: Select the **obj_collider.**

Step 13: Place colliders along the bottom of the grass tiles so that your level looks similar to **Figure 3.35**. For some colliders you may need to hold down the Alt key to get them to line up with the edge of the hole. Make sure the colliders all line up flat across the top; otherwise the dog will have collision issues while running.

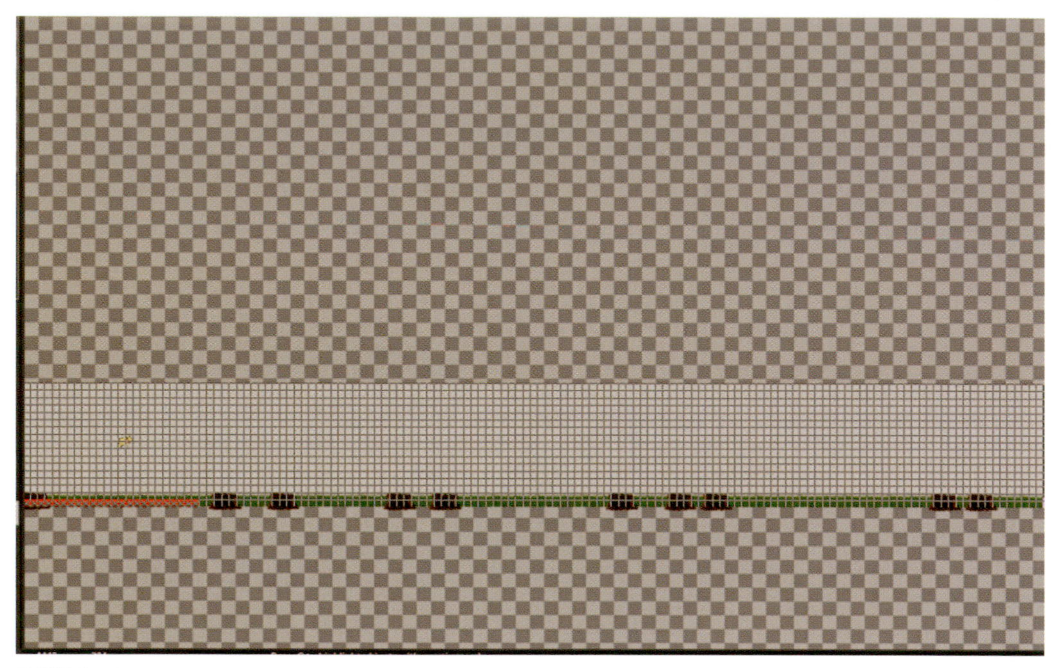

FIGURE 3.31

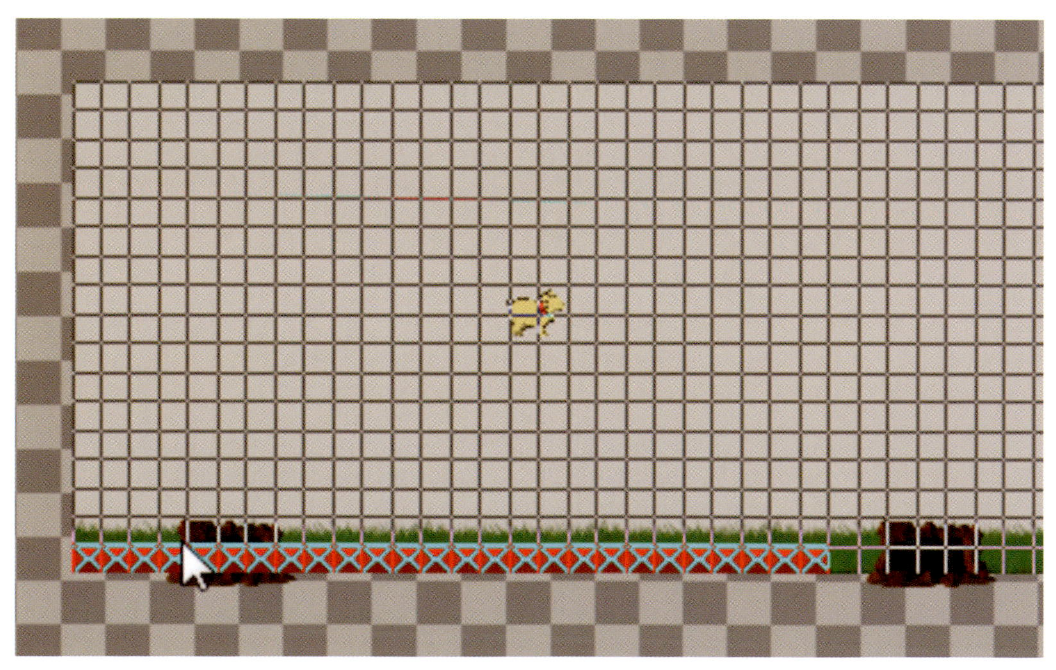

FIGURE 3.32

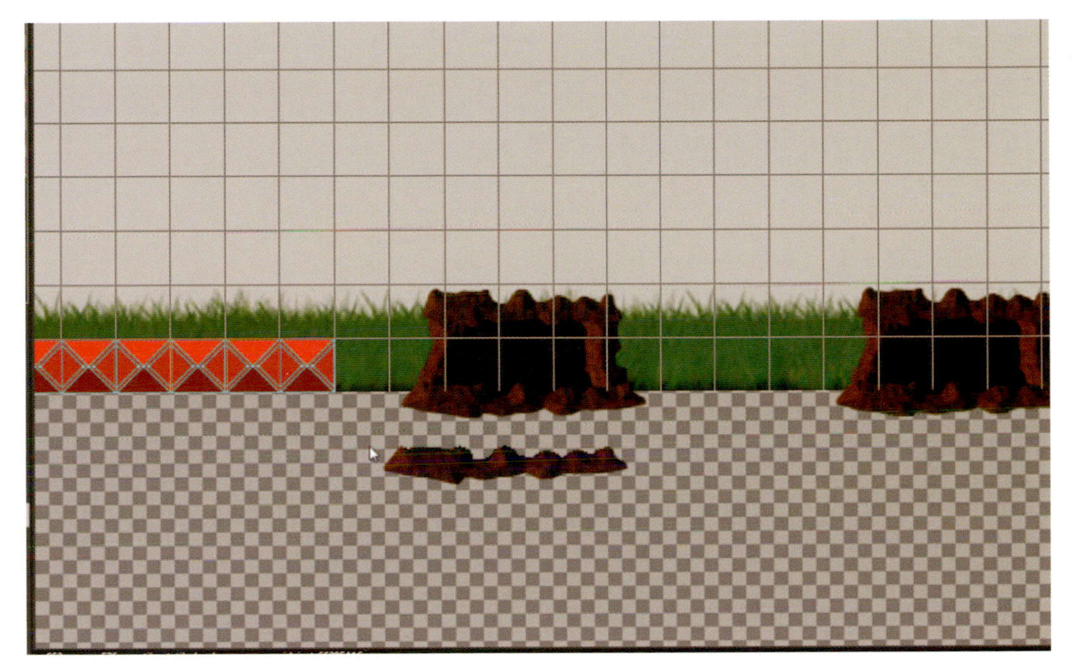

FIGURE 3.33

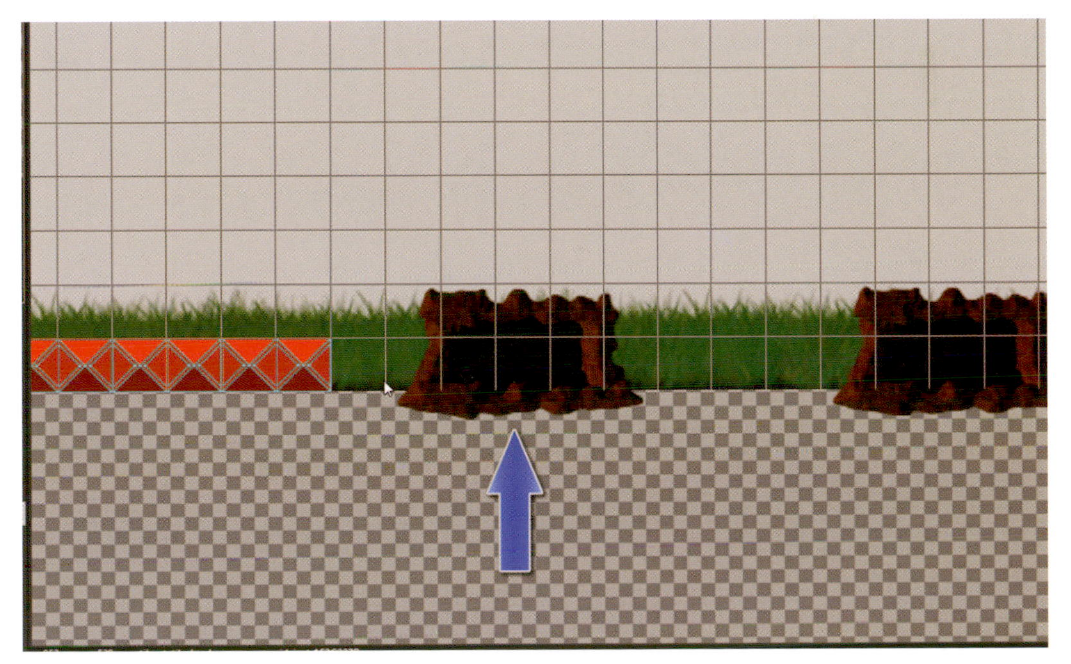

FIGURE 3.34

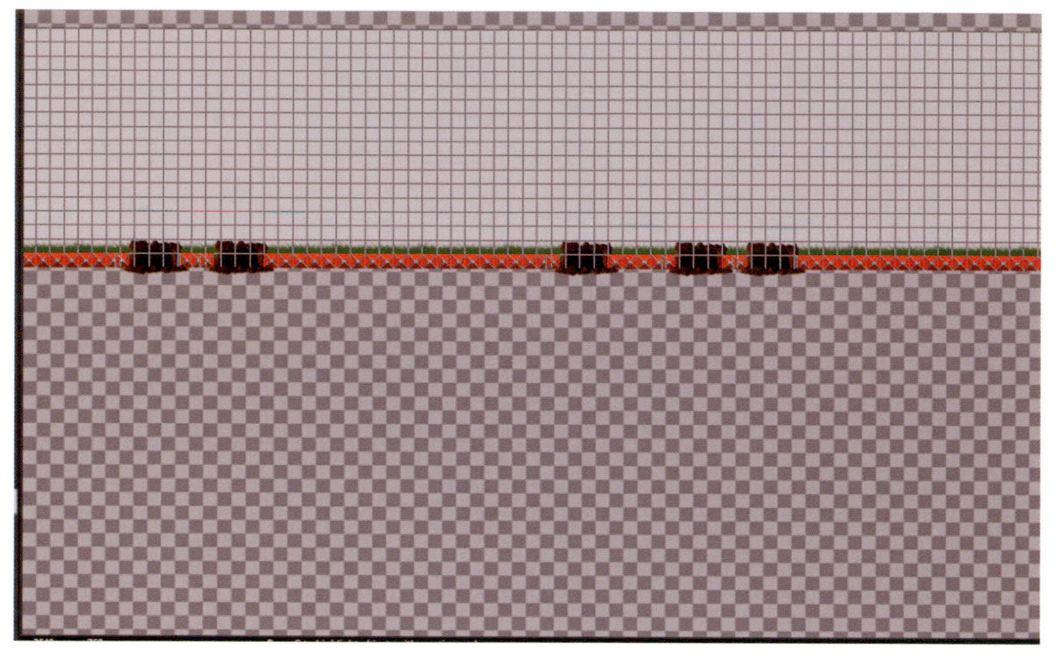

FIGURE 3.35

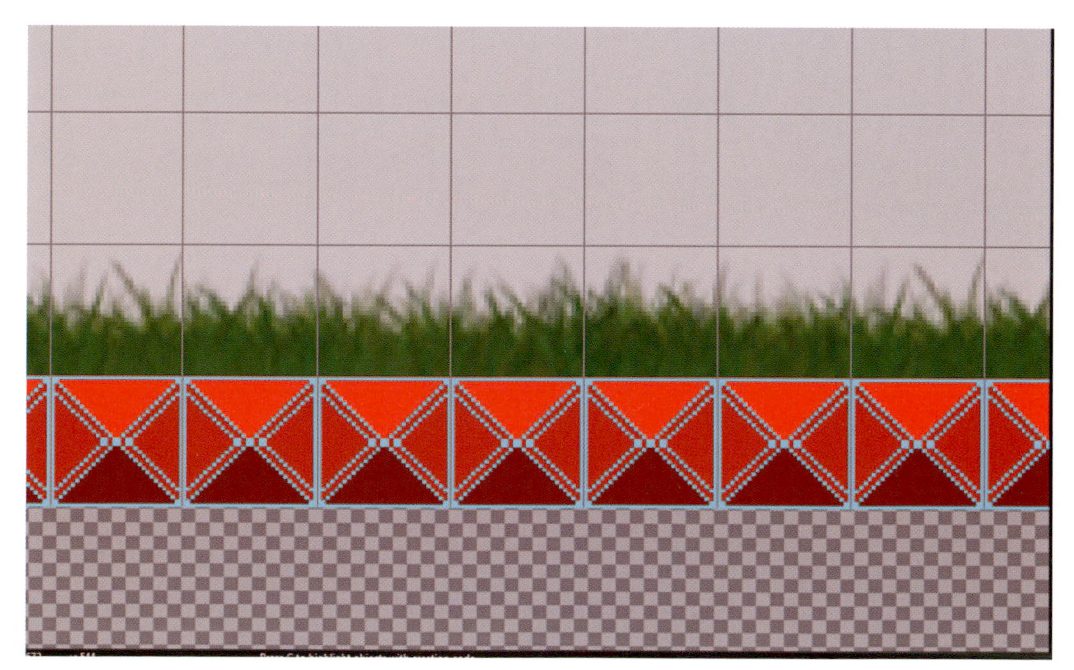

FIGURE 3.36

Now you can test the game. Run along the grass and jump over holes. Before quitting be sure to jump into or fall into a hole. It should now appear that the dog is falling into the hole; however, when it does you will notice that nothing happens. We need to add an event to the dog that will restart the game when the dog is no longer visible on the screen.

Restarting Game When Dog Disappears

Step 1: Open the **obj_dog.**

Step 2: Click **Add Event** and select **Other Event** and then **Outside Room.**

Step 3: In the **Main1** tab drag a **Restart Room** Action into the Actions window.

Whenever the dog falls through a hole the room will now reset. Our game is coming along nicely, but it looks a bit plain. Let's add a scrolling graveyard background to our level.

Adding a Scrolling Background

Step 1: Open **room_level_one.**

Step 2: Select the **Backgrounds** tab.

Step 3: Click the drop down box and choose **bg_level_one**. This background is made to tile itself across the room no matter the size.

To give the graves a more authentic look we will now add some tombstones behind the grave openings.

Adding Tombstones

Step 1: Open **room_level_one.**

Step 2: Select the **Tiles** tab and choose **tile_level_one.**

Step 3: Add a new layer and type **1001** into the box labeled **Depth** and hit **OK**. This will place the tile depth between the grass and the open grave.

Step 4: Highlight the tombstone graphic.

Step 5: While holding down the Alt key, place the tombstone behind the open grave so that it looks similar to **Figure 3.38**.

FIGURE 3.37

FIGURE 3.38

Our graveyard is going to be haunted by ghosts. We do not want our dog to get too close to these ghosts so we are going to add some brick walls that the player can use strategically to avoid the ghosts.

Adding Brick Walls to the Level

Step 1: In the **Backgrounds** folder open the **tile_bricks.**

Step 2: Click the **Use as tile set** box and click **OK**.

Step 3: Open **room_level_one** and go to the **Tiles** tab.

Step 4: Choose **tile_level_one_wall.**

Step 5: Select layer 1001.

Step 6: Place the wall in the two spots on the level indicated in **Figure 3.39.**

Step 7: Click the **Objects** tab and select the collider.

Step 8: Place the collider along the wall as shown in **Figure 3.40**.

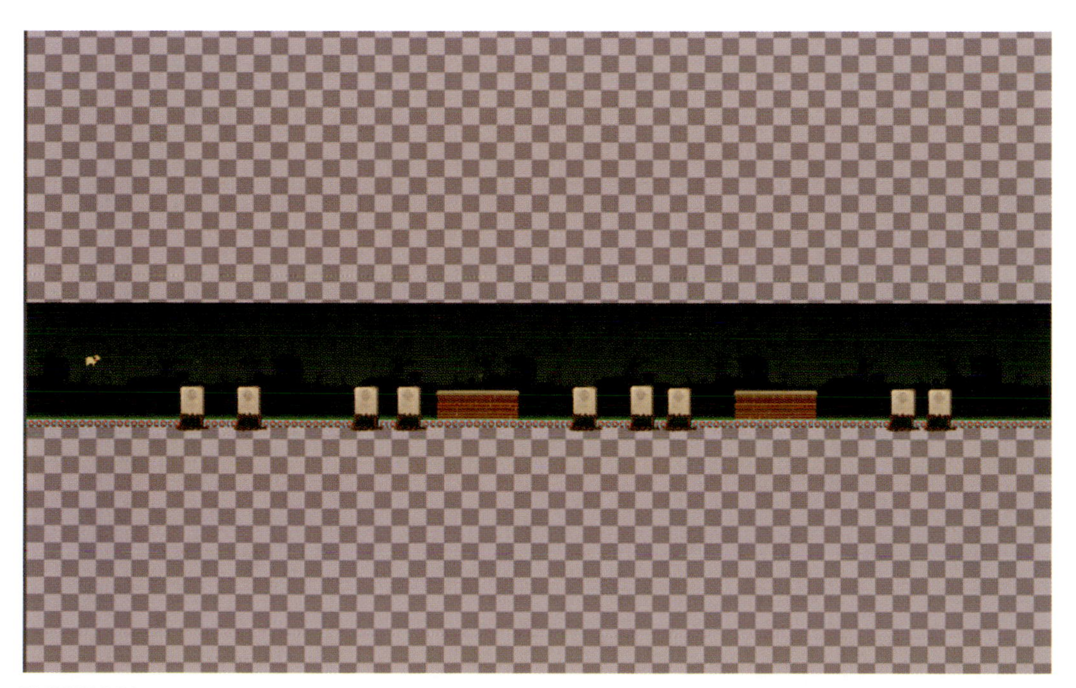

FIGURE 3.39

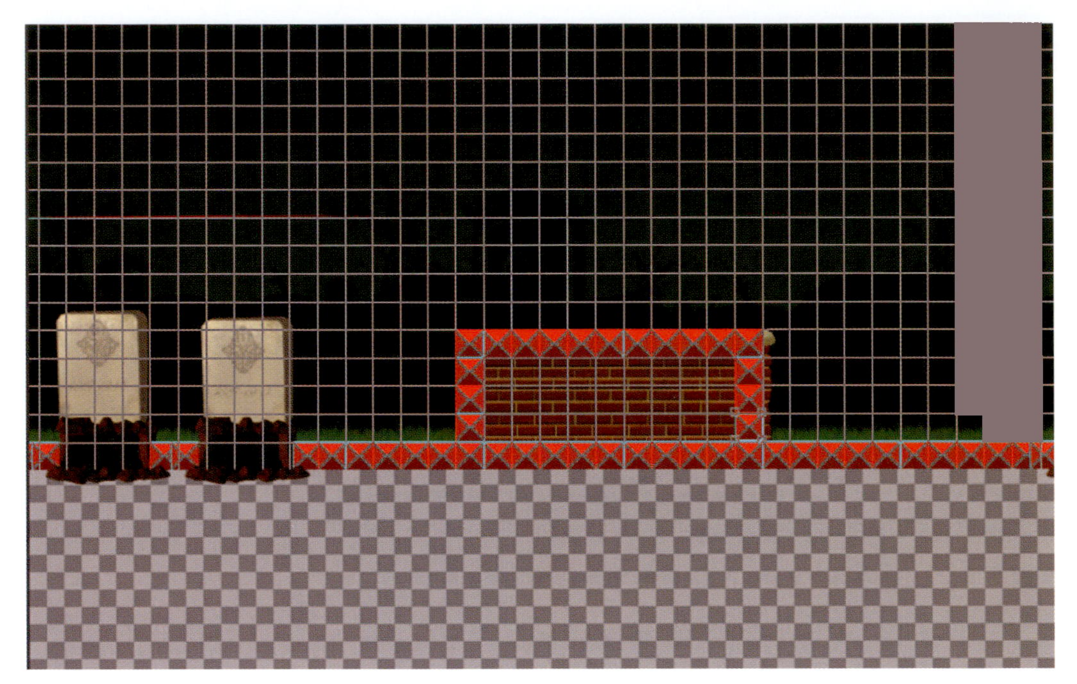

FIGURE 3.40

This will give the illusion that the dog can run into and jump on top of the wall. The player will now be able to use the spaces between the walls to avoid the ghosts. Of course this tactic will only work if there are actual ghosts in our game.

Adding Ghosts to the Level

Step 1: Create a new object and name it **obj_ghost**.

Step 2: Set the object's sprite to **spr_ghost_strip**.

Step 3: Add a **Create** Event. In the **Create** Event under the **Main2** section drag in a **Set Alarm** and set the following:

Number of steps: 1
In alarm no: Alarm 0

Step 4: Create an **Alarm** Event with **Alarm 0**.

Step 5: Drag a **Move Fixed** into the **Alarm** Event and set its arrow to the left and a speed to 4.

Step 6: Drag a **Change Sprite** into the Actions window with the following settings:

Sprite: spr_ghost_strip
Subimage: 0
Speed: 0

Step 7: Drag a **Set Alarm** below the **Move Fixed** and set the following:

Number of steps: 120
In alarm no: Alarm 1

Step 8: Create an **Alarm** Event with **Alarm 1.**

Step 9: Drag a **Move Fixed** into the Alarm Event and set its arrow to the right and a speed to 4.

Step 10: Drag a **Change Sprite** into the Actions window with the following settings:

Sprite: spr_ghost
Subimage: 1
Speed: 0

Step 11: Drag a **Set Alarm** below the **Move Fixed** and set the following:

Number of steps: 120
In alarm no: Alarm 0

This will make the ghosts move left for a few seconds, then turn and move right. The ghosts will always start by moving left, which is good to keep in mind when placing them into the game. Now we will make the ghosts lethal to the dog.

Making the Ghosts Lethal

Step 1: Create a new object and name it **obj_dog_dead**.

Step 2: Choose the sprite **spr_dead**.

Step 3: Make a **Create** Event**.**

Step 4: Drag a **Set Alarm** Event into the Actions window and set the following:

Number of steps: 60
In alarm no: Alarm 0

Step 5: Create an **Alarm** Event using **Alarm 0.**

Step 6: In the Alarm 0 Event drag a **Restart Game** Action, which is located in **Main2**.

Step 7: Close the **obj_dog_dead.**

Step 8: Open **obj_dog.**

Step 9: Add a collision with the **obj_ghost** Event.

Step 10: In the **Main1** drag an **Instance Change** Event into the Actions window. Set the following:

Change into: obj_dog_dead
Perform events: yes

Now when you place the **obj_ghost** in the room and run into it with the dog, the dog will flip over and fall, thus restarting the game.

Place the ghosts throughout the level in places that would add more difficulty to the player. One option that can make the game challenging is by placing a ghost on a brick wall. As the ghost turns away from the dog the player must follow the ghost and time their movements so they can jump down off the wall before the ghost returns. Be careful not to make the game impossible to beat. A challenging game is fun, an unbeatable game is not.

This game will consist of two levels. Once the player has navigated through the graveyard successfully, they can enter a teleporter to move to the next level. A teleporter can be anything such as a door, an elevator, or a giant pipe in the ground like those seen in the Mario universe. Once a player's character comes in contact with a teleporter, it is transported to the next level. We are going to add a cave at the end of our first level, which will lead to the second level of our game.

Creating a Teleporter

Step 1: Create a new object and call it **obj_level_collider**.

Step 2: Set the new object's sprite to **spr_collider** and click the box next to Visible so it is unchecked.

Step 3: Add a **Collision** Event with **obj_dog.**

Step 4: In **Main1**, drag a **Next Room** Action into the Actions window.

Step 5: Click **OK** and open the background named **tile_cave_one**.

Step 6: Check the **Use as tile set** box and click **OK**.

Step 7: Open **room_level_one.**

Step 8: Adjust your view so you can see the end of the level and place the cave using the tile system we have learned. Use layer 1000001. Your screen should now look similar to **Figure 3.41**.

Step 9: Open the **Objects** tab and place the **obj_level_colider** on the cave so it will appear the dog is about to run through the cave. Use the squares around the object after it is placed in the room to increase the scale of it.

Do not attempt to play the game yet. If you did and ran into the next level collider it would cause an error and crash the game. This is because we do not have a room for the game to load after **room_level_one**. Before creating the second level, however, we are going to add a start menu screen and an end game menu.

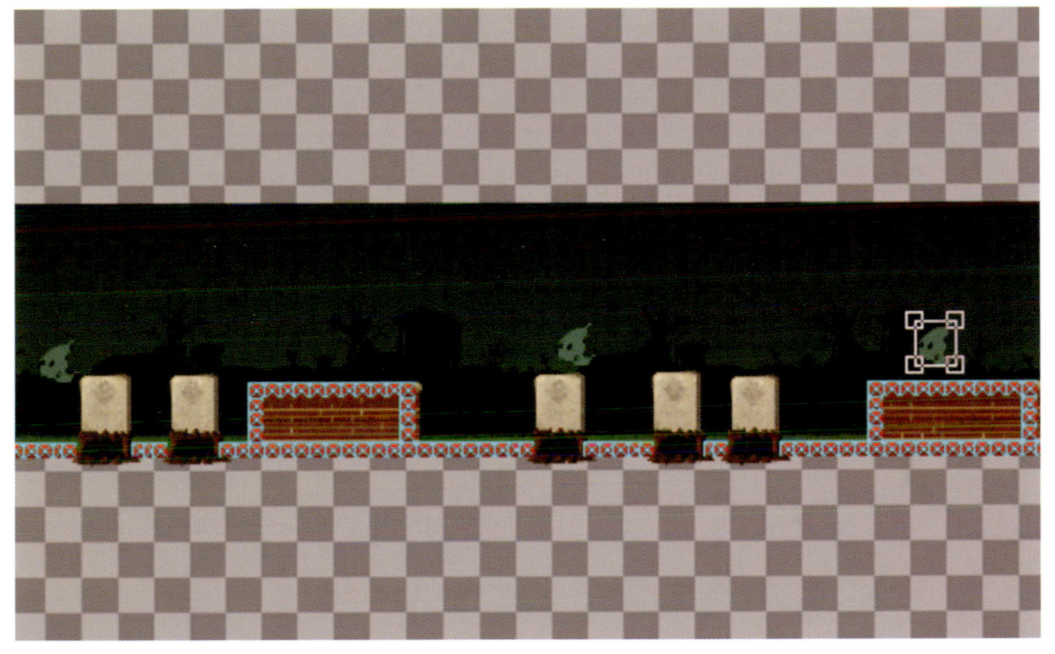

FIGURE 3.41

FIGURE 3.42

Adding Start and End Game Menus

Step 1: Create two new rooms and name them **room_title** and **room_end**.

Step 2: Leave the width the same but change the height of both rooms to **544**.

Step 3: Set the background of **room_title** to **bg_title**, and **room_end** to **bg_end.**

Step 4: Select the green checks on the top left of both rooms to save and close the windows.

On the start menu we will have two options for the player to choose from. The player will be able to start the game or exit the game. On the end menu the options are the same, but rather than use the word *start* we will be using the word *replay*.

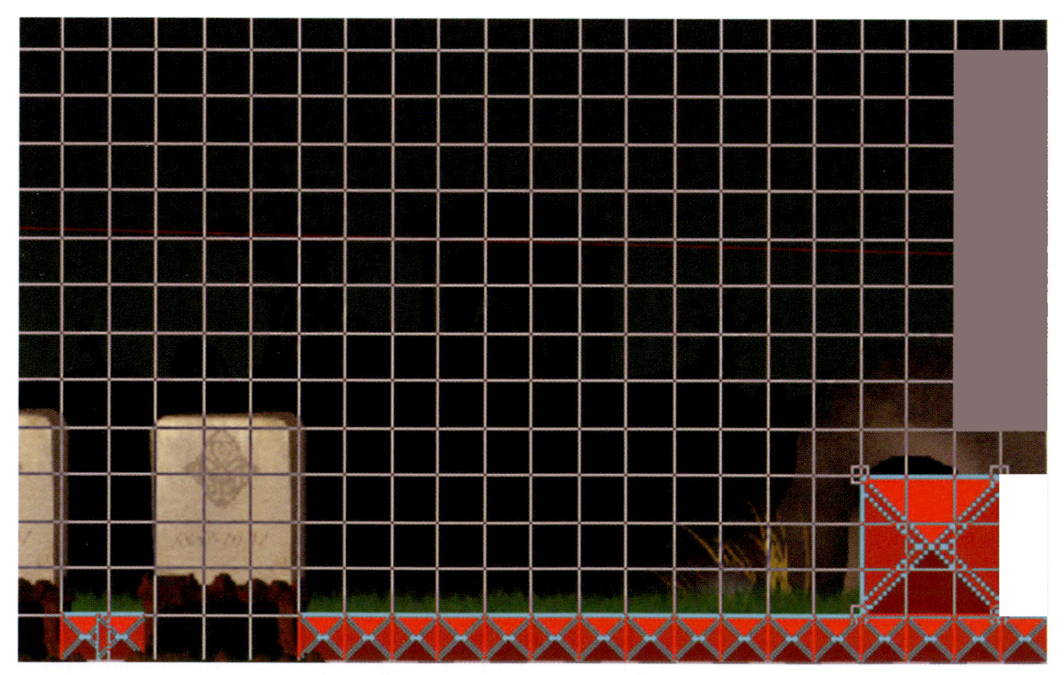

FIGURE 3.43

Adding Buttons to Menus

Step 1: Create two **New Objects** and name them **obj_play** and **obj_quit.**

Step 2: Assign the **spr_button** sprite to both and uncheck the **Visible** option.

Step 3: With **obj_play** selected add a **Mouse>Left Button** Event and under the **Main1** tab add a **Different Room** Action to it. Set the new room to **room_level_one.**

Step 4: With **obj_quit** selected add a **Mouse>Left Button** Event and under **Main2** add an **End Game** Action to it.

Step 5: Drag the rooms up and down in the room's folder so they are in the following order: **room_title**, **room_level_one**, **room_end**.

Step 6: Open **room_title** and in the **Objects** tab select the **obj_start** button and drag it into the appropriate location. Scale the button to fit over the word **Play** completely.

Step 7: In the **Objects** tab select the **obj_quit** button and drag it into the appropriate location over the **Quit** text. Click the green check to close the **room_title** window.

Step 8: Open **room_end** and place **obj_start** and **obj_quit** over the appropriate trash cans.

FIGURE 3.44

Run the game and test the Start and Quit buttons. The Start button should activate level one and the Quit button should close out the game. Rather than having level one restart when the dog falls or gets hit by a ghost, we are going to have the game go to the title screen instead. This will allow the player to either start the game over or quit playing altogether.

Resetting Game Restart to Title Screen

Step 1: Open **obj_dog.**

Step 2: Click the **Outside Room** Event and delete the **Restart the Room** Action.

Step 3: Drag a **Different Room** Action into the window to replace it. Set the following:

New room: Room_title

Step 4: Select **OK**.

Step 5: Open **obj_dog_dead** and select the **Alarm 0** Event.

Step 6: Delete the **Restart the Game** Action and place a **Different Room** in to replace it. Set the following:

New room: Room_title

To add to the creepiness of the graveyard we are going to add some ambient music and some sound effects to our game. Each level will have a different background song and sound effects so we will import all the sounds at once and apply them to the correct levels.

Importing Music and Sounds

Step 1: Find the *Lost Dog* assets folder and locate the sounds folder.

Step 2: Drag all the sound files from the sounds folder into the GameMaker window just as you did earlier for the sprites and backgrounds.

Step 3: Click the **OK** box for all the windows that pop up.

Step 4: Remove the **sound1_ portion** from all of the sounds so that they end up being named as follows:

Snd_end_screen
Snd_level_one
Snd_level_two
Snd_dog_yelp
Snd_splash

Adding Music

Step 1: Create three new objects and name them as follows:

obj_snd_end
obj_snd_one
obj_snd_two

We'll use these to control which song plays on each level. None of these objects will use sprites.

Step 2: Open **obj_snd_one** and add a Create Event. Reminder, all sound actions are found under the Main1 tab.

Step 3: Drag a **Play Sound** Action into the Actions window and set the following:

Sound: snd_level_one
Loop: true

Step 4: Add a **New Event**, Other>Room end.

Step 5: Drag a **Stop Sound** into the Actions window and set the following:

Sound: snd_level_one

Step 6: Click **OK** and open the **obj_snd_two**.

Step 7: Use snd_level_two and repeat the previous steps.

Step 8: Open **obj_snd_end** and use **snd_end_screen**. Repeat the steps for the **Create** Event, however, this time set **loop** to **false** and do not create the **Room End** Event.

Placing Sound Objects in the Game

Step 1: Open **room_level_one** and place the **obj_snd_one** anywhere in the room. The location is not important. When the player enters level one they will hear the level one music.

Step 2: Obj_snd_two is for the music the player will hear on level two. Add **obj_snd_two** to **room_level_two**.

Step 3: Open **room_end** and place the **obj_snd_end**. Again, location is not important. If the player completes the game they will go to **room_end** and hear the **obj_snd_end** music play.

Adding the Dog Yelp

Now we will make the dog yelp when it hits a ghost which will give the player an audio cue in addition to the visual cue of the dog falling, emphasizing that this is something the player will want to avoid doing in the future.

Step 1: Open obj_dog.

Step 2: Select the collision with **obj_ghost** Event.

Step 3: Drag a **Play Sound** Action **above** the change instance and set the following:

Sound: snd_dog_yelp
Loop: false

Applying Your Knowledge

Now it is time to apply the knowledge you have acquired thus far in the chapter. Following written instructions can assist game developers when learning new skills, however, it is necessary to practice these steps with limited instructions for the steps to become second nature. If what you are attempting is not working you can review the material discussed earlier in this book. Over time you will need to do this less and less. The goal is to eventually not need any written instructions at all so you will be able to create the games you imagine on your own in the future.

Step 1: Attempt to completely design the second level using the tiles and colliders.

Step 2: Level two should be named **room_level_two.**

Step 3: In the rooms folder **room_level_two** should be located below **room_level_one**.

Step 4: Use the following images provided in the assets folder.

Background: **bg_level_two**

Tiles used: **Tile_level_two_broken**

Tile_level_two_cave
Tile_level_two_ground
Tile_level_two_slime
Tile_level_two_unbroken

Step 5: Create the level so that it looks similar to **Figure 3.45** below.

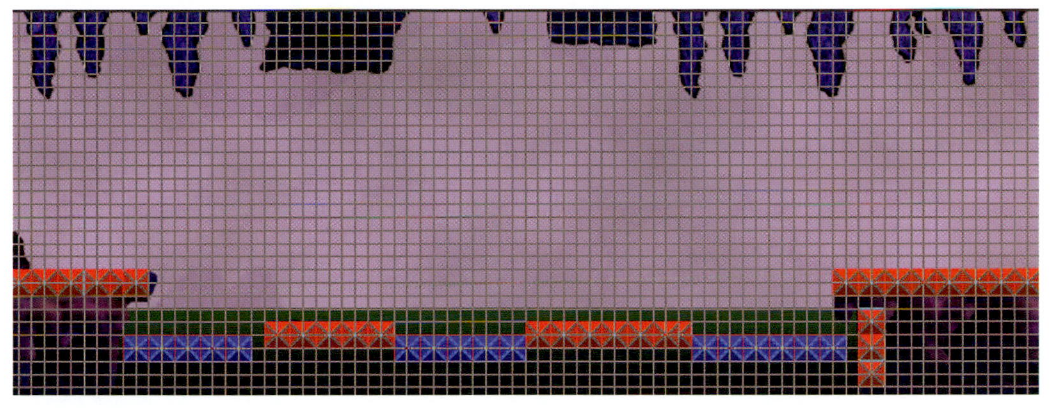

FIGURE 3.45

Incorporating Puzzle Elements

Level two has our dog entering a cave environment. The nice thing about the *Lost Dog* premise is that hundreds of levels can be created in which the dog has to navigate through ever stranger environments. For our purpose of learning GameMaker we will only be creating these two levels, however. In level two the objective is for the player to look at the broken stalactites at the top of the screen and envision where the other broken part is under the slime. This is where the dog will be able to jump and not fall into the slime. We will have the first platform in the slime obvious so that the player can figure out the puzzle of looking at the top of the screen to see where to jump in the slime. The player will then attempt to make their way to the end of the level while avoiding any ghosts.

Creating the Illusion of Falling into the Slime

In order to give the appearance that the dog is falling into the slime we will place the top layer of the slime on a high layer and then place the rest on a layer that is lower than the dog. For example, if the dog is at a depth of 0 then the slime should be at −1. The platforms that the dog will land on would then be set to −2. Use **Figures 3.46** through **3.50** below as a guide when creating your level.

FIGURE 3.46

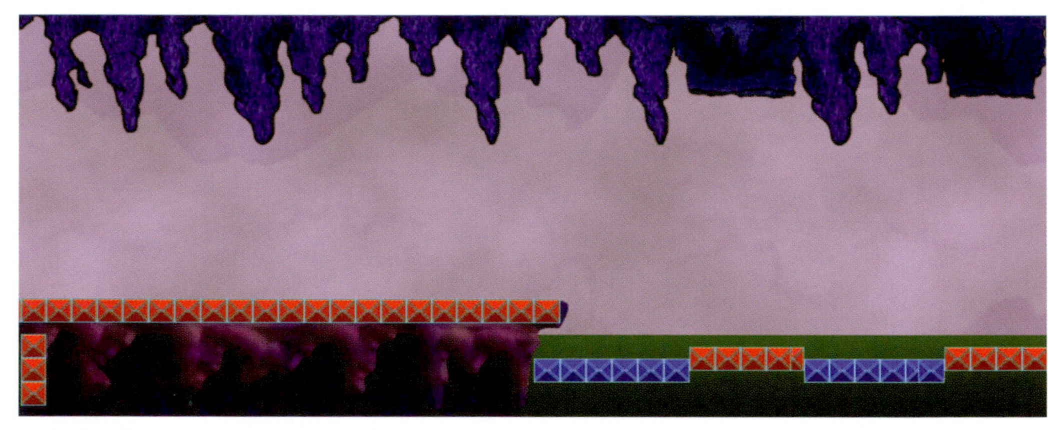

FIGURE 3.47

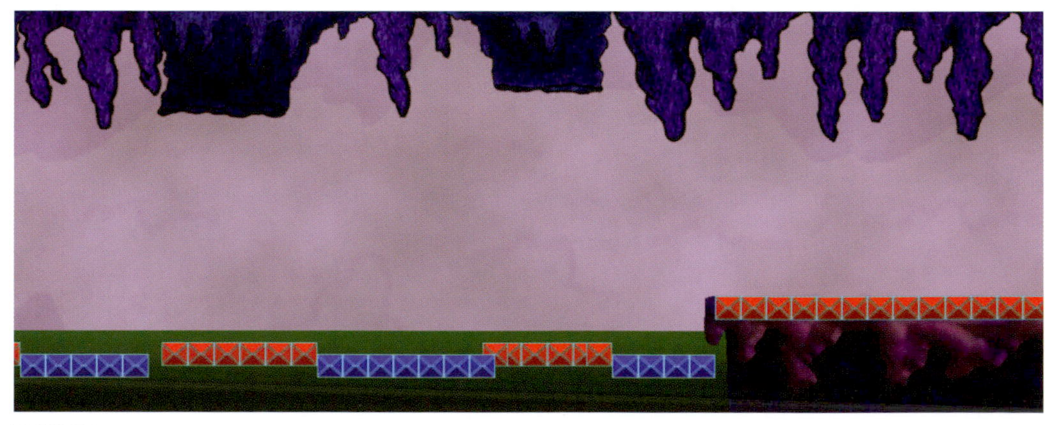

FIGURE 3.48

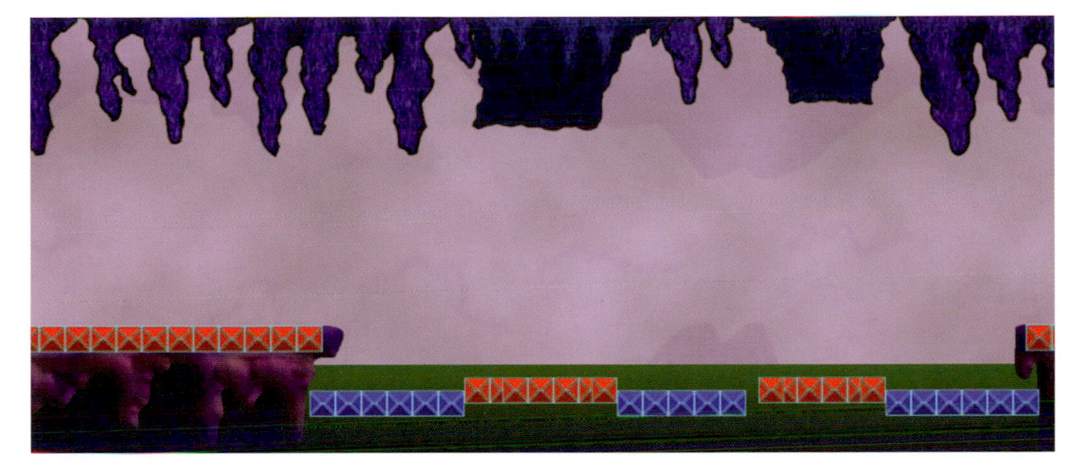

FIGURE 3.49

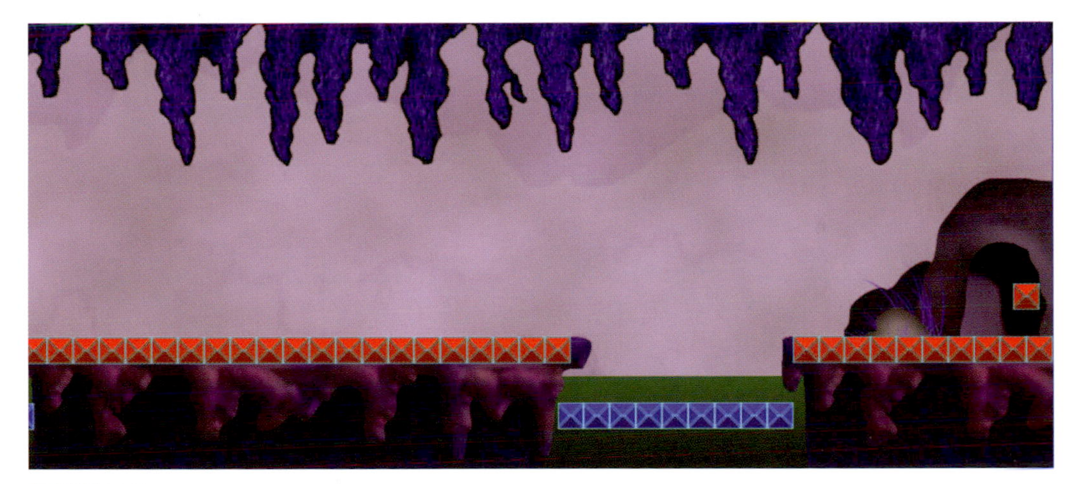

FIGURE 3.50

Step 1: Place the **obj_snd_two** in the level.

Step 2: Add both caves from the **tile_level_two_cave** at the start and end of the level. On the end cave add an **obj_level_collider** so the player can complete the game.

Creating a Water Collider

If the player jumps into the slime in an area where there is not a hidden platform, the dog will fall into the slime and the level will restart. To create this we need to add one final object which will be a collider that will play the splash sound and restart the level.

Step 1: Create a new object named **obj_water_collider**.

Step 2: Set the sprite to **spr_water_collider.**

The following steps will create the splash animation.

Step 3: Create a new object called **obj_splash**.

Step 4: Set the sprite to **spr_splash**.

Step 5: Add a **Create** Event.

Step 6: Place a **Move Fixed** Event into the Actions window and set the following:

Click the square in the center.
Speed: 0

Step 7: Add a Set Gravity below the **Move Fixed** Action and set the following:

Direction: 0
Gravity: 0

Step 8: Create an **Animation End** Event and drag a **Restart Game** into the actions window.

Step 9: Open the **obj_dog** object.

Step 10: Add a **Collision** Event with **obj_water_collider.**

Step 11: Drag a **Play Sound** Action into the event and set the following:

Sound: **snd_splash**
Loop: **false**

Step 12: Drag a **Stop Playing** Action below the **Play Sound** Action and set the following:

Sound: **Snd_level_two**

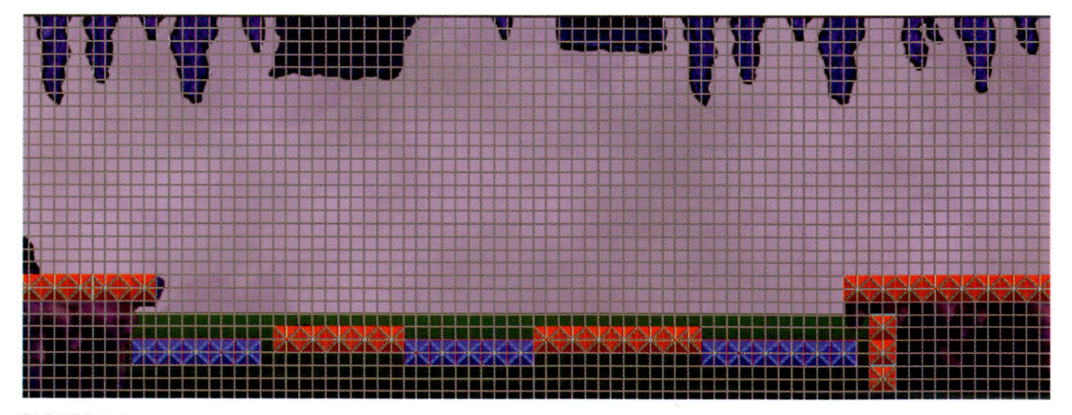

FIGURE 3.51

Step 13: Drag a **Change Instance** below the **Stop Playing** Action.

Change into: **obj_splash**
Perform events: **yes**

Step 14: Place the obj_water_collider along the edge of the slime as it appears in **Figure 3.51**.

Game Play Through and Bug Testing

Congratulations, you have now created a multi-level game and incorporated simple puzzle elements into it. You have also introduced simple artificial intelligence elements to control the patrol routes of the ghosts. Try playing your game to see if you can spot any elements that are not working. Those in the game development field call these problems bugs. Usually a bug can be easily fixed by rechecking the settings you typed in for certain actions. If you cannot find any bugs, then it is time to have someone else play your game to see if they can find any. Since you are the developer of the game, it is easy to overlook something because you already know how the game is supposed to work. People not involved in the game development process will often try to do things in a game we never thought about and thus uncover some bugs for us to fix. If you have not already, you may wish to add some ghosts to level two to make it a bit more challenging. You may wish to create additional levels using the assets provided for you. Experimenting with different puzzle ideas can be a lot of fun.

Two Player Games

Learning Objectives—Upon completion of Chapter 4 readers will be able to:

- Map control keys and identify which keys are commonly used and which should be avoided
- Create two player games
- Include pick-up items that can be stored and used later in the game
- Create contrails behind player characters
- Include pick-up items that change the behaviors of player character and opponent
- Include multiple rounds and track winnings that total to reveal game winner
- Work with parent objects
- Include persistent objects that remain across multiple levels

Project Overview: *Snail Trail*

Snail Trail is a two player competitive game in which two people play against each other with the goal of winning two out of three rounds. Each player controls their own snail which must avoid objects in the game while continually moving. Players use the contrail created by their snail to trap the other player's snail by attempting to get the other player to collide with either a snail trail or another object in the game. Players can also pick up different colored mushrooms in the game, which allows the player to either freeze the other player temporarily or allow their own snail to be indestructible

FIGURE 4.1

for a limited time. The player who wins two out of three matches wins the game.

To begin creating the *Snail Trail* game, first download the *Snail Trail* game assets at www.thegamemakerstandard.com/snailtrail; after downloading the assets folder read over the updates.pdf document which contains any changes since the publication of this book, then create a new project in GameMaker.

Creating a New Project and Importing Assets

Step 1: Create a new project in GameMaker Studio and name it: **Snail Trail.**

Step 2: Import the sprites, backgrounds, and sounds and name them similar to those shown in **Figure 4.1**.

Creating Groups

We will be creating two different characters for the game: a yellow snail and a purple snail. One player will control the yellow snail, while the other player will control the purple snail. By creating groups we can keep the different files used for each snail separate and organized.

Step 1: Right click on the **Sprites** folder in the left side of the GameMaker editor.

Step 2: Choose **Create Group** from the options.

Step 3: Name the group: **Yellow Snail**.

Step 4: Repeat **Steps 1–3** under the **Creating Groups** heading, but this time name the group: **Purple Snail**.

Step 5: Drag the four yellow snail images: **spr_yellow_down**, **spr_yellow_left**, **spr_yellow_right,** and **spr_yellow_up** into the **Yellow Snail** folder.

Step 6: Do the same for the **Purple Snail** images and place them in the Purple Snail folder.

Mapping Keys

For this particular project the game will be played using one keyboard that both players will share. Game developers can later map the key controls to two separate USB game controllers, but for this particular project we will be sticking with just the keyboard. The player on the right side of the keyboard will use the arrow keys to control their player. The player on the left side of the keyboard will use the W, A, S, and D keys to control their player. Certain keys are frequently used when mapping keys to control games. The arrow keys are common as are the W, A, S, and D keys. The Space bar is frequently used for repeated keystrokes such as shooting and the number keys such as 1, 2, and 3 are typically used to switch weapons or activate different menus in a game. Other keys should not be used for some game actions because the keys may have different computer functions when held down for several seconds or if tapped multiple times. An example of a key that you would not want to use to fire weapons in a game is the Shift key. Although the location of the Shift key is near both of the movement keys areas we mentioned earlier, which would make it easy to reach, hitting the Shift key five times in a row will activate the sticky key option which would disrupt the game. The right Shift key would be a poor choice if used as an accelerator for a car racing game because holding down the right Shift key for eight seconds activates filter keys. When choosing to map keys for a game that may be outside of what many games typically use, be sure to test your games using those keys to ensure that they do not have any other hidden computer functions you did not know about.

Creating the Right Side Player Character

We will now create the first of two snails for the players to use and add an empty level to test the snail movement.

Step 1: Create a **New Object** and name it: **obj_yellow_snail**.

Step 2: Set the Sprite to **spr_yellow_right**.

This will be the character that the player on the left side of the keyboard uses. We will use the W, A, S, and D keys to move the yellow snail.

Step 3: Create a separate **Key Press** Event for the **W** key, the **A** key, the **S** key, and the **D** key.

Step 4: In the **Press W-Key** Event drag in a **Move Fixed** Action and set the following:

Click the Up arrow
Speed: 2

Step 5: In the same event drag in a **Change Sprite** Action and set the following:

Sprite: spr_yellow_up
Subimage: 0
Speed: 0

This will switch the snail sprite from facing right to facing up when the W key is pressed.

Step 6: Now that we have set the **W** key to move the yellow snail up, use what we have learned to make the **S** key switch the sprite so that it is facing down, make the

FIGURE 4.2

A key so that it switches the sprite to facing left, and set the **D** key so that it switches the sprite to facing right. Review Steps 4 and 5 if you need to while adding the change sprite actions. When you are done you should have a change sprite event that moves the player and changes the sprite to face the direction they are moving based on the key that is being pressed.

Step 7: To get the snail moving we need to add a Create Event that starts it moving to the right at a speed of 2. In the snail object add a **Create** Event.

Step 8: Add a **Move Fixed** Action to the Create Event and set the following:

Click the Right arrow
Speed: 2

Now when the game starts the snail will automatically start moving toward the right. To test this out we will need to create an empty room.

Step 9: Create a **New Room** and name it **room_level_one**.

Step 10: Click the **Objects** tab and place the **obj_snail_yellow** on the far left side of the room. Run the game and make sure the snail can be controlled with the **W, A, S,** and **D** keys and that the snail is facing the correct direction when moving. Although our player character is a snail, we would like for it to move a bit faster than it is currently to make the game more challenging.

Step 11: Open the **Room Settings** tab for **room_level_one** and change the speed to **60.**

Creating the Contrail

We have the snail, now we need the trail. Each snail is going to leave a colored trail behind them. Not only can the opponent not cross over this trail, but the player cannot cross over their own trail either without being destroyed. The yellow snail will create a yellow trail on the screen and the purple snail will leave a purple trail on the screen. The yellow snail cannot collide with either of these trails and neither can the purple snail.

Step 1: Close the room options and create a **New Object** called **obj_yellow_trail**.

Step 2: Set the Sprite to **spr_yellow_trail**.

Step 3: Click **OK** and open the **obj_yellow_snail** object.

Step 4: Create an **Alarm, Alarm 0** Event.

Step 5: Add a **Create Instance** to the Alarm Event and set the following:

Object: obj_yellow_trail
x: 0

y: 0
Relative: checked

Step 6: Under the **Main2** tab, drag a **Set Alarm** Action below the **Create Instance** Action and set the following:

Number of steps: 2
In alarm no: Alarm 0

Step 7: Click the **Create** Event, add a **Set Alarm**, and set the following:

Number of steps: 1
In alarm no: Alarm 0

If you were to run the game now you would notice that the yellow trail is off to the left side of the snail. We will now center the trail so that it is always created from the center of the snail.

Step 8: Open **spr_yellow_trail** and click the **Center** button, then select **OK**.

Step 9: You will now want to open the four yellow snail sprites and do the same.

When you run the game now you will see a trail following from the center of the snail. The trail is actually a series of yellow circles that are created quickly and placed on top of each other so that it gives the illusion that there is a solid trail following the snail rather than a series of yellow circles.

Creating the Right Side Player Character

If we were creating a single player game we would now be finished setting up our player character. *Snail Trail* is a two player game so we now need to set up our second player character. This is an opportunity to practice what you have learned thus far in the chapter with the creation of the yellow snail. You will be completing the same steps to create the purple snail, but making changes where appropriate so that the snail is purple, starts from the right side of the screen moving toward the left, has a purple trail that is centered, and moves correctly when the player presses different **arrow keys**.

Now you should have a yellow and a purple snail in the game that move and leave a trail behind them. If we played the game now it would look more like a two player cooperative drawing game than a competitive to-the-death race. Time to make the trails lethal.

Setting Colliders on the Snails

You may have been wondering why we have four separate sprites for each snail instead of using subimages. This is so we can use separate colliders for each direction the snail is facing. The colliders will be located on the snails' head, this way the snails will not die immediately after they spawn. If the collider was not on the snail's head and was instead on its whole body, then as soon as the trail started to form it would destroy the snail because the trail would be touching the back of the snail.

Step 1: Open **spr_yellow_right** and click the **Modify Mask** option.

Step 2: Click the magnifying glass icon with the + in it to zoom in a bit.

Step 3: Check the manual box.

Step 4: Click and drag the mouse over the snail's head so it looks similar to **Figure 4.3**.

Step 5: The dark-colored box is the snail's new collider; if this comes in contact with any of the trails it will destroy the snail and the player will lose that round.

Step 6: Select the **OK** box and repeat the process for all the yellow and purple snail images. The results should look similar to **Figures 4.4** and **4.5**.

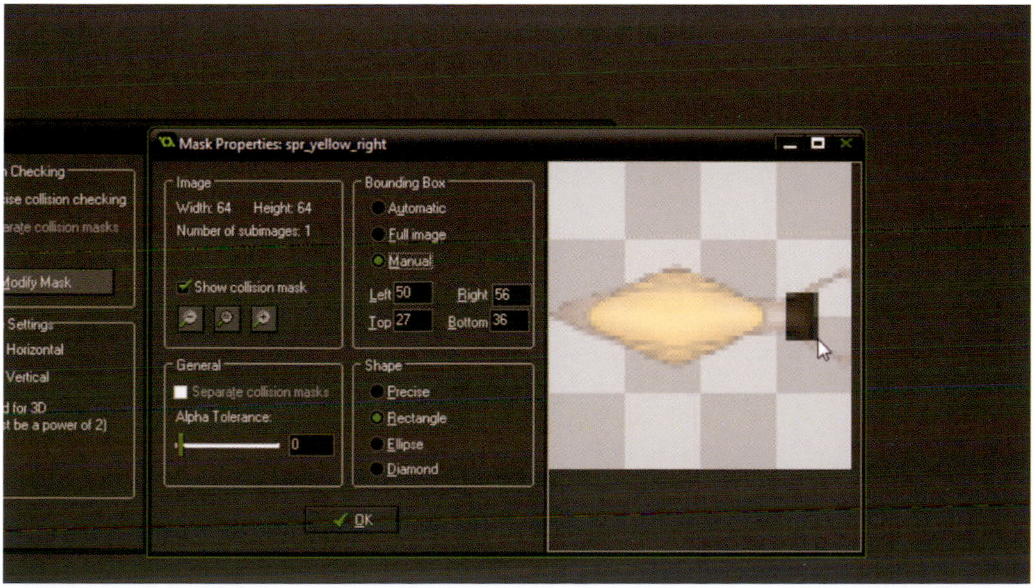

FIGURE 4.3

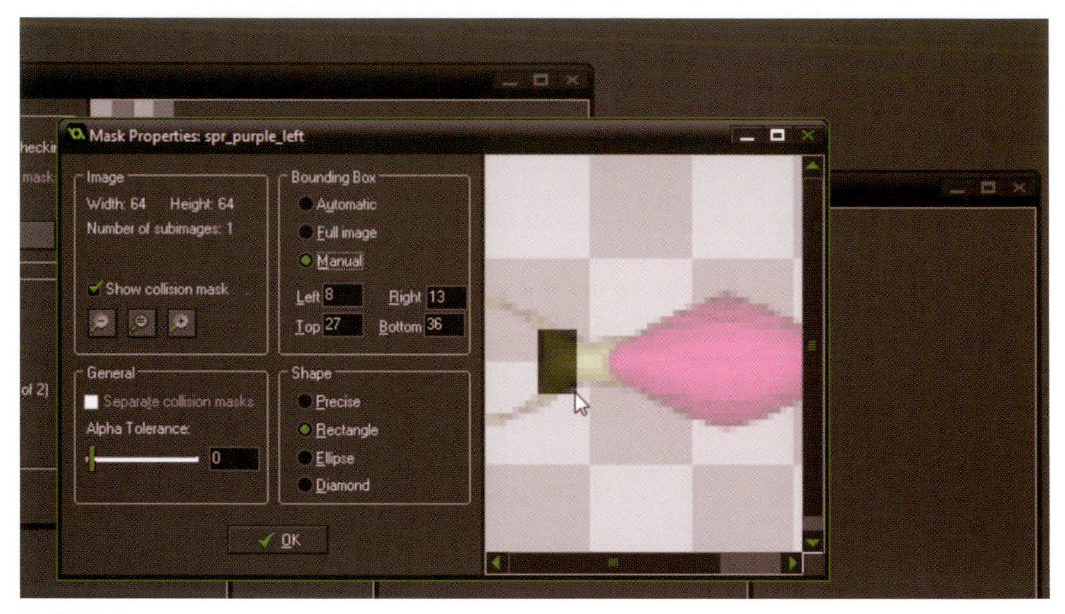

FIGURE 4.4

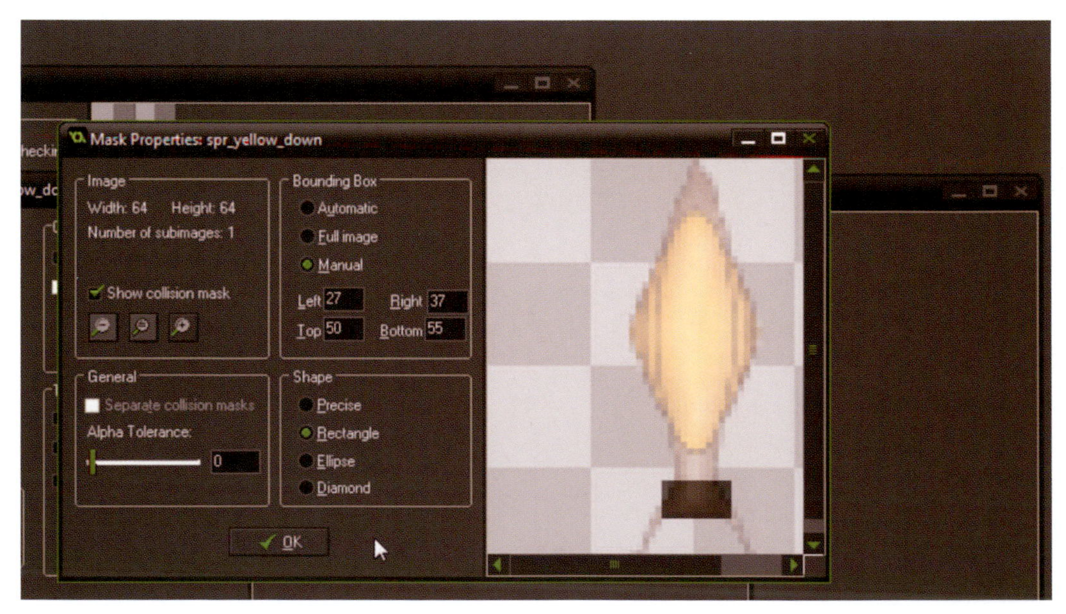

FIGURE 4.5

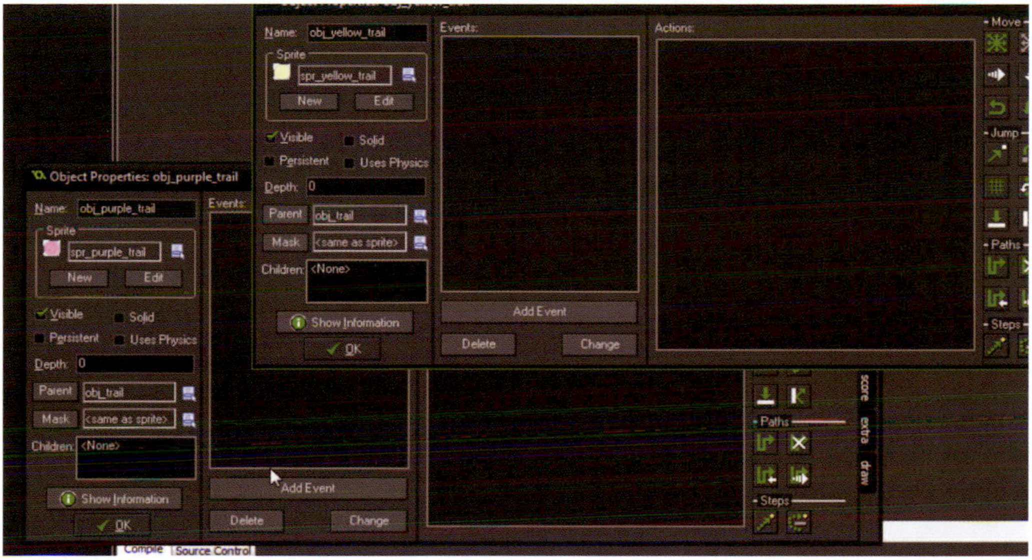

FIGURE 4.6

Creating a Parent Object

With all the colliders in place we will set up a parent trail so we do not need to make a collision event with both trail objects for both snails. This is a time-saving technique that reduces the amount of redundant collision events needed.

Step 1: Create a **New Object** named **obj_trail** with no sprite.

Step 2: Open both **obj_yellow_trail** and **obj_purple_trail** and set the parent option of each to **obj_trail** as shown in **Figure 4.6**.

Now we will be able to set up one collision event for the trails of both snails at the same time.

Step 3: Open both of the snail objects and add a **Collision** Event to each with the **obj_trail**.

Step 4: Add a **Destroy Instance** Action to the collision events for both snails.

Testing the Snail Trails

Test your game and watch to see that when a snail collides with a trail, that snail is destroyed. If a snail is destroyed without hitting a trail, you will want to go back and check the collision mask to be sure the images are centered.

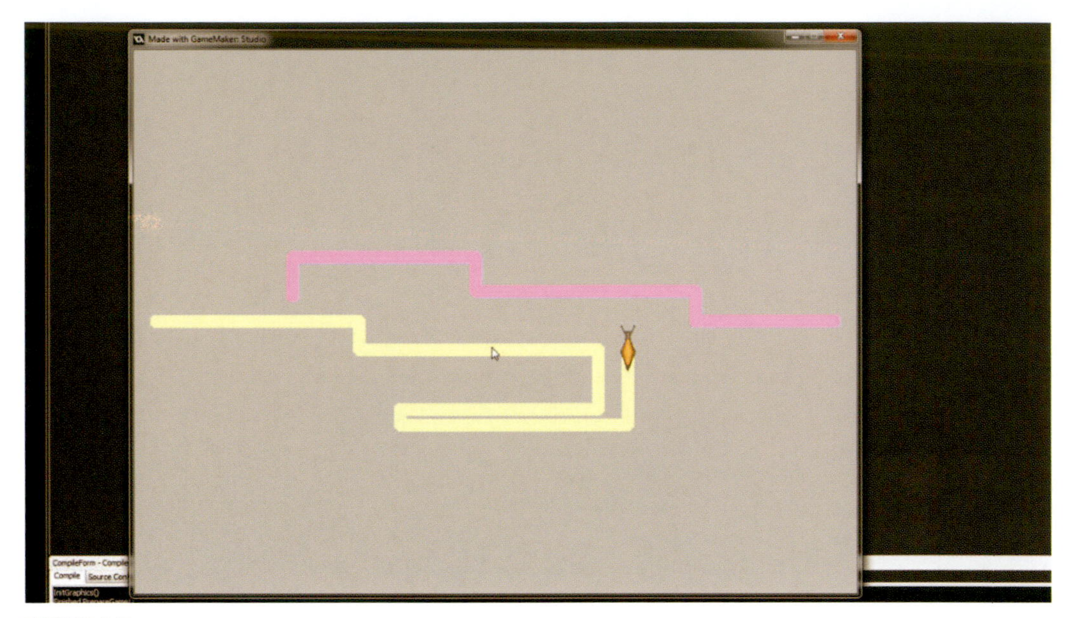

FIGURE 4.7

Adding Pick-Up Items

The game as it currently stands is pretty challenging but we want to add some elements that will add a bit of strategy to the gameplay. We will now add two different items that the players can pick up. These items will be in the form of different colored mushrooms. If a play picks up a red mushroom they will be able to turn their snail invulnerable for a limited time. This will allow that player to move their snail over trails without being harmed. This type of pick-up item is different than the power-ups we used in the *Scout* game because in the *Scout* game the power-ups were activated immediately upon the player getting them. In *Snail Trail* the player can choose when to activate the item they are holding. This option becomes more relevant when it comes to the second pick-up item, which is a blue mushroom. The blue mushroom allows the player that picked it up to freeze the other player's character when the blue mushroom item is activated. When used strategically, the player could pick up the mushroom and save it until they are near the other player. Then they can freeze the other player and move in front of them so that when the other player starts moving again they would have no choice but to collide with the other player's trail. To make the decision process on when to use the picked-up item more challenging, each player can only hold on to one item at a time. So if a player picks up a red mushroom and then picks up a blue mushroom without first using the red one, they will lose the red mushroom.

Earlier in this chapter we discussed keys that are commonly used for games and keys that are frequently not used because they can activate options on the computer.

The Shift key was the example we used as a key not to use. For this game we will be using two of the most commonly used keys: the Space bar and Enter keys, to activate carried items. The Enter key is located in close proximity to the arrow keys on a keyboard so it makes a good option for the player on the right side of the keyboard to use. In addition, the **Enter** key is normally a larger key than the arrow keys, thus making it easier to strike quickly. The left-hand side of the keyboard does not have an Enter key so we will be using the Space bar for the player on the left to use. The Space bar is the largest button and thus can easily be hit by the player on the left side without the player having to look down and search for a particular button.

Step 1: Create two new objects named **obj_shroom_blue** and **obj_shroom_red.**

Step 2: Set the sprites to **spr_shroom_blue** and **spr_shroom_red,** respectively.

Step 3: Set the following variable for both Snail objects. In the **Create** Event of each, add a **Set Variable** Action which is found under the Control tab. Set the following:

Variable: powerupOne
Value: 0

Step 4: Add a second **Set Variable** below that for each. Set the following:

Variable: powerupTwo
Value: 0

Step 5: Add one last **Set Variable** for each below that and set the following:

Variable: powerupOne_active
Value: 0

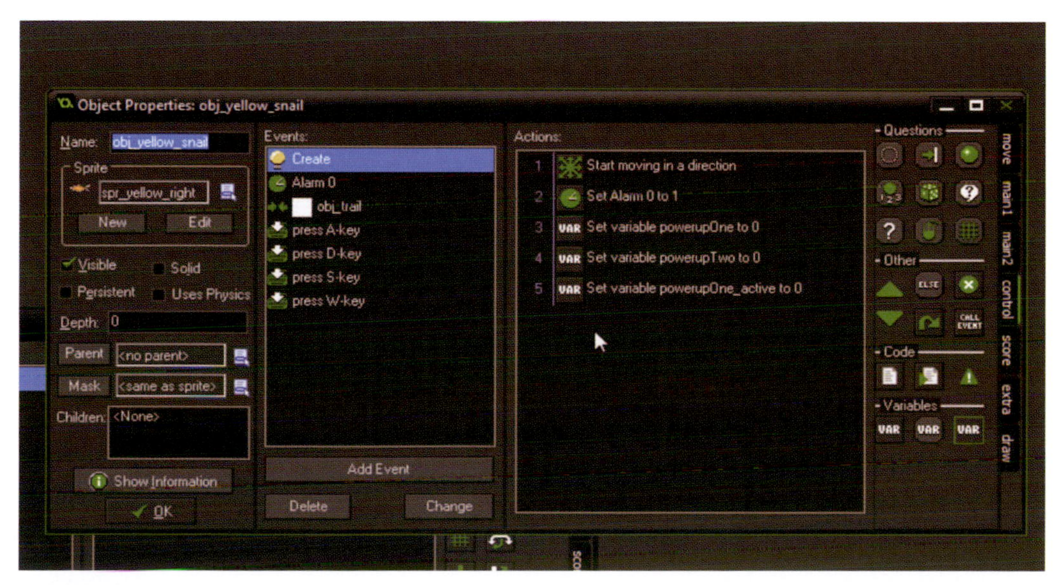

FIGURE 4.8

We will use the values 0 and 1 to represent when a picked-up object is active or not. We will need to create two variables. One with a value of zero indicating that the picked-up object is not active and a second variable with a value of one which indicates the picked-up object has been activated. The instructions below will show how to tell GameMaker that an object is picked up and, based on the value, if that object has become active or not.

Picking Up and Activating Objects

Step 1: For both snail objects add a **Collision** Event with both mushrooms.

Step 2: For both snail objects add a **Destroy Instance** Action in both of the Collision Events. At the top check the **Other** option so that the mushrooms will disappear rather than the snails disappearing.

Step 3: In both snail objects, for the Collision with the **Red** Mushroom Event selected, add a **Set Variable** Action and set the following:

Variable: powerupOne
Value: 1

Step 4: In both snail objects add a second **Set Variable** below that with the following settings:

Variable: powerupTwo
Value: 0

Step 5: In both snail objects, for the Collision with the **Blue** Mushroom Event selected, add a **Set Variable** Action and set the following:

Variable: powerupTwo
Value: 1

Step 6: In both snail objects add a second **Set Variable** below that with the following settings:

Variable: powerupOne
Value: 0

Setting the Invulnerable Ability for the Yellow Snail

Step 1: Open the **obj_yellow_snail** object.

Step 2: Add an **Alarm** Event using **Alarm 1**.

Step 3: Add a **Key Press** Event using **<Space>**.

Step 4: In the **Press<Space>** Event add a **Test Variable** Action, which can be found under the Control tab. Set the following:

Variable: powerupOne
Value: 1
Operation: Equal to

Step 5: Drag a **Start of a Block** arrow below the **Test Variable** Action. You may recall from previous chapters that the **Start of a Block** is a green up arrow.

Step 6: Drag a **Set Variable** Action below the **Start of a Block** and set the following:

Variable: powerupOne_active
Value: 1

Step 7: Drag a **Set Alarm** below the **Set Variable** Action and set the following:

Number of steps: 180 (Note: The room speed is 60, 60 = 1 second, therefore, 60 * 3 = 180, which would equal 3 seconds.)
In alarm no: Alarm 1

Step 8: Drag another **Set Variable** beneath the **Set Alarm** we just added. We will be adding this second **Set Variable** to prevent players from constantly reactivating the picked-up item. Set the following:

Variable: powerupOne
Value: 0

Step 9: Drag an **End of a Block** arrow beneath the **Set Variable** Action we just added so that the Actions window looks similar to **Figure 4.9**.

FIGURE 4.9

When the **Space** key is pressed the game will look to see if powerupOne is equal to 1. This will tell the game that the yellow snail collided with the red mushroom at some point. If powerupOne is equal to 1 the game will set the powerupOne_active variable to 1, which will start a 3-second timer. After the timer runs out it will activate the Alarm 1 Event. Next we will need to make an Alarm 1 Event that will set the powerupOne_active back to 0.

Step 10: In the **Alarm 1** Event drag a **Set Variable** Action into the Actions window and set the following:

Variable: powerupOne_active
Value: 0

We now need to make it so that the trail will not destroy the player while the picked-up object is active, thus making the player invulnerable for a set amount of time.

Step 11: In the **Collision** Event with **obj_trail** drag a **Test Variable** Action above the **Destroy Instance** Action and set the following:

Variable: powerupOne_active
Value: 0
Operation: equal to

This will test to make sure **powerupOne_active** is equal to 0.

Step 12: Drag a **Start of a Block** in between the **Test Variable** and **Destroy Instance** Action blocks.

Step 13: Drag an **End of a Block** below the **Destroy Instance** Action so that your Action window looks similar to the one in **Figure 4.10**.

FIGURE 4.10

Setting the Invulnerable Ability for the Purple Snail

Step 1: Open the **obj_purple_snail** object.

Step 2: Add an **Alarm** Event using **Alarm 1**.

Step 3: Add a **Key Press** Event using **<Enter>**.

Step 4: In the **Press<Enter>** Event add a **Test Variable** Action, which can be found under the Control tab. Set the following:

Variable: powerupOne
Value: 1
Operation: Equal to

Step 5: Drag a **Start of a Block** arrow below the **Test Variable** Action.

Step 6: Drag a **Set Variable** Action below the **Start of a Block** and set the following:

Variable: powerupOne_active
Value: 1

Step 7: Drag a **Set Alarm** below the **Set Variable** Action and set the following:

Number of steps: 180
In alarm no: Alarm 1

Step 8: Drag another **Set Variable** beneath the **Set Alarm** we just added. Set the following:

Variable: powerupOne
Value: 0

Step 9: Drag an **End of a Block** arrow beneath the **Set Variable** Action.

When the **Enter** key is pressed the game will look to see if powerupOne is equal to 1. This will tell the game that the purple snail collided with the red mushroom at some point. If powerupOne is equal to 1 the game will set the powerupOne_active variable to 1, which will start a 3-second timer. After the timer runs out it will activate the Alarm 1 Event. Next we will need to make an Alarm 1 Event that will set the powerupOne_active back to 0.

Step 10: In the **Alarm 1** Event drag a **Set Variable** Action into the Actions window and set the following:

Variable: powerupOne_active
Value: 0

We now need to make it so that the trail will not destroy the player while the picked-up object is active, thus making the player invulnerable for a set amount of time.

Step 11: In the **Collision** Event with **obj_trail** drag a **Test Variable** Action above the **Destroy Instance** Action and set the following:

Variable: powerupOne_active
Value: 0
Operation: equal to

This will test to make sure powerupOne_active is equal to 0.

Step 12: Drag a **Start of a Block** in between the **Test Variable** and **Destroy Instance** Action blocks.

Step 13: Drag an **End of a Block** below the **Destroy Instance** Action.

Testing the Picked-Up Item

Place two red mushrooms in the game and test to see that when the **Enter** or **Space** key is pressed for the appropriate snail that it allows the snail to move across the trails without being destroyed.

Setting the Freeze Ability for the Blue Mushroom

The blue mushrooms when picked up will allow a player to freeze the other player's snail. Since a snail can only hold one item at a time, we will use the same **Space** and **Enter** keys to activate the blue mushroom.

Step 1: We will start by creating two new snail objects. Create two objects and name them **obj_yellow_frozen** and **obj_purple_frozen**.

Step 2: Set the depth for both to −1.

Step 3: Set the sprite for the **obj_yellow_frozen** to **spr_yellow_frozen** and set the sprite for the **obj_purple_frozen** to **spr_purple_frozen**.

Step 4: In both objects, set up a **Create** Event and a **Step** Event which you will want to set as Step 0.

Step 5: In both Create Events drag a **Set Alarm** Action into the Actions window and set the following:

Number of steps: 180
In alarm no: Alarm 0

Step 6: In both Create Events drag a Moved Fixed Action and set the following:

Select the middle square in the center.
Speed: 0

Step 7: In the Alarm Event for obj_purple_frozen add a **Change Instance** Action in the Actions window and set the following:

Change into: obj_purple_snail
Perform events: yes

Step 8: In the Alarm Event for obj_yellow_frozen add a **Change Instance** Action in the Actions window and set the following:

Change into: obj_yellow_snail
Perform events: yes

Step 9: Open both of the snail objects and in the Press<**Space**> and Press<**Enter**> add a **Test Expression** Action to the bottom and set the following:

Variable: powerupTwo
Value: 1
Operation: equal to

Step 10: For both objects drag a **Start of a Block** beneath the **Test Expression**.

Step 11: Drag a **Change Instance** Action below the Start of a Block in each object and set the following.

Check the **Object** circle and set it to the **Opposite** snail.
Change into: The **Opposite** snails **Frozen Object.**
Perform events: yes

Step 12: Drag a **Set Variable** below the **Change Instance** Action for each object and set the following:

Variable: powerupTwo
Value: 0

Step 13: For both objects drag an **End of a Block** below the **Set Variable** Action we just added to each.

When the game is played now and a player picks up a blue mushroom and activates it the opposing player's snail will freeze for 3 seconds. This can allow the player that activated the picked-up item to navigate in front of the frozen snail so that when the frozen snail unfreezes after 3 seconds they will immediately slam into the trail left by the opponent's snail. At this time you will want to place a few mushrooms around the room and test to make sure the blue mushroom items work as intended.

Creating Multiple Levels

Step 1: Create two more rooms and name them **room_level_two** and **room_level_three.** This will give us a total of three rooms now. These will be our three playing levels. Set the room speed for each room to 60.

Step 2: Set the backgrounds for all three rooms we have created. The background for **room_level_one** should be **bg_level_one**. The background for **room_level_two** should be **bg_level_two,** and the **room_level_three** background should be set to **bg_level_three**.

Around the perimeter of each level are graphics that represent areas snails cannot go. At the moment these are simply graphics and a snail could easy move on top of them. We need to set up colliders so that the snails cannot leave the room, and if they hit one of the perimeters, they will be destroyed.

Adding Colliders to Each Level

Step 1: Create three new objects and name them as follows:

obj_collider_square
obj_collider_circle
obj_collider

Step 2: Set the sprite for the **obj_collider_square** to **spr_collider_square**. Set the sprite for **obj_collider_circle** to be **spr_collider_circle**. We will not be adding a sprite for the **obj_collider**.

We will be doing the same things for the colliders that we did for the trails earlier in the chapter. In fact we could just use the **obj_trail** as the parent for the colliders; however, that would limit any extra features that would make a collision with a wall different from a collision with a trail. First we need to make some changes to the Collider Properties.

Adjusting Collider Properties

Step 1: With the **obj_collider_square** and the **obj_collider_circle** open, uncheck the **Visible** option.

Step 2: Parent the **obj_collider_square** and the **obj_collider_circle** to the **obj_collider** as shown in **Figure 4.11**.

Adding Colliders to the Levels

Step 1: Open **room_level_one.**

Step 2: Click and place an obj_collider_square in the top left corner similar to that shown in **Figure 4.12**.

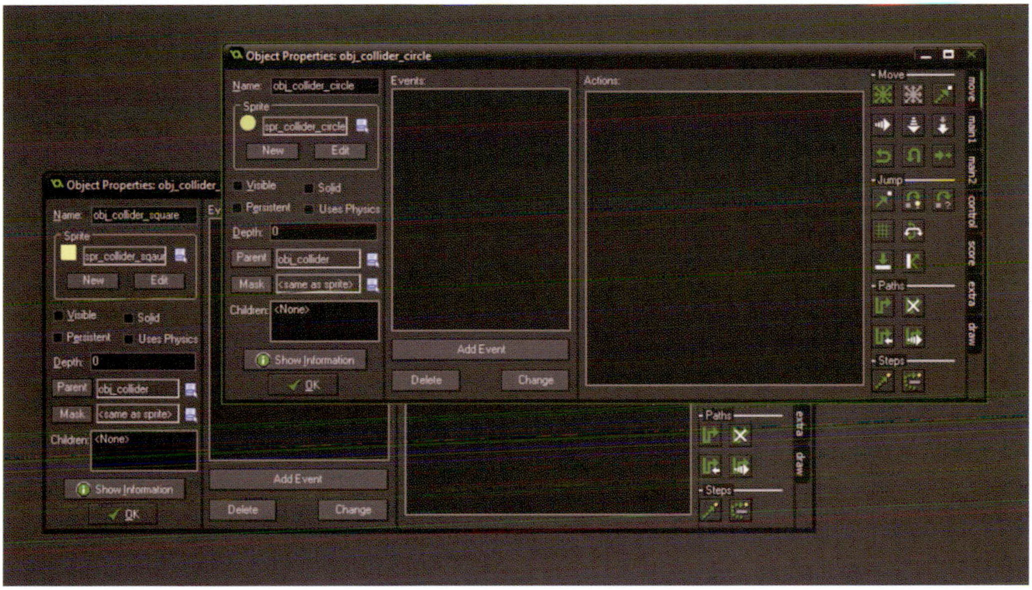

FIGURE 4.11

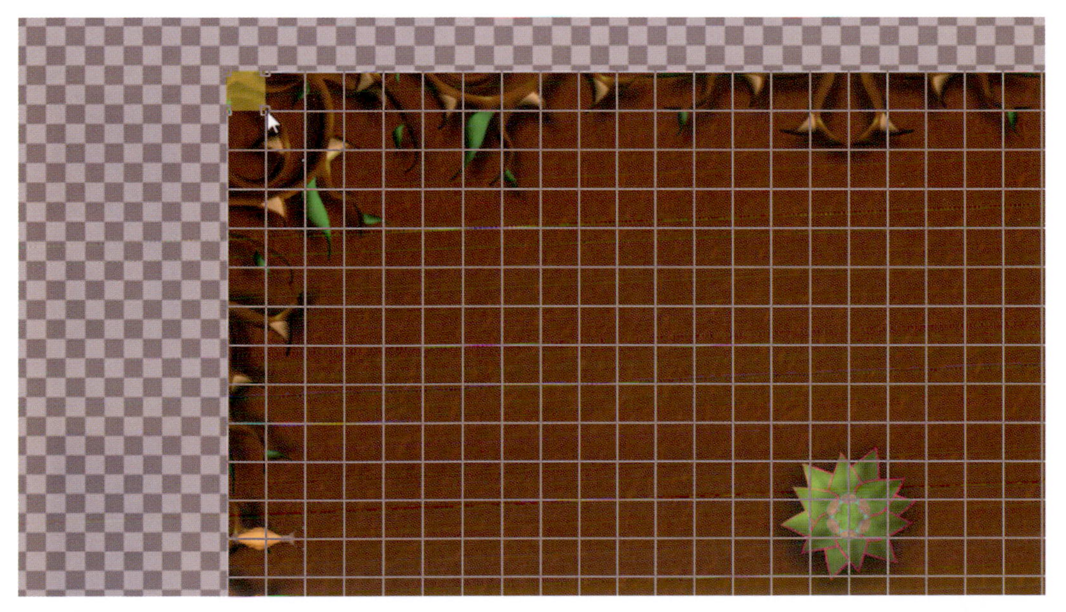

FIGURE 4.12

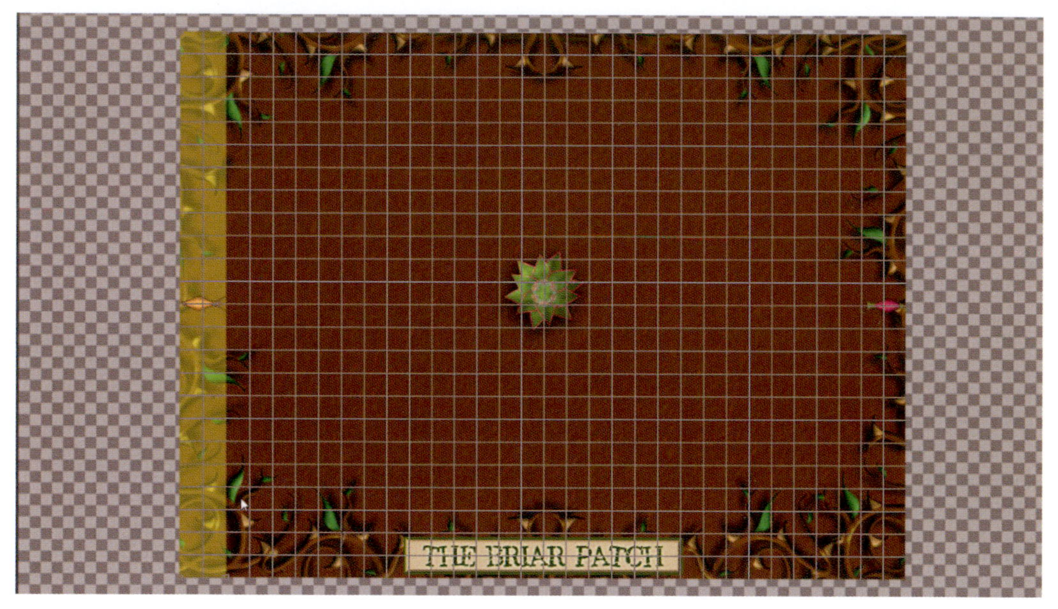

FIGURE 4.13

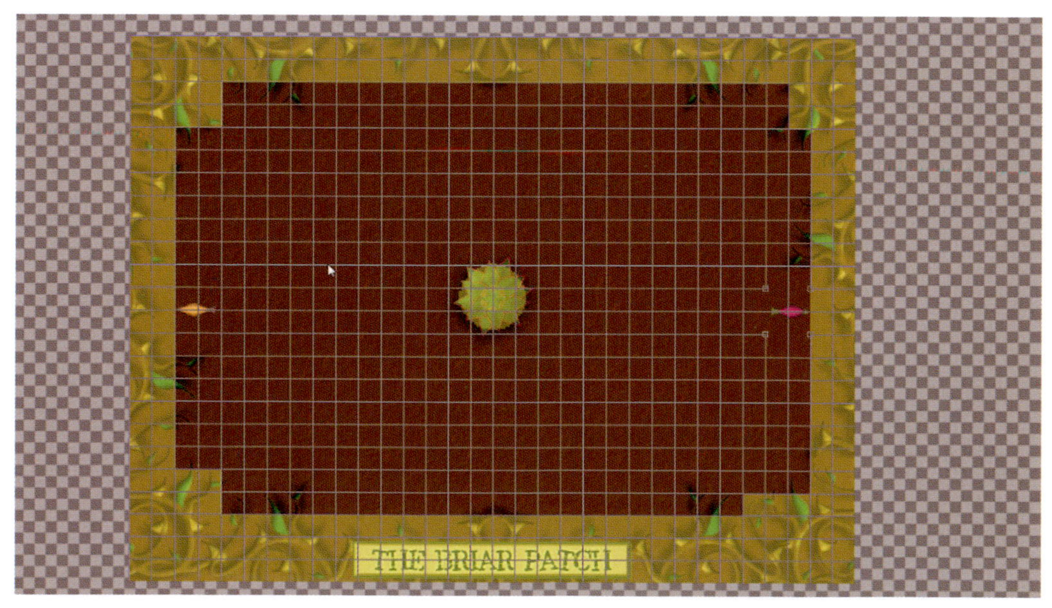

FIGURE 4.14

Step 3: Click and drag the small square shape on the bottom right of the object. This will allow you to scale the object.

Step 4: Scale the collider by holding down the **ALT** key so that it looks similar to the one shown in **Figure 4.13**. When scaling objects the object scales from the top left corner down.

Step 5: Place colliders and the snail objects in the rest of the levels so that your level looks similar to **Figure 4.14**. We will be setting up the collision events with the colliders later in this chapter.

Calculating Who the Winner Is

For the players to keep track of who has won each level we will be creating an object that will display text on each level of who the winner of that level is. The winner of the game is the player that wins two out of three games.

Step 1: Create a new object and name it **obj_winner_text.** Set the sprite to **spr_winner_text**.

Step 2: Add a Create Event and in the Create Event place a **Change Sprite** Action and set the following:

Sprite: spr_winner_text
Subimage: 2
Speed: 0

These settings will make it so that the image is blank while the match is being played. We will be setting up an event later in the chapter that will cause the blank image to change to a different subimage that reveals who the winner of the match is.

Step 3: Place the image on each level wherever you would like the text to appear.

Step 4: Next we will set up an object which will keep track of who wins. Create a new object and name it **obj_scorekeeper**. This object will not need a sprite.

Step 5: Add an **Other: Game Start** Event.

Step 6: In the **Game Start** Event add two **Set Variables** Actions and set them as follows:

Variable: global.purpleWins
value: 0
Variable: global.yellowWins
value 0

The **global.** tells the game that this variable can be accessed by any other object in the room. For this game object we will need it to store the values of the variables until the last room. In order to accomplish this we will need to make it **persistent,**

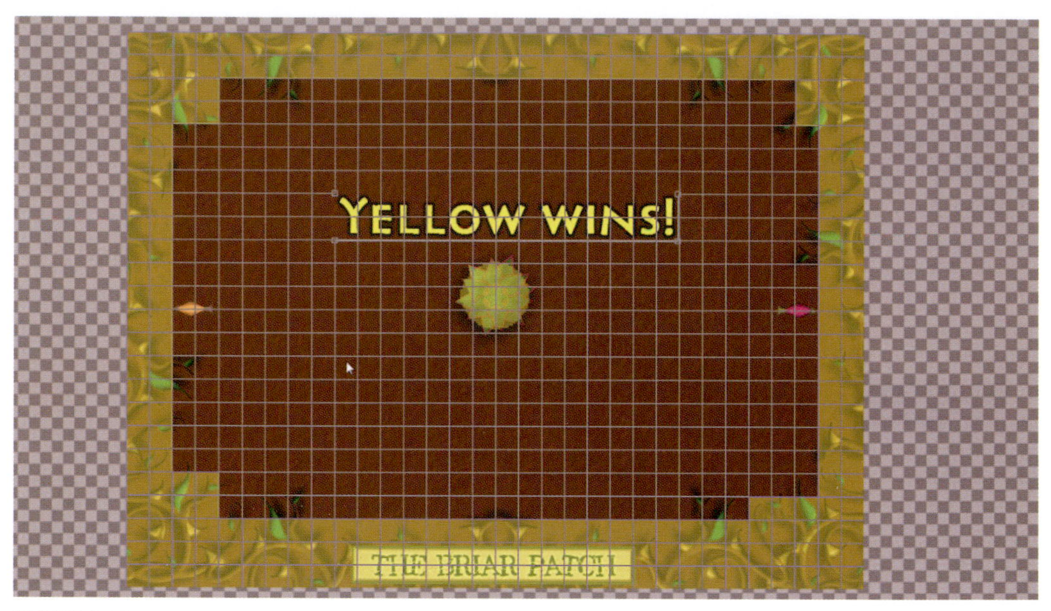

FIGURE 4.15

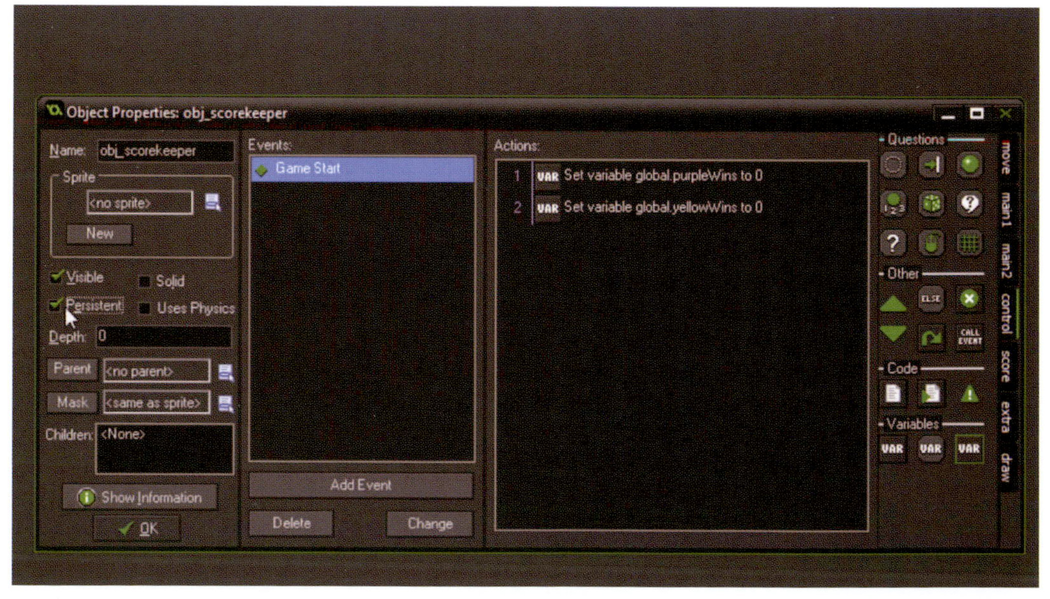

FIGURE 4.16

which means it will not be destroyed when a new room is loaded. This persistent game object will continue to the next room with the same values it stored from the previous room.

Step 7: Click the **Persistent** checkbox.

Step 8: We will now place obj_scorekeeper in room_level_one. The position you place this object in is not important.

What Are Parent and Child Objects?

Using parent objects can save game developers a lot of time. Parent objects are used for a variety of purposes, but to define what makes them special we will use an imaginary game as an example. Imagine we created a game in which a character jumps over fire pits and if the player's character lands in a fire pit they will be destroyed. One method of setting this up would be to create a collision event with each of these fire pits. Although this would work it could take a lot of time to set up. By using a parent object, we can set up the parent object with all of the information relating to the collision and then share that information with all the child objects, which in this case would be the fire pits. By doing this we only need to set up the collision information once in the parent object and then place as many child objects in the game as we want. This allows developers to save a lot of time when creating games and also allows each child object to have different attributes if desired since they are still separate objects.

Setting Up a Parent Object

To save time when adding colliders to our game we are going to set a parent for the snails that will hold the events that should be executed when a snail collides with a trail or a collider.

Step 1: Create a new object and name it **obj_snail_parent**. This object will not need a sprite.

In the parent object we will set up two alarm events that the snail will access to determine the winner. We will also want to check that the alarm number is not used by any of the other snail objects. We have already used Alarm 0 and Alarm 1. This lets us know that Alarms 2 and up are still available.

Step 2: Create an **Alarm 2** Event in the **obj_snail_parent**.

Step 3: Place a **Set Variable** Action and set the following:

Variable: global.yellowWins
Value: 1
Relative: checked

This will add one to the **yellowWins** variable. We will want to do the same for purple. Since we have just used Alarm 2 we will now want to use the next consecutive number for purple.

Step 4: Create an **Alarm 3** Event and drag in a **Set Variable** and set the following:

Variable: global.purpleWins
Value: 1
Relative: checked

Step 5: Press **OK** to save the **obj_snail_parent** and then open **obj_yellow_snail** and **obj_purple_snail**.

Step 6: For both snail objects, in the Collision Events with **obj_trail** we will now replace the **Destroy Instance** Action with a **Set Alarm** Action. Right-click and delete the **Destroy Instance** located between the green arrows for both objects.

Step 7: For both objects drag a **Set Alarm** Action where the **Destroy Instance** was and set the following:

Number of steps: 1
In alarm no: Alarm (**3** for **obj_snail_yellow**, **2** for **obj_snail_purple**)

Step 8: Now we will set up the Collision Event with the **obj_collider**. For both objects create a new **Collision** Event with the **obj_collider**.

Step 9: For both objects drag a **Set Alarm** Action in and set the following:

Number of steps: 1
In alarm no: Alarm (**3** for **obj_snail_yellow**, **2** for **obj_snail_purple**)

Step 10: For both objects click the **Parent** drop down box and select **obj_snail_parent,** then select the **OK** button for both snails.

Step 11: We will want to create two new versions of the snail, one for victory and another for defeat. Create two new objects and name them **obj_snail_winner** and **obj_snail_defeat**.

Step 12: Set the **obj_yellow_frozen** sprite for both of these; we will be changing the sprite later.

Step 13: For both the **obj_snail_winner** and the **obj_snail_defeat** objects add a Create Event.

Step 14: Drag in a **Move Fixed** Action to both of these objects and set the following:

Click the square in the middle.
Speed: 0

Step 15: Click **OK** and close only the winner snail.

Step 16: Add an **Other: Animation End** Event to the **obj_snail_defeat.**

Step 17: Drag a **Destroy Instance** Action into the event and click **OK** and close the object.

Here is a quick recap of what we have just accomplished in the **Setting Up a Parent Object** section:

- We created an object that will store how many wins each snail has.
- We created an object that will hold the events that are triggered when a snail collides with a trail or collider.
- We changed the collision with the **obj_trail** Event for both snails so that it now calls the previously stated events.
- We set up a Collision Event with the **obj_collider** that will also call the previously stated events.
- We created two separate objects that will be used after a snail collides and the player loses.

Setting Yellow as the Winner

In this next section we not only get to set up our game so that it calculates who the winner is, but we also get to explode the sprite of the loser so there is no question who the victor is for each round.

Step 1: Open the **obj_snail_parent** object and click on the **Alarm 2**. **Alarm 2** is called when yellow wins so let's make the purple snail explode and the yellow snail stops moving. In the rare occurrence that a snail has been frozen at the time the other player dies, we will need to test for both the frozen and normal snail objects. We will be using a **Test Instance Count** found in the Control tab to do it.

Step 2: Drag in a **Test Instance Count** Action and set the following:

Object: obj_yellow_frozen
Number: 1
Operation: equal to

Step 3: Drag in a **Start of a Block**.

Step 4: Drag in a **Change Instance** Action and set the following:

Click the Other checkbox and select obj_yellow_frozen
Change into: obj_snail_winner
Perform events: yes

Step 5: Drag in a second **Change Instance** Action and click the **Object checkbox** and select **obj_purple_snail**. Set the following:

Change into: obj_snail_defeat
Perform events: yes

Step 6: Drag in an **End of a Block**.

Step 7: Drag in an **Else** Action (this will occur only if the frozen snail does not exist).

Step 8: Drag in a **Start of a Block**.

Step 9: Drag in a **Change Instance** Action, click the **Object checkbox,** and select: **obj_purple_snail.** Set the following:

Change into: obj_snail_defeat.
Perform events: yes

Step 10: Drag in an **End of a Block**.

Step 11: Drag in an **Else** Action (this will occur only if the frozen snail does not exist).

Step 12: Drag in a **Start of a Block**.

Step 13: Drag in a second **Change Instance** Action, click the **Object checkbox,** and select: **obj_purple_snail.** Set the following:

Change into: obj_snail_defeat
Perform events: yes

Step 14: Drag in an **End of a Block**.

At the present we do not have sprites that correlate to **obj_spr_winner** and **obj_spr_defeat**. Nor have we added the text sprite that will appear declaring the winner of the round. We will now set the sprites for when yellow wins a round.

Setting the Sprites for When Yellow Wins

Step 1: With the **obj_snail_parent** object still open and the **Alarm 2 chosen,** drag in a **Change Sprite** and set the following:

Object: obj_spr_winner
Sprite: spr_yellow_frozen
Subimage: 0
Speed: 0

Step 2: Drag in a second **Change Sprite** and set the following:

Object: obj_spr_defeat
Sprite: spr_purple_explode
Subimage: 0
Speed: 0.2

Step 3: Drag in a final **Change Sprite** and set the following:

Object: obj_winner_text
Sprite: spr_winner_text
Subimage: 0 (yellow)
Speed: 0

At this moment our game is not very fair because we have not made it possible for the player controlling the purple snail to win. We will now add the same information for Alarm 3 so that purple can win as well.

Setting Purple as the Winner

Step 1: Open the **obj_snail_parent** object if it is not already open and click on the **Alarm 3**. **Alarm 3** is called when purple wins, causing the purple snail to stop moving and the yellow snail to explode.

Step 2: Drag in a **Test Instance Count** Action and set the following:

Object: obj_yellow_frozen
Number: 1
Operation: equal to

Step 3: Drag in a **Start of a Block**.

Step 4: Drag in a **Change Instance** Action and click the **Object checkbox,** then select: **obj_yellow_snail**. Set the following:

Change into: obj_snail_defeat
Perform events: yes

Step 5: Drag in an **End of a Block**.

Step 6: Drag in an **Else** Action (this will occur only if the frozen snail does not exist).

Step 7: Drag in a **Start of a Block**.

Step 8: Drag in a **Change Instance** Action, choose the **Object checkbox,** and select: **obj_purple_snail**. Set the following:

Change into: obj_snail_winner
Perform events: yes

Step 9: Drag in a **Change Instance** Action, click the **Object checkbox,** and select: **obj_purple_snail.** Set the following:

Change into: obj_snail_winner.
Perform events: yes

Step 10: Drag in a second **Change Instance** Action, click the **Object checkbox,** and select: **obj_yellow_snail.** Set the following:

Change into: obj_snail_defeat
Perform events: yes

Step 11: Drag in an **End of a Block**.

Setting the Sprites for When Purple Wins

Step 1: With the **obj_snail_parent** object still open and the **Alarm 3** chosen, drag in a **Change Sprite** and set the following:

Object: obj_spr_winner
Sprite: spr_purple_frozen
Subimage: 0
Speed: 0

Step 2: Drag in a second **Change Sprite** and set the following:

Object: obj_spr_defeat
Sprite: spr_yellow_explode
Subimage: 0
Speed: 0.2

Step 3: Drag in a final **Change Sprite** and set the following:

Object: obj_winner_text
Sprite: spr_winner_text
Subimage: 1 (purple)
Speed: 0

Progressing to the Next Level

We will now add another Alarm Event. Just as we did with Alarm 2 and 3, we will need to name this alarm for the next consecutive number that has not been used, which is 4. This alarm will have two functions. The first function for this alarm is to pause the game for 3 seconds after a round is finished; it will then see what level the players are on. If they are on level three it will calculate who the winner is and move the players to the winner screen. If the players are on one of the previous levels, it will advance the players to the next level.

Step 1: Open the **obj_snail_parent** object if it is not already open and create an **Alarm** Event which will be called after **Alarm 2** or **Alarm 3** has been executed. Name this alarm: **Alarm 4**.

Step 2: Alarm 4 will be activated 3 seconds (180 steps) after Alarm 2 or 3 has been called. You will want to add this setting now. This will give the appearance of the game being paused for 3 seconds. When **Alarm 4** is called it will decide if the players just finished level three or if they need to move to the next level. If the players have not yet completed level three, it will figure out who wins and go to the appropriate winner screen. Before we can do this we need to finalize the hierarchy of the Rooms folder by creating the additional rooms needed and placing them in the appropriate order.

Creating Two Different Winning Screens

We need two separate winning screens that will signal the end of the game. One winning screen will inform the players that yellow won and the other will be used when purple wins. The winning screens will be created using two new rooms that can be called in the actions we will be creating.

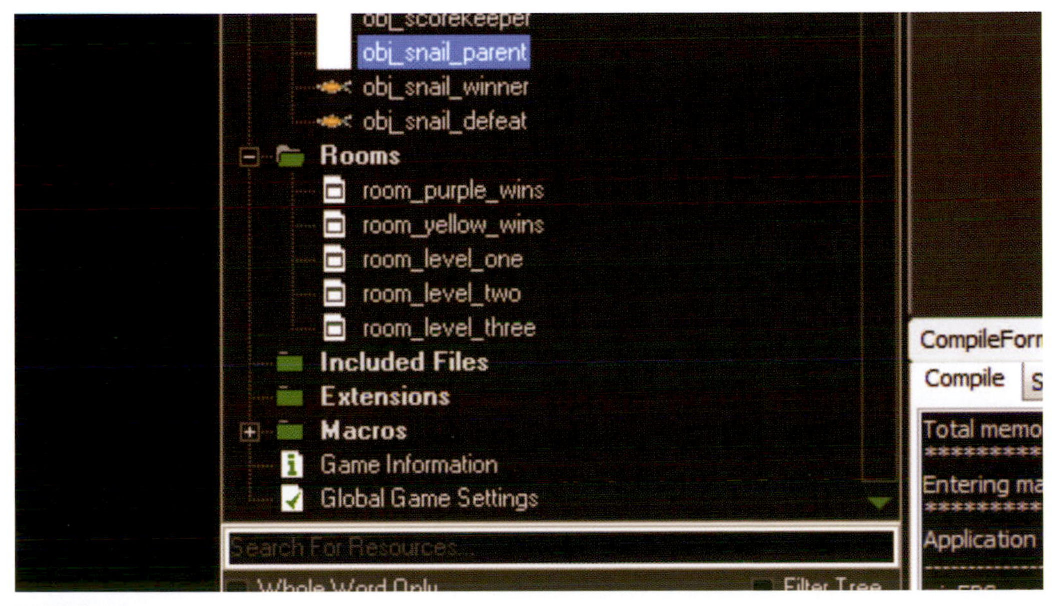

FIGURE 4.17

Step 1: Create two new rooms and name them **room_purple_wins** and **room_yellow_wins**.

Step 2: Click and drag each of these new rooms and place them above **room_level_one** in the list.

Step 3: We will now set the background for **room_purple_wins** as **bg_purple_wins** and the background for **room_yellow_wins** as **bg_yellow_wins**. Select the green check when complete.

Programming the Alarm 4 Event

Step 1: Open the **obj_snail_parent** object if it is not already open and in the **Alarm 2** and **3** Events, add a **Set Alarm** Action to the bottom of both lists and set the following:

Number of steps: 180
In alarm no: Alarm 4

Step 2: Select the **Alarm 4** Event. Earlier we placed the winner rooms above our level rooms in the list. We did this so that we can use an action which will locate the room our players are in and if another room exists after the room they are currently in. If another room does not exist, then we are clearly on level three because there will not be any additional rooms in the list.

Step 3: Drag in an **If Next Room Exists** Action.

Step 4: Place a **Start of a Block** Action below the **Check Next** Action.

Step 5: Drag a **Go to Next Room** Action below the **Start of a Block**.

Step 6: Drag an **End of a Block** beneath the **Go to Next Room** Action.

Step 7: Drag an **Else** Action below the **End of a Block,** which can be located on the **Control** tab.

Step 8: Drag in another **Start of a Block**. We will next add a variable that will test to see who the winner is.

Step 9: Drag in a **Test Variable** Action and set the following:

Variable: global.yellowWins
Value: global.purpleWins
Operation: greater than

This operation is basically asking: "Are the yellow wins greater than the purple wins?"

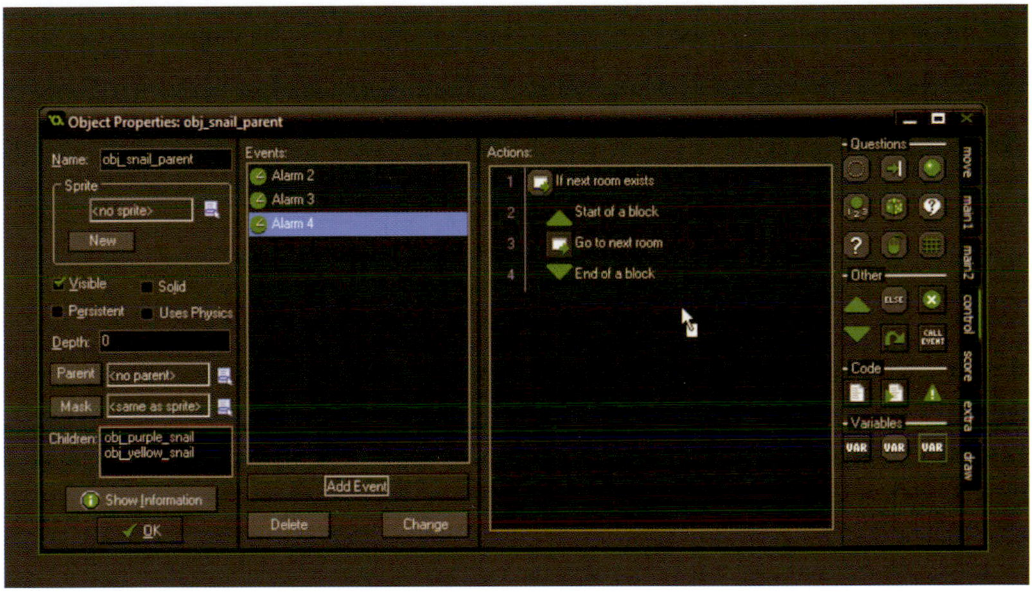

FIGURE 4.18

The formula GameMaker is following is: "**is variable > value?**".

Step 10: Drag a **Start of a Block** below the **Test Variable** Action.

Step 11: Drag a **Different Room** Action and place it under the **Start of a Block** and set the following:

New room: **room_yellow_winner**

Step 12: Drag an **End of a Block** below the **Different Room** Action.

Step 13: Drag an **Else** Action below the **End of a Block**. This **Else** Action will call any of the actions below it when the **Test Variable** Action we created is not true.

Step 14: Drag in a **Start of a Block** beneath the **Else** Action.

Step 15: Drag in a **Different Room** Action and set the following:

New room: room_purple_winner

Step 16: Drag in two **End of a Block** Actions.

Now when GameMaker sees that yellow has won more rounds than purple has, it will load a screen that reads "Yellow Wins!" If purple has won more games than yellow has won, then the game will load a screen that reads "Purple Wins!"

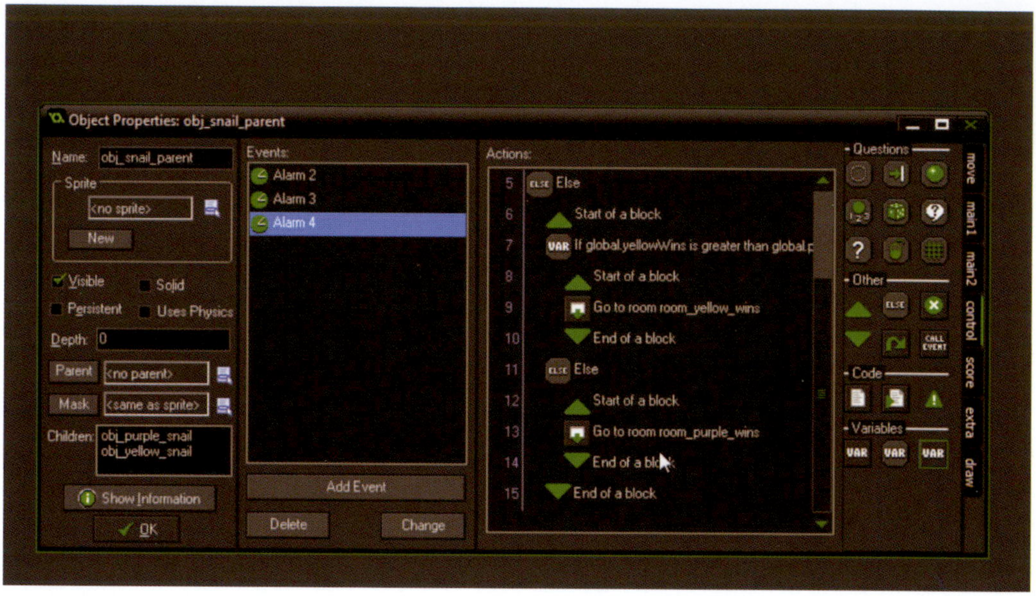

FIGURE 4.19

Finalizing the Title and Win Screens

In order for the players to start playing the game, quit the game, or replay the game after the game is complete, we need to create a title screen and add buttons to our win screens.

Step 1: Create a new room and name it **room_title,** then set the background to **bg_title**. Drag the room_title above all the other rooms in the Rooms folder. For the buttons on these screens we are going to use the scalable objects feature that we used previously on the colliders.

Step 2: Create two new objects and name them **obj_start** and **obj_quit**. Use the **spr_collider_square** sprite for both of these objects.

Step 3: In the **obj_start** object add a **Mouse: Left Button** Event.

Step 4: Drag in a **Go to Room** Action and set the following:

Room: room_level_one

Step 5: Click **OK** and then open the **obj_quit** object.

Step 6: Add another **Mouse: Left Button** Event and drag in an **End Game** Action.

Step 7: Go through **room_title**, **room_purple_wins,** and **room_yellow_wins** and position the **obj_quit** objects over the Quit buttons and scale it so it fits. Do the same with the **obj_start** for the start and replay graphics.

FIGURE 4.20

Adding Music and Sound Effects

Step 1: First we will add an explosion sound to the **obj_snail_defeat** object. Open **obj_snail_defeat** and click the Create Event, then add a **Play Sound** Action. Set the following:

Sound: snd_explosion
Loop: false

Step 2: Now we will create a sound effect so a player that is frozen will hear a sound indicating that they cannot move. Open both frozen snail objects and click the Create Event in both and add a Play Sound Action for both. Set the following in both frozen snail objects:

Sound: snd_snail_freeze
Loop: false

Step 3: We will want a sound effect to play when a snail is protected by the shield item. Open both snail objects. In the **<Enter>** and **<Space>** Events for both snail objects, drag a **Play Sound** Action between the **Set the variable powerupOne to 0** and the **End of a Block** Actions. Set the following:

Sound: snd_shield
Loop: false

Step 4: When a player picks up a mushroom we will have the game create a pick-up sound. Open both snail objects and in the collision events with blue and red mushrooms, drag a **Play Sound** Action below the **Set Variable** Action that is already there. Set the following for both snail objects:

Sound: snd_mushroom_pickup
Loop: false

Step 5: Each level will have its own background music. Create three new objects and name them: **obj_music_one**, **obj_music_two,** and **obj_music_three**.

Step 6: Open each of these objects and add a **Create** Event and an **Other: Room End** Event. In the Create Events for each of these three objects, add a **Play Sound** Action and set the following:

For **obj_music_one** set:

Sound: snd_level_1
Loop: true

For **obj_music_two** set:

Sound: snd_level_2
Loop: true

For **obj_music_three** set:

Sound: snd_level_3
Loop: true

Step 7: We will want only one background sound file to play at a time so that two songs are not playing at once. In the **Other: Room End** Event for all three objects, add a **Stop Sound** Action and set the following:

For **obj_music_one** set:

Sound: snd_level_1

For **obj_music_two** set:

Sound: snd_level_2

For **obj_music_three** set:

Sound: snd_level_3

Step 8: With all of our background music files set we will want to place them in the appropriate rooms. Place the **obj_music_one** object in **room_level_one**. Place the **obj_music_two** object in **room_level_two**. Place the **obj_music_three** object in **room_level_three**.

Testing the Final Game

Snail Trail is a two player competitive game in which two people play against each other with the goal of winning two out of three rounds. In order to test this game you will want to find another player to play against. Rather than playing the game from the GameMaker program you can export your game as a stand-alone executable file by clicking on **File,** then **Create Executable**. The drop down box below **File Name** should be set to **Single runtime executable (*.exe)**. This will allow you to play your game on another computer, even if that computer does not have GameMaker installed. Test to make sure that each player can control their own snail and that each snail is in a continuous state of movement. Test to make sure that when each snail collides with a solid object, the snail is destroyed. This should also include if the snail turns back upon its own trail and if the two snails collide with one another. You and the other player should practice using the snail contrails to trap one another and that the game scores who the winner is appropriately. If all of those controls are working properly, then you will want to test that the picked-up items are working as they are designed to. If one player wins two out of three matches, the game should then go to the winner screen. Once you have tested the game with a friend and everything appears to be working correctly, have two more players that have not played the game play against each other while you observe. This can sometimes reveal bugs that you would not have found on your own because different players may try things in a game that you never would have thought of trying.

Pixel Art

Learning Objectives—Upon completion of Chapter 5 readers will be able to:

- Create pixel art sprites and import them into their games
- Set the visual area of a room different from the actual area of the game
- Create multiple spawning alarms for different objects
- Use irandom to create random variables within a set range
- Use Mouse: Left Button Events so the game can be played on a touch screen
- Automatically remove a game object after a set time period

Project Overview: *Candy Catch*

The objective for the *Candy Catch* game is simple. The player will want to collect as much candy as possible while simultaneously squashing all the pumpkins. Pumpkin items will spawn randomly and travel down from the top of the screen to the bottom of the screen along with a variety of candy pieces. The challenge of the game is to only click on the pumpkins and not on the candy pieces. Doing so will result in a loss of points for the player. The player will also lose one of their three lives each time a pumpkin travels all the way to the bottom of the screen without being squashed. After creating this game we will then replace the pumpkin and candy graphics with pixel art.

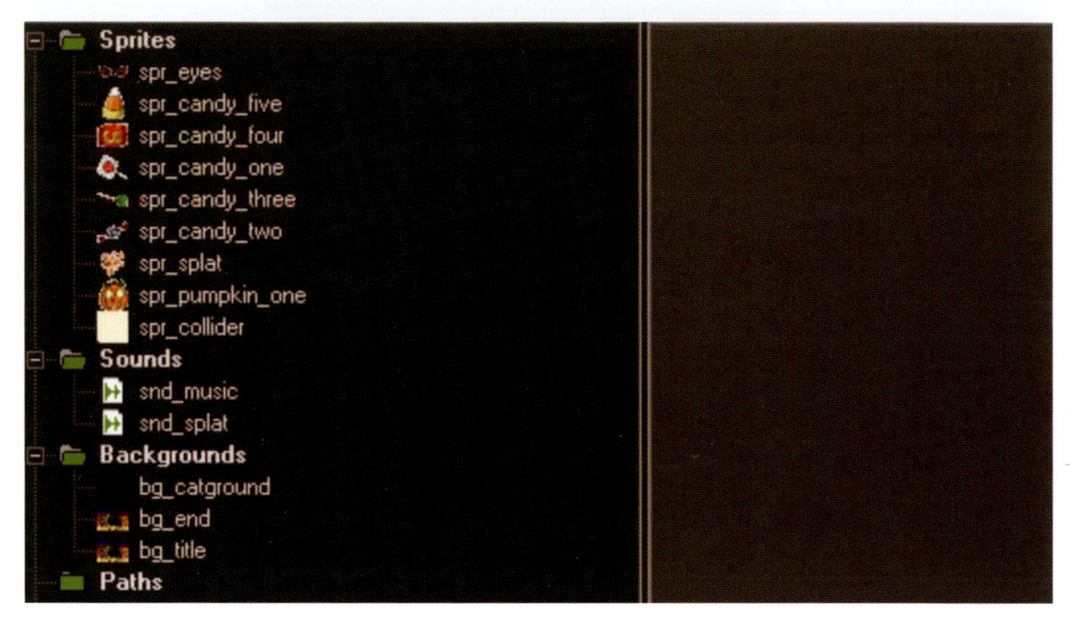

FIGURE 5.1

Go to www.thegamemakerstandard.com/candycatch and download the Candy Catch Game Asset zip file. After downloading the assets folder read over the updates.pdf document, which contains any changes since the publication of this book.

Creating a New Project

Step 1: Create a new game and name it **Candy Catch**.

Step 2: Import all the assets for the *Candy Catch* game and name them appropriately so they appear similar to **Figure 5.1.**

Step 3: Create a new room and name it room_gameplay. This particular game will only have one level so we will not need to make multiple room levels.

Step 4: Set the background to **bg_catground**.

Setting the Visual Game Play Area

The visual game play area is the area that the player sees while playing a game. In this case, the actual game will be taller than what the player will actually see. This way we can have objects falling into the field of view of the player. In order to have objects spawn and start falling before the player sees the objects, we will need to have the actual height of the game higher than the area the player can see. The area that the objects will spawn and start falling will be slightly above where the player can see.

Step 1: In the **Settings** tab for the rooms change the **Height** to **964.**

Step 2: Click the **Views** tab and check **Enable the Use of Views.**

Step 3: Check **Visible When Room Starts** and then set the **View in Room** settings as follows:

x: 0 W: 1024
y: 0 H: 768

Step 4: Set the **Port on Screen** settings as follows:

x: 0 W: 1024
y: 0 H: 768

Step 5: Click the green check to close the room.

Preparing the Sprites and Objects

Step 1: Open all the candy and pumpkin images and press the **Center** button. Then click the **Modify Mask** option and set the following for each:

Bounding box: Automatic
Shape: Precise

Step 2: Now that the sprites settings are correct we need to make our pumpkin and candy objects. Start by creating two objects and name them **obj_candy** and **obj_pumpkin.**

Step 3: Set the obj_pumpkin object's sprite to **spr_pumpkin.** Next set the **obj_candy** sprite to one of the five candy images. We will later set this up so it will pick a random candy image.

Setting the Objects to Spawn

We will now create an object that will spawn pumpkins and candy. For this we will be using two different Alarms. We will create an Alarm 0 which will be in charge of spawning the pumpkins that the player must destroy. We will then create an Alarm 1 which will be in charge of spawning the candy that the player will want to avoid touching so that it can be collected in their bag at the bottom of the screen.

Step 1: Create a new object and name it **obj_spawner**.

Step 2: Create three new events in the **obj_spawner** object. Add a **Create** Event, an **Alarm 0** Event**,** and an **Alarm 1** Event.

Step 3: In the **Create** Event add a **Set Alarm** Action and set the following:

Number of steps: 1
In alarm no: Alarm 0

Step 4: Below the **Set Alarm** Action add another **Set Alarm** Action and set the following:

Number of steps: 1
In alarm no: Alarm 1

Step 5: In **Alarm 0** we will be setting the location that each object will spawn and the speed in which it will fall from the top of the screen to the bottom. We will be creating the spawn points and the speed randomly so that the player will not be able to predict where the next item will appear or how fast it will be moving. In **Alarm 0** add a **Create Moving** Action and set the following:

Object: **obj_pumpkin**
x: irandom(980)+32 (This will pick a random x value between 0 and 980, then add 32 to it. **Figure 5.2** illustrates the area of the room this relates to.)
y: –64
Speed: irandom(5)+2 (This will pick a random speed between 0 and 5, then add 2 to it.)
Direction: 270
Relative: checked

Step 6: We will now create a time delay so that no two pumpkins will appear at the same time and avoid them appearing on top of each other. Drag a **Set Alarm** below the Create Moving Action and set the following:

Number of steps: irandom(15)+15 (This will give us a time delay of 15 to 30 steps before spawning a new pumpkin.)
In alarm no: Alarm 0

Now that we have completed all the settings for **Alarm 0** we can turn our attention to setting up **Alarm 1,** which is in charge of spawning the candy and randomly setting the candy falling speed.

Step 7: For the **Alarm 1** Action, add a **Create Moving** Action and set the following:

Object: obj_candy
x: irandom(980)+32
y: –64
Speed: irandom(5)+2
Direction: 270
Relative: checked

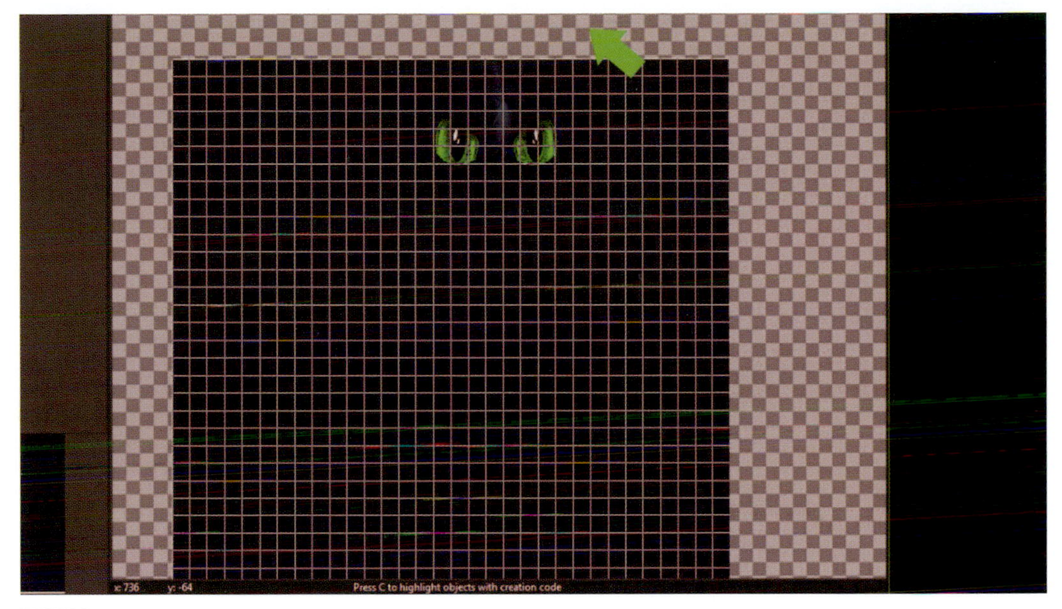

FIGURE 5.2

Step 8: Below the **Create Moving** Action add a **Set Alarm** Action and set the following:

Number of steps: 20
In alarm no: Alarm 1

Spawning Different Types of Candy

We can now place the **obj_spawner** in our **room_gameplay** room and observe as the pumpkin and candy objects fall from the top of the room at random speeds. We currently have only one type of candy falling from the top. A variety of different types of candy will make the game more visually exciting and will make spotting the pumpkins a bit more difficult. We will now change the settings in our obj_candy object so that it will randomly spawn different candy sprites rather than the same one over and over.

Step 1: Open the **obj_candy** object and add a **Create** Event.

Step 2: Drag in a **Set Variable** Action and set the following:

Variable: myImage
Value: irandom(4)+1

For the value we are using irandom. The irandom picks a whole number between the range of 0 and the number in the parenthesis. For this particular irandom function we want a number between one and five. To accomplish this we put the number four in parenthesis and then added one. This way if a zero is selected it will automatically convert to the number one. The number generated will never be over five nor less than one.

We need to set five **Test Variables** and change sprite actions. Each **Test Variable** will relate to a different candy sprite. Below are the steps to create two of the five variables. These steps provide all the information needed to create the other three. Make sure you create all five **Test Variables** by modifying the information from the instructions for the first two below. When complete you may wish to double check to ensure you made the appropriate changes to each so all five images will work correctly in the game.

Step 3: Drag in a **Test Variable** Action and set the following:

Variable: myImage
Value: 1
Operation: Equal to

Step 4: Drag in a **Start of a Block.**

Step 5: Drag in a **Change Sprite** Action and set the following:

Sprite: **spr_candy_one**
Subimage: 0
Speed: 0

Step 6: Drag in an **End of a Block**.

We will now repeat Steps 3 through 6 for the four other candy images. We will walk through with the second **Test Variable** so the changes that need to be made to this second **Test Variable** compared to the first one are apparent.

Step 7: Drag in a **Test Variable** Action and set the following:

Variable: myImage
Value: **2**
Operation: Equal to

Step 8: Drag in a **Start of a Block.**

Step 9: Drag in a **Change Sprite** Action and set the following:

Sprite: **spr_candy_two**
Subimage: 0
Speed: 0

Step 10: Drag in an **End of a Block.**

Complete the next three **Test Variables** with the appropriate changes for each and run the game. You should now see that the candy images are random. There should be five different candy sprite images being generated randomly.

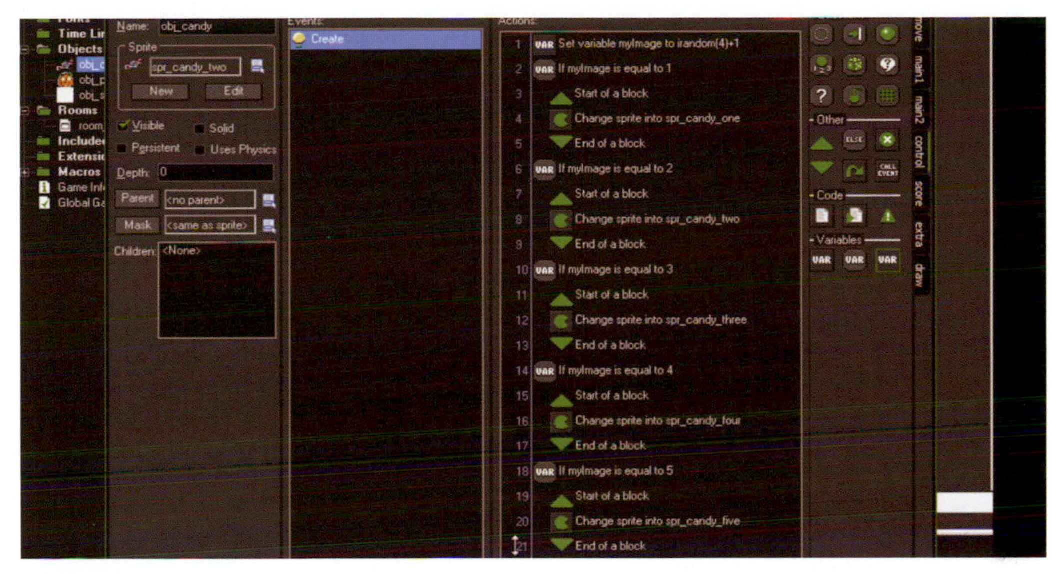

FIGURE 5.3

Destroying the Pumpkin and Candy Objects

As the candy and pumpkin objects leave the screen at the bottom after falling they seem to disappear. GameMaker is still calculating these objects, however, and will continue to calculate their movements as long as the game is running. Since the player can no longer see these objects it is a waste of computer resources for them to continue existing. With all of the on screen objects being calculated and all of the objects no longer on screen being calculated, we face a good possibility of the game crashing after a while because so many items are being tracked. It is therefore necessary to destroy the candy and pumpkin instances as soon as they leave the viewable area. This way the only items using resources are those in the visible area of the screen.

Step 1: Create a new object and name it **obj_collider** and use **spr_collider** as the sprite. Uncheck the Visible option in the **obj_collider.**

Step 2: Place the **obj_collider** at the bottom left corner of the **room_gameplay** screen.

Step 3: Change the **x scale** so that the **obj_collider** covers the bottom of the screen as shown in **Figure 5.5**.

Step 4: We will now create the collision events that will destroy a pumpkin object or a candy object when either of them hits the object collider. Open **obj_pumpkin** and add a **Collision** Event with the **obj_collider** Event.

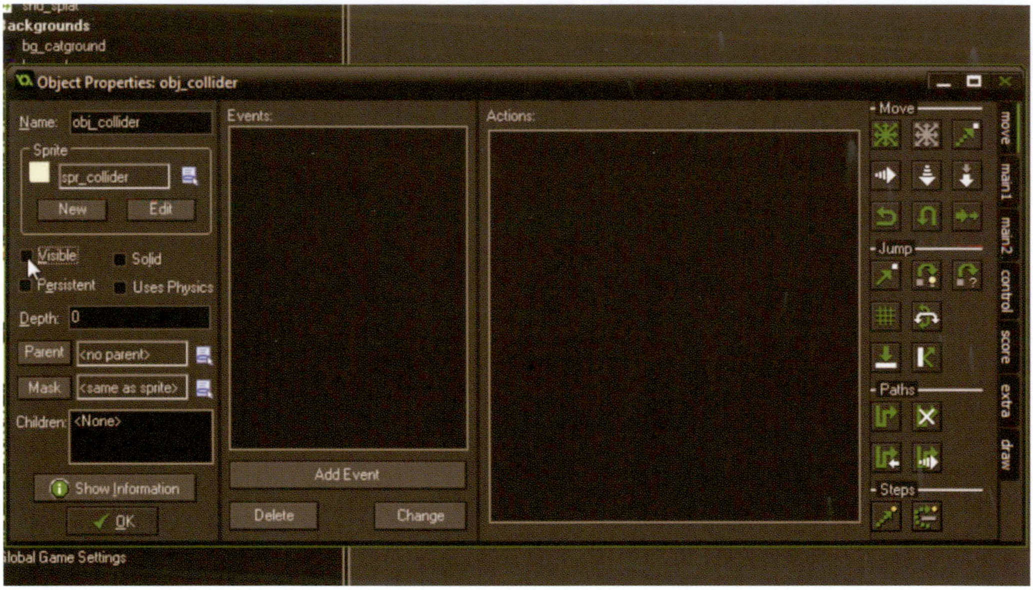

FIGURE 5.4

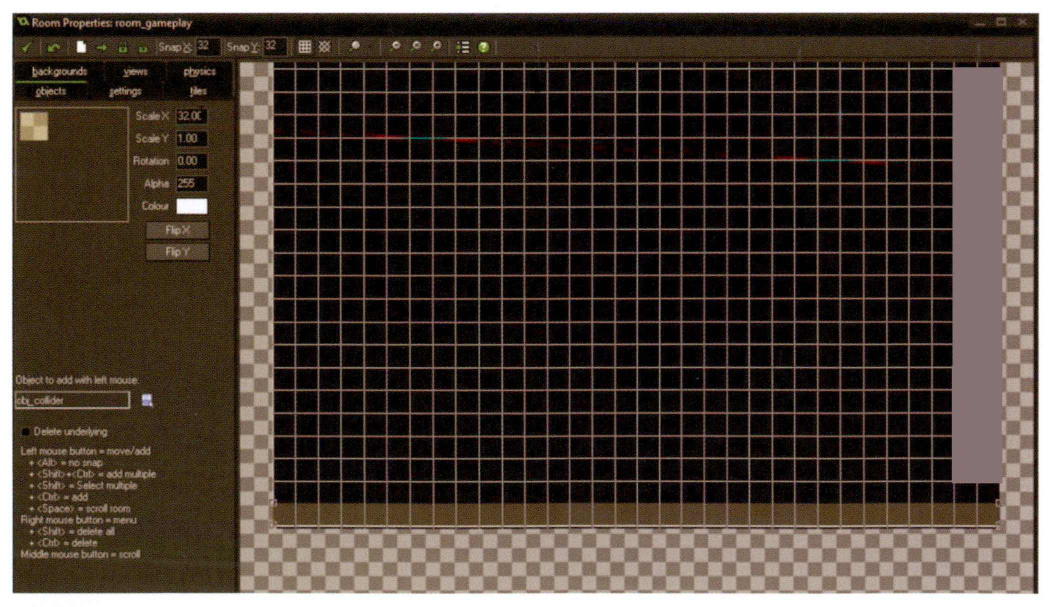

FIGURE 5.5

Step 5: Add a **Destroy Instance** Action to the event.

Step 6: Open **obj_candy** and add a **Collision** Event with the **obj_collider** Event.

Step 7: Add a **Destroy Instance** Action to the event.

Adding a Mouse: Left Button Event

The player will attempt to squash the pumpkins before the pumpkins reach the bottom of the screen. We will be using a **Mouse: Left Button** Event which will allow players to use their mouse to cursor over the pumpkin images to squash them, which will also play a sound effect. If a player is using a touch screen on a tablet they would be able to squash the pumpkins by touching the screen in the same type of movement they would use to double click an icon to activate a program. By using this type of control it allows users with touch screens to play using the touch screen options while also allowing users with a traditional mouse to play the game as well.

Step 1: Open the **obj_pumpkin** object and add a **Mouse: Left Button** Event.

Step 2: Once the pumpkin is clicked we will want it to stop moving. Drag a **Move Fixed** Action and set the following to stop the pumpkin:

Square in the middle pressed
Speed: 0

Step 3: Now that the pumpkin has stopped moving, we will set it so that the pumpkin sprite switches to that of a squashed pumpkin. Drag in a **Change Sprite** and set the following:

Sprite: spr_splat
Subimage: 0
Speed: 0

Step 4: We will now add a sound effect that will play when the pumpkin is being squashed. Drag in a **Play Sound** Action and set the following:

Sound: snd_splat
Loop: false

Setting the Sprite Depth

If you were to play the game at present and started clicking pumpkins you would find that the squashed pumpkin sprite is not lined up correctly with the original pumpkin image. Both images must be lined up for the effect to work. We also need the squashed pumpkin image to appear behind all the candy images so that once a pumpkin is squashed the candy that is falling above it will pass in front of it.

Step 1: Open the **spr_splat** sprite and press the **Center** button. Then select **OK**.

Step 2: Now that the image is centered we will give the game the ability to change the depth of the squashed pumpkin image as soon as it appears. Open the Object **obj_pumpkin** and select the **Mouse Click** Event. Using the **Set Variable** Action we can access GameMaker's built-in depth variable. Add a **Set Variable** below the **Play Sound** Action and set the following:

Variable: depth
Value: 5

Now if we run the game we will see that the splat images are behind all the other images. We will next want to set a timer that will remove the squashed pumpkin images after a certain number of steps. If we did not add a timer the game screen would quickly become cluttered with squashed pumpkins, which would not only make the game more difficult to play than we want, but it would also use up computer resources by keeping those images visible.

Destroying an Instance After a Set Number of Steps

Step 1: In the **obj_pumpkin** object add an **Alarm: Alarm 0** Event.

Step 2: Add a **Destroy Instance** Action to the **Alarm 0** Event.

Step 3: Select the **Mouse: Left Button** Event and add a **Set Alarm** Action in it and set the following:

Number of steps: 15
In alarm no: Alarm 0

In GameMaker, 15 steps equals half a second. Now after a pumpkin object is clicked, the object will disappear after 0.5 seconds. We will now add a Destroy Instance Action to the candy object as well so each candy will disappear after being clicked on.

Step 4: Open the **obj_candy** object and add a **Mouse: Left Button** Event.

Step 5: Add a **Destroy Instance** Action to the **Mouse: Left Button** Event.

Setting the Player's Lives

In its current state the game allows the player to destroy the candy and pumpkin objects without any rewards or punishments. We will now set the game goals and rules so that if a pumpkin reaches the bottom of the screen the player will lose a life. If candy reaches the bottom of the screen the player's score will increase; however, if the player accidentally clicks on one of the candy objects the player will lose points. We will first start with setting up the player's lives.

Step 1: Create a new object and name it **obj_control**. This object will not need a sprite.

Step 2: Add a **Create** Event and drag in a **Set Lives** Action and set the following:

New lives: 3

Step 3: Now that the player has three lives the game will want to check to make sure that the player's lives are not less than one. If the player's lives are less than one, it means that the player has used up all of their lives and the game is over.

Step 4: Create a **Step: Step** Event then drag in a **Test Lives** Action and set the following:

Value: 1
Operation: smaller than

Step 5: Drag in a Start of a Block.

Step 6: Drag in a **Display Message** below the **Start of a Block**. Set the following:

Message: Game over!

Step 7: Drag in a **Restart Room** Action below the **Display Message** and then drag in an **End of a Block**.

FIGURE 5.6

Step 8: Close the **obj_control** object, then open **room_gameplay** and place the **obj_control** anywhere in the room.

Step 9: To set the **obj_pumpkin** to remove a player's life if a pumpkin falls off the screen, we will open the **obj_pumpkin** and select the **Collison** Event.

Step 10: Drag in a **Set Lives** Action below the **Destroy Instance** Action and set the following:

New lives: –1
Relative: Checked

Notifying the Player That They Have Lost a Life

This particular type of game requires the player to constantly remain focused on what objects are currently on the screen. We need to set up something that notifies the player they lost a life without disrupting the player's concentration or requiring them to look outside the main playable area of the screen. The background of the playable area of the game is an image of a cat with vibrant green eyes. The rest of the cat almost blends in with the dark background so as not to make the game objects difficult to see and also to bring attention to its eyes. To inform the player that they have just lost one of their lives we will have the cat's eyes turn red for a brief moment. This way the player can be informed that they lost a life in a subtle way that does not break their concentration.

Step 1: Create a new object and name it **obj_eyes**. Set the sprite for the **obj_eyes** to be spr_eyes.

Step 2: Add an **Other: Animation End** Event and drag in a **Destroy Instance** Action, then close the object.

Step 3: Reopen the **obj_pumpkin** object and select the **Collision** Event. Add a **Create Instance** Action and set the following:

Object: obj_eyes
x: 446
y: 87

Creating the Game Score System

Step 1: Open the **obj_control** object and select the **Create** Event.

Step 2: Drag in a **Set Score** Action and set the following:

New score: 0

Step 3: Open the **obj_candy** object and select the **Collision** Event. Add a **Set Score** Action and set the following:

New Score: 100
Relative: checked

The player will now receive points for every candy object that crosses the bottom of the screen. Next we will set the game to take away points if the player accidentally clicks on a candy object.

Step 4: Select the **Mouse: Left Button** Event and drag in a **Set Score** Action and set the following:

New score: –500
Relative: checked

Step 5: In order for the player to see their score we will set up an event which will draw the score on the screen. Open the **obj_control** and add a **Draw Event: Draw.**

Step 6: Drag in a **Draw Score** Action and set the following:

x: 0
y: 0
Caption: Score:

Step 7: Select the **Create** Event and drag in a **Set Color** Action. Select the color you would like the text to be.

Setting the Background Music

A music loop will play in the background of our game. The music is a simple loop that will continue over and over while the game is being played. This type of song will eventually be tuned out by the player but adds a whimsical feel about the game. The player should not be surprised if they find the song playing in their head long after they have stopped playing the game. Simple loops such as this can linger with a person when heard over and over. We will be using a .wav file for the background music so that the music will loop without any audible gaps. For our sound effects we typically use compressed MP3 files because they are much smaller files than uncompressed .wav files; however, MP3 files may cause a moment of silence when looping as the MP3 file reloads.

Step 1: Open the **obj_control** object and select the Create Event.

Step 2: Drag in a **Play Sound** Action and set the following:

Sound: snd_music
Loop: true

Step 3: Add an **Other: Room End** Event and drag a **Stop Sound** into the event and set the following:

Sound: snd_music

Setting the Title and End Game Screen

Step 1: Create two rooms and name them **room_title** and **room_end.** Set the background for **room_title** to **bg_title** and set the background for **room_end** to **bg_end.**

Step 2: Drag the **room_title** and place it above **room_gameplay**.

Step 3: When the game is over the Game Over screen will appear. To set this, open the **obj_control** and select the **Step** Event.

Step 4: Delete the **Restart Room** Action we added previously and add a **Next Room** Action in its place.

Step 5: Setting up the buttons is all that is left to do for the title and end screens. Create two objects and name them **obj_play** and **obj_quit**.

Step 6: Set the sprite for both **obj_play** and **obj_quit** to **spr_collider**

Step 7: Open the **obj_play** object and add a **Mouse: Left Button** Event.

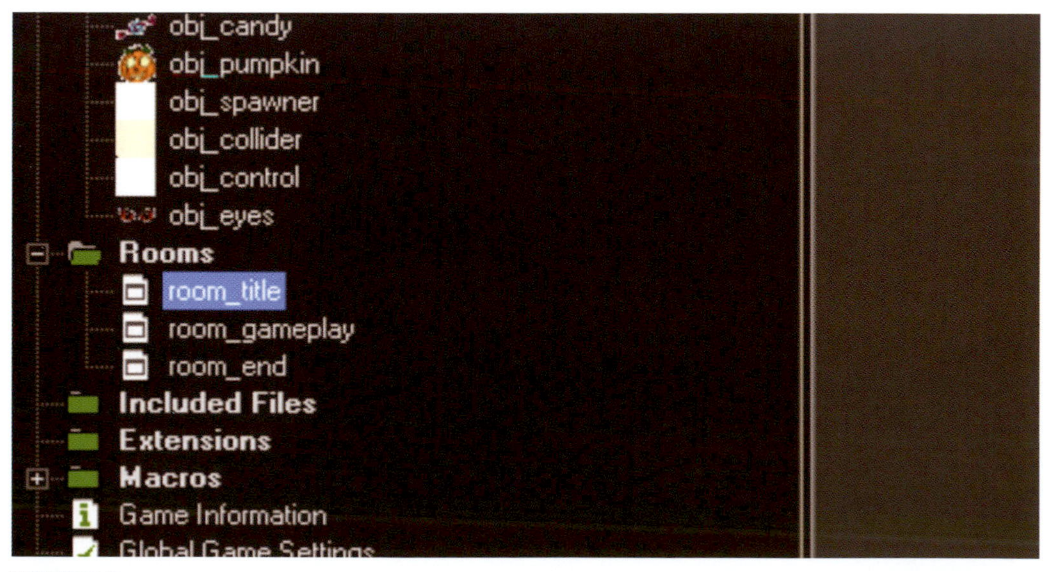

FIGURE 5.7

FIGURE 5.8

FIGURE 5.9

Step 8: Drag in a **Different Room** Action and set it to **room_gameplay.**

Step 9: Open the **obj_quit** object and add a **Mouse: Left Button** Event.

Step 10: Add an **End Game** Action.

Step 11: Open the title and end rooms and place the Play button and Quit button in the appropriate spots, scaling them as needed.

Creating Pixel Art

Pixel art is a popular style of game graphic art that is reminiscent of the 8- and 16-bit games from the early 1980s. Although pixel art games could invoke a feeling of nostalgia, there is a growing fan base for this style of game art among players that were not even born when these original games were released.

There are many different methods of creating pixel art for games. Some artists will draw a high resolution graphic and then reduce the number of pixels in a graphic editing software program such as Adobe Photoshop. Others will create graphics using basic drawing tools like Microsoft Paint. There is not a right or wrong way to create pixel art so long as the end result is to your liking. For our game we will be using the image editor in GameMaker to pull in candy and pumpkin images, deleting them, and then drawing our own version. The main purpose of this portion of the game development is not to become an expert in designing pixel art as that takes time and practice, but rather to be familiar with the term, how pixel art can be created in GameMaker, as well as introducing the drawing tools in GameMaker.

Step 1: Open the **spr_pumpkin_one** sprite.

Step 2: Select **Edit Sprite**. This will open up the **Sprite Editor**.

Step 3: On the **Sprite Editor toolbar** click on **Edit**. Then select **Edit** from the drop down list.

Step 4: This will open up the **Image Editor** allowing you to change the way the sprite looks. You can zoom in on the image by using the center mouse button or scroll wheel.

Step 5: Use the **Eraser Tool** to erase the existing pumpkin image. You can also use the **Selection Tool** to select the entire pumpkin and then press the **Delete Key** on your keyboard to delete the current image.

Step 6: Use the drawing tools to draw the outline of a new pumpkin. As you hover over each tool a label will pop up telling what the tool does. Experiment with the different tools. For the pumpkin you may wish to start with a circle tool and then use the fill tool to fill in the color for the pumpkin.

Step 7: Add the pumpkin's face and details. To add shading, use a color slightly darker than the color you are shading.

Step 8: When your pumpkin is complete, go to **File>Close Save Changes**. This will replace the original pumpkin with the new pixel art drawing you just made. You do

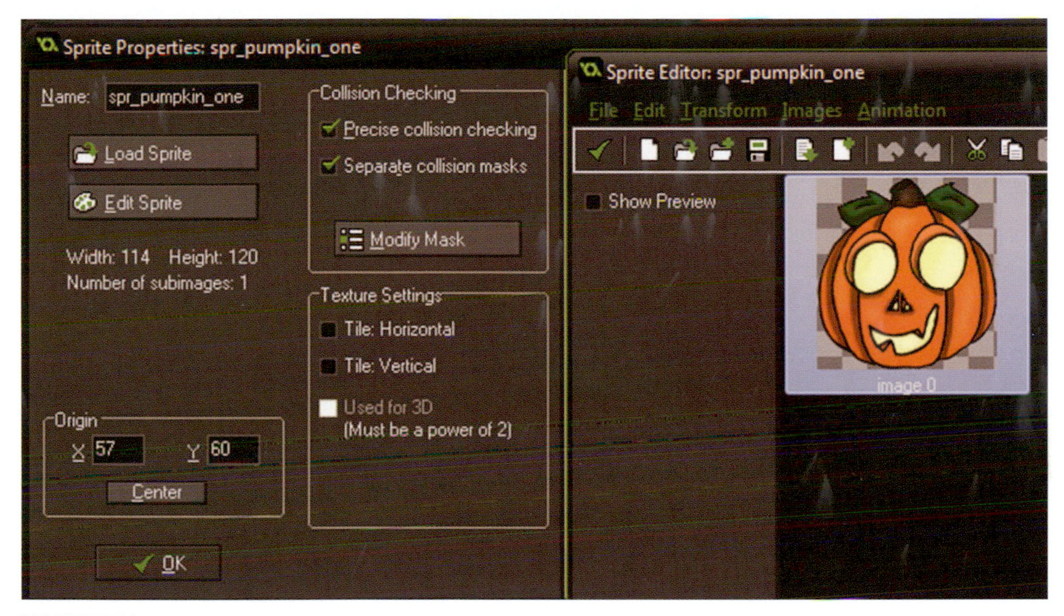

FIGURE 5.10

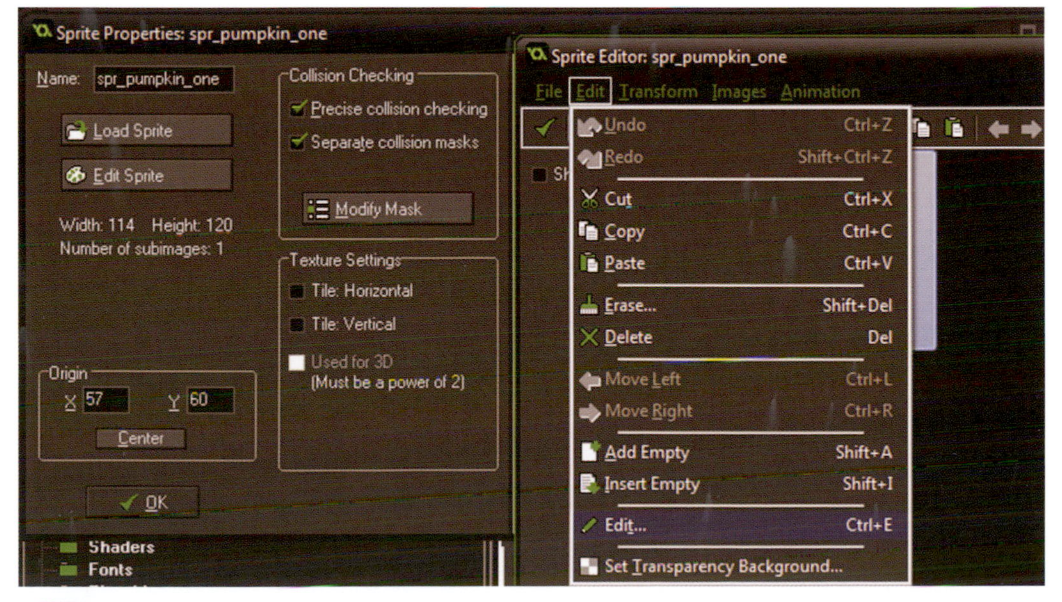

FIGURE 5.11

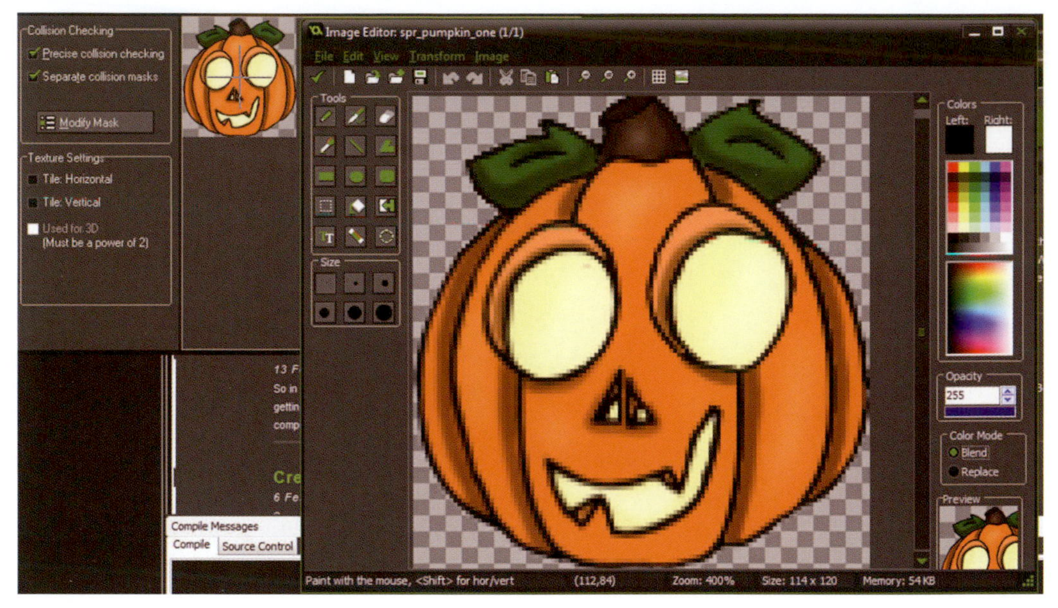

FIGURE 5.12

FIGURE 5.13

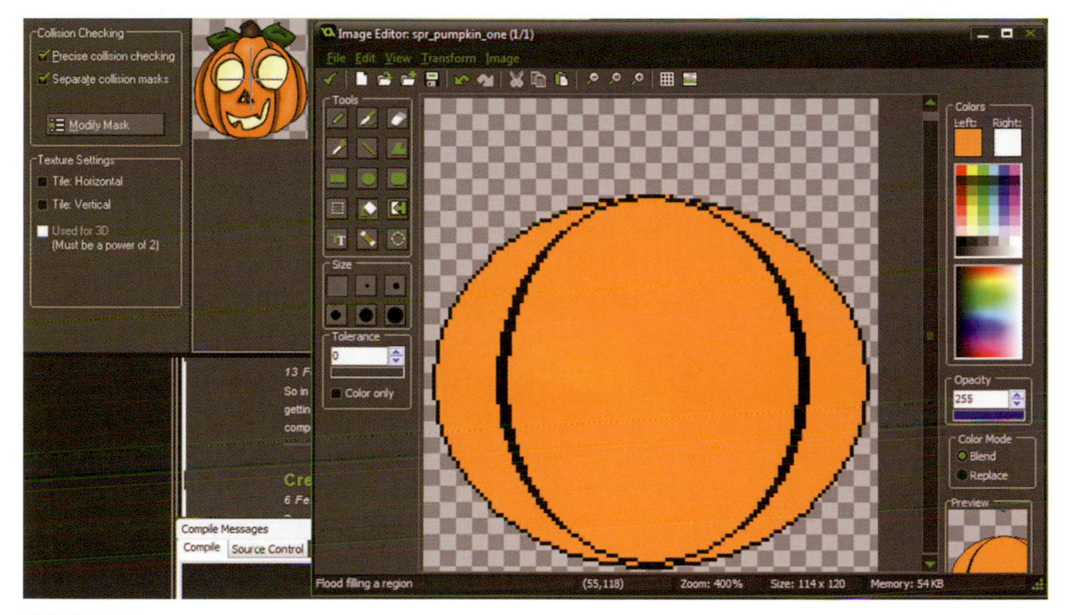

FIGURE 5.14

FIGURE 5.15

not have to make your pumpkin look the same as the one in the game; however, make sure any item you create fits within the same space as the original so that it will show up correctly in the game.

Step 9: Open up all of the other candy items one at a time and replace them with pixel art. Since our background changes when the player lets a pumpkin hit the bottom of the screen, we will not be changing the background image for this game.

Testing the Final Game

The *Candy Catch* game is almost complete. The final step in creating any game is testing it. Play the game by yourself first to make sure everything is working as it should and that the newly created pixel art graphics are appearing. Check to see if you need to create a pixel art version of the pumpkin being squashed or if you picked up on the fact that the squashed image needed to be turned into pixel art as well to fit in with the game. As with any art form, whether it is creating games or creating pixel art, continuing to practice will help you develop new skills that you can implement in future projects.

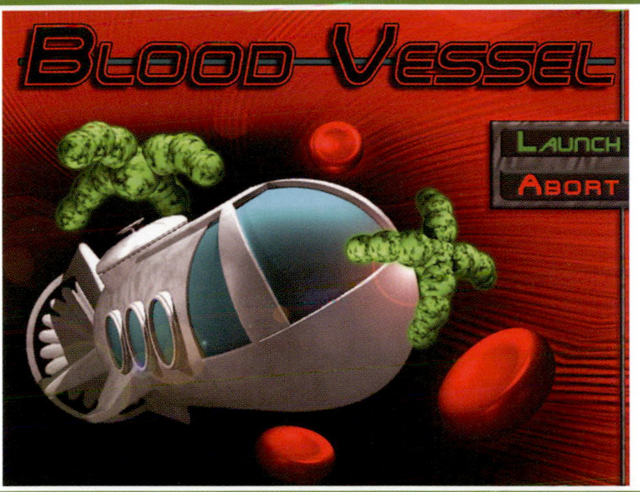

2.5D—Simulating a 3D Look in a 2D Game

Learning Objectives—Upon completion of Chapter 6 readers will be able to:

- Define what a 2.5D game is and how it differs from 2D and 3D games
- Illustrate techniques used to create the illusion of depth
- Use sprite sheets to create three-dimensional-looking objects
- Define what an optical illusion is and how it can be incorporated into game design
- Understand how the human eye sees objects in a three-dimensional space
- Create an in-game health bar

Project Overview: *Blood Vessel*

In *Blood Vessel* the player is piloting a microscopic vehicle which is traveling through another person's bloodstream. The player will want to blast antiviral charges at the green viruses which have found their way into the victim's bloodstream. The player will also want to avoid destroying the healthy blood cells. A health bar at the top of the screen will track the player's progress. For each virus that is destroyed the green portion of the health bar at the top of the game will increase showing that the person is becoming healthier. In contrast for every virus that is missed and for every healthy cell that is destroyed the red portion of the health bar will increase indicating that the person is getting sicker. This game uses a series of optical illusions to create the impression that the blood cells and viruses are moving toward the player's ship in a 3D space. We will go into further detail for each of these illusions as we add them to the game. First we will want to download the Blood Vessel asset files from www.thegame makerstandard.com/bloodvessel. After downloading the assets folder read over the updates.pdf document which contains any changes since the publication of this book.

Creating the 2.5D Effect

An optical illusion is when you look at one thing but your brain perceives it differently than it actually is. By understanding the way the human eye distinguishes

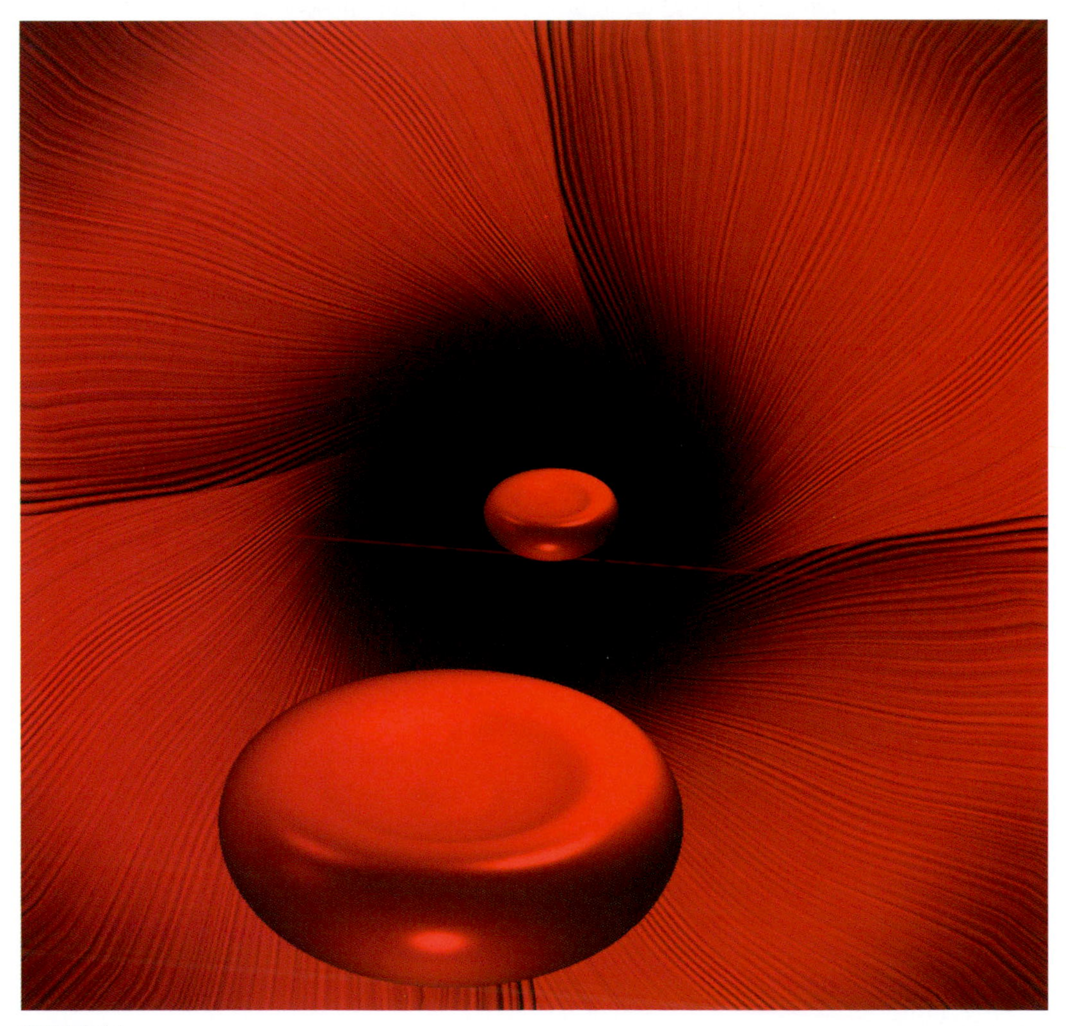

FIGURE 6.1

the distance of objects we can trick the player of our game into thinking the two-dimensional game they are playing is actually a three-dimensional game. In the world of game design this technique is called 2.5D. 2.5D uses two-dimensional images in such a way that they create the illusion they are moving in a three-dimensional space. Before computer technology allowed designers to create fully three-dimensional games, 2.5D was a common technique used to simulate a 3D environment. Before starting, however, we must have a basic understanding of how we perceive objects in the world. **Figure 6.1** simulates two objects in a 3D space.

The object in the bottom of the image appears to be closer to us while the object higher up appears to be farther way. In actuality both images exist the same distance away from you on a flat page in this book. Why do we then perceive the object at the bottom of the image to be closer to us? The reason we do is because this image shows objects on the page in a way that our brain would perceive them to be in real life. If you look around your environment you will find that objects that are closer to you appear larger and with more detail. Objects that are closer to you also appear lower on the horizon than objects farther way. If you were to look at two street signs that were of identical size but one is farther away, the sign that is farther away will appear to have less detail, appear smaller, and appear to be higher on the horizon than the sign closer to you. We will be using this technique to trick our eyes while creating the *Blood Vessel* game.

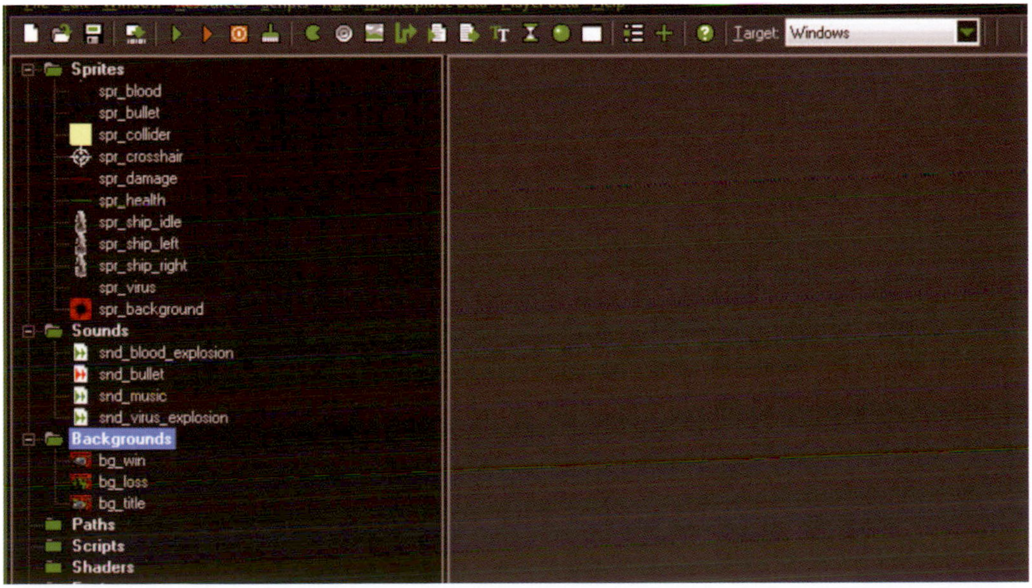

FIGURE 6.2

Creating a New Project and Importing Assets

Step 1: Create a new project and name it **bloodvessel**.

Step 2: Import the assets from the Blood Vessel asset folder.

Step 3: Rename each of the game assets so they appear similar to those shown in **Figure 6.2.**

Inserting the Player's Ship and a Spinning Background

The background image for our game as shown in **Figure 6.1** is specially created to simulate the illusion of the player moving toward the center or moving away from the center depending on which way the graphic is spinning. The player will actually control which direction the background is spinning depending on what movements are required by the player at that particular moment of the game. The background is a graphical representation of what it would appear like to travel through the bloodstream. The dark center of the image creates the illusion that the center is farther away from the player than the edges because it contains less detail and is not as well lit as the edges of the graphic. In order to reinforce the illusion that the center of the image is farther way we will provide an additional object that our brain understands. This additional object will be our player's ship. The ship will show the scale of which we are seeing something in this environment, and the size of the ship compared to the size of the graphic gives our brains more information to determine how far away the center of the background is from our ship.

Step 1: Open the three different ship sprites and select the center button.

Step 2: Create a new object named **obj_ship.**

Step 3: Set the sprite to **spr_ship_idle**.

Step 4: Add a **Create** Event for the **obj_ship**.

Step 5: Using a resolution of 720 x 720 will cause some scaling issues with the ship which we can counteract by adding a Transform Sprite Action. Add a Transform Sprite Action and set the following:

xscale: 0.4
yscale: 0.5
Angle: 0
Mirroring: no mirroring

Step 6: To create the background open **spr_background** and press the **Center** button, then click **OK**.

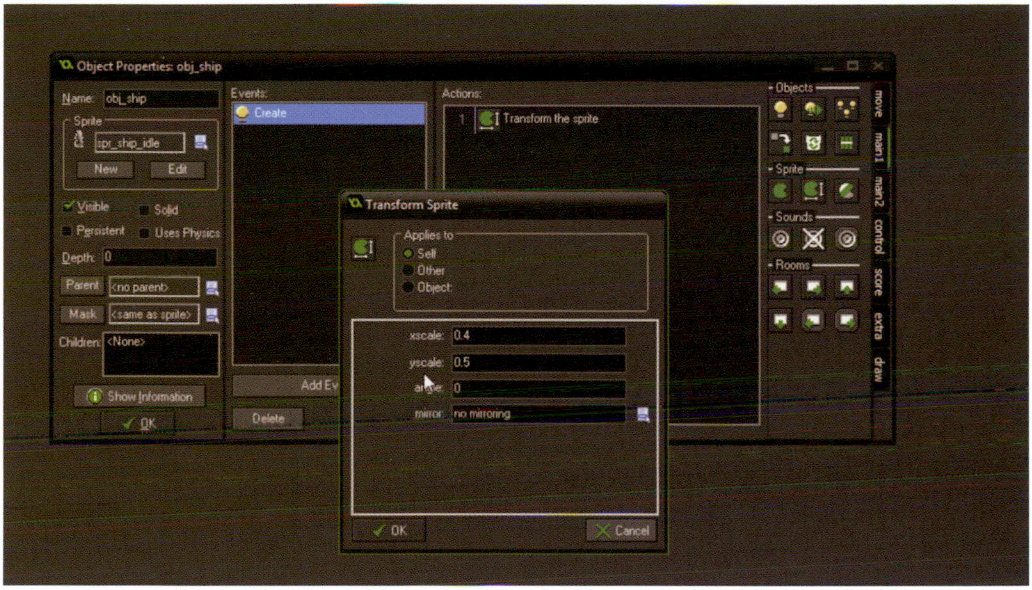

FIGURE 6.3

Step 7: Create a new object named **obj_background** and set the sprite to **spr_background**.

Step 8: Set the depth to **5**.

Step 9: To create the spinning motion create a **Keyboard: Right** Event and a **Keyboard: Left** Event in the **obj_background** object.

Step 10: In order to rotate the **obj_background** object we will change the values of **image_angle**. In the **<Left>** Event drag a **Set Variable** Action in and set the following:

Variable: image_angle
Value: 1
Relative: checked

Step 11: In the **<Right>** Event drag a **Set Variable** Action in and set the following:

Variable: image_angle
Value: –1
Relative: checked

Step 12: We will now place the background in our game. Create a new room named **room_gameplay** and under the Settings tab for **room_gameplay** change the following to:

Width: 720
Height: 720
Speed: 60

Step 13: Trying to drag and place the **obj_background** perfectly in the center would be tedious and time-consuming. Instead we will let the game place the background in the precise location for us automatically when the room starts. To set this open the **obj_background** object and add another **Room Start** Event.

Step 14: Drag a **Jump to Position** Action into the event and set the following, which will place the **obj_background** exactly in the center of the room.

x: 360
y: 360

Step 15: Reopen the room and place the **obj_background** off the screen to the left so the game will know where to find it.

Step 16: Place the **obj_ship** object down at the bottom of the screen in the center similar to how it is positioned in **Figure 6.5**.

Step 17: Run the game and test to see if the **obj_background** object is in the center of the room and that it spins when the left and right arrow keys are held down. Note: If a dialog box pops up reading "There are instances outside the room," select **No**.

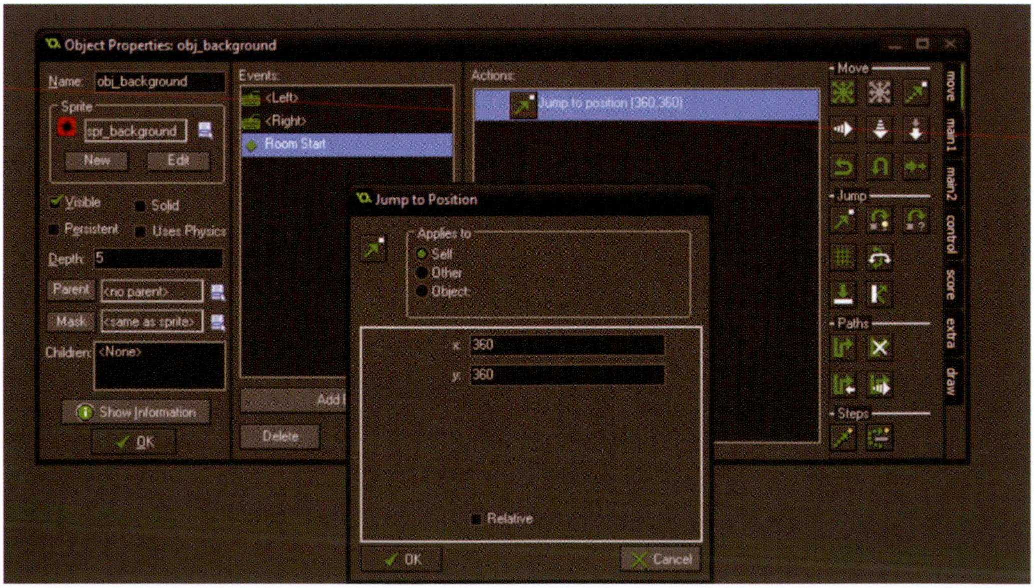

FIGURE 6.4

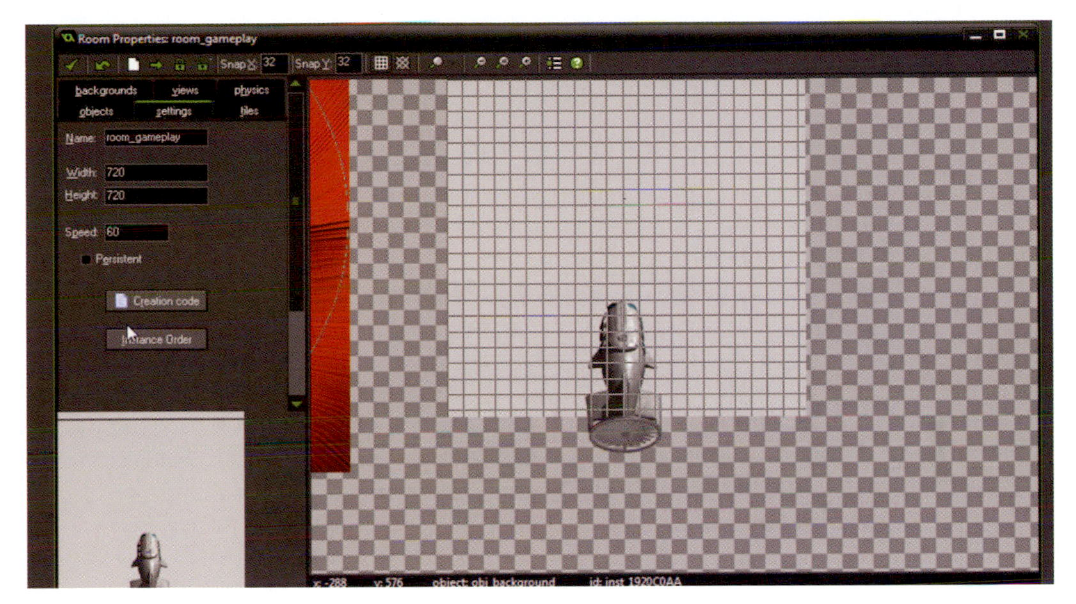

FIGURE 6.5

Animating the Ship

Our ship is going to stay at the bottom center of the screen as the camera perspective is focused on the camera. The ship will appear to bank left and right by switching image states. As the ship does this, the entire game environment will rotate. This provides the player with an interesting vantage point. They can see the world around them spinning while they appear sitting still, when it is actually the ship that is moving. Since the camera perspective is following the ship, when the player uses the arrow keys to move, it appears as if the environment is turning rather than the ship.

Step 1: Open the **obj_ship** object. We will change the ship so it appears to tilt left and right when the keys are pressed. Since the ship is not an actual 3D model, but rather a flat 2D image, we will be replacing the ship with different images when the player presses the left and right keys. This will make it appear as if the ship is a 3D object and is actually pivoting left and right.

Step 2: Add a **Key Press: Left** Event and **Key Press: Right** Event. In the **<Press Left>** Event add a **Change Sprite** Action and set the following:

Sprite: spr_ship_left
Subimage: 0
Speed: 1

Step 3: In the **<Press Right>** Event add a **Change Sprite** Action and set the following:

Sprite: spr_ship_right
Subimage: 0
Speed: 1

Step 4: In order for this effect to work we also need the ship to switch back to an idle animation when no keys are pressed. Create a **Key Release: Right** Event and a **Key Release: Left** Event.

Step 5: In **the Key Release<Right>** Event add a **Test Expression** Action and set the following:

Expression: keyboard_check(vk_left) || keyboard_check(vk_right)
Not: checked

This will check to make sure the left and right arrow keys are not being held down.

Step 6: Drag in a **Start of a Block** below the **Key Release <Right>** Event, then drag in a **Change Sprite** and set the following:

Sprite: spr_ship_idle
Subimage: 0
Speed: 1

Step 7: Drag in an **End of a Block**.

Step 8: Repeat **Steps 6 and 7** for the **Release<Left>** Event.

FIGURE 6.6

FIGURE 6.7

At this point you will want to test the game to make sure the ship animates properly. When the right button is pressed it should appear that the ship is banking toward the right and when the left button is pressed the ship should appear as if it is banking toward the left. If no buttons are pressed, the ship should appear as if it is flying straight.

Moving Objects Toward the Player

Earlier in the chapter we discussed how objects that are farther away appear higher in the horizon, less defined, and smaller than objects closer to us. We are going to use this information to trick the brain of the player into thinking that there are actual 3D models moving toward the player's ship. We will do this by putting in graphics that are designed to show an object starting off with little detail and gaining detail and size while moving downward on the horizon. This will make the object appear to be moving toward the player. We will also have these objects constantly switch images so that the flat 2D sprites will appear as if they are rotating 3D models.

Step 1: Open the **spr_blood** sprite and in the **Origin** section set **x** to **100** and **y** to **0**.

Step 2: Click the **Modify Mask** option.

Step 3: Check the **Precise** option.

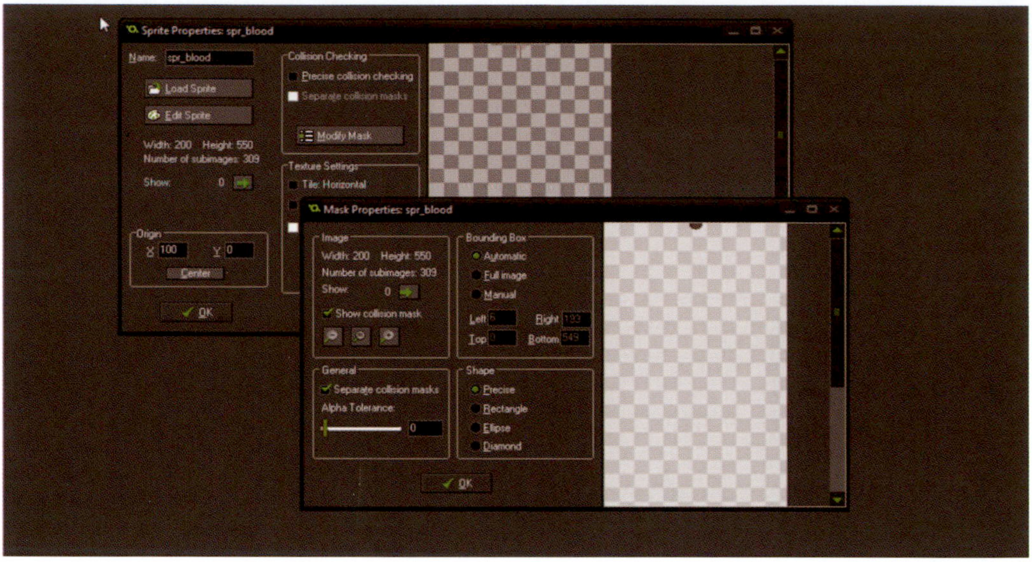

FIGURE 6.8

Step 4: Repeat **Steps 1 through 3** for the **spr_virus** sprite. This ensures that the collider is always on the visible image as it moves toward the edge of the screen. By doing this we can destroy any of these objects no matter how close or far away they are from the center of the screen and it will appear as though we are hitting the visible version of the object rather than where the object was a moment ago or where it will be in a few seconds. We also set the center point to the top in the middle of the image.

Spawning Objects

In order for the blood cells and viruses to appear, a new object will need to be created that will spawn the objects. This object will be responsible for spawning the blood cells and the viruses. The object will spawn either a virus or blood cell at random so that the player will not know which type of object will be appearing next. The human brain is quite remarkable and if we set a particular pattern of spawning many players would be able to figure it out and predict which type of object will appear next. Keeping the objects random keeps the game interesting and unpredictable.

Step 1: Create a new object named **obj_spawner**. This object will not have a sprite attached to it.

Step 2: Add a **Create** Event and an **Alarm: Alarm 0** Event to the **obj_spawner** object.

Step 3: In the **Create** Event add a **Set Alarm** and set the following:

Number of steps: 15
In alarm no: Alarm 0

Step 4: In the **Alarm 0** add a **Create Random** Action which is found under the **Main1** tab and set the following:

Object1: obj_virus
Object2: obj_blood
Object3: No object
Object4: No object
x: 360
y: 360

Step 5: In the **Alarm 0** add a **Set Alarm** Action and set the following:

Number of steps: 60
In alarm no: Alarm 0

Step 6: Open the **room_gameplay** room and place the **obj_spawner** object anywhere in the room. Test the game to ensure that every second a blood cell or virus object should spawn in the center of the screen and move toward the player. The game still needs quite a few modifications before the environment begins to look as it should. The animation speed is at present too fast and the objects only spawn in one direction. The objects also will not rotate with the background when the player presses the left and right arrows.

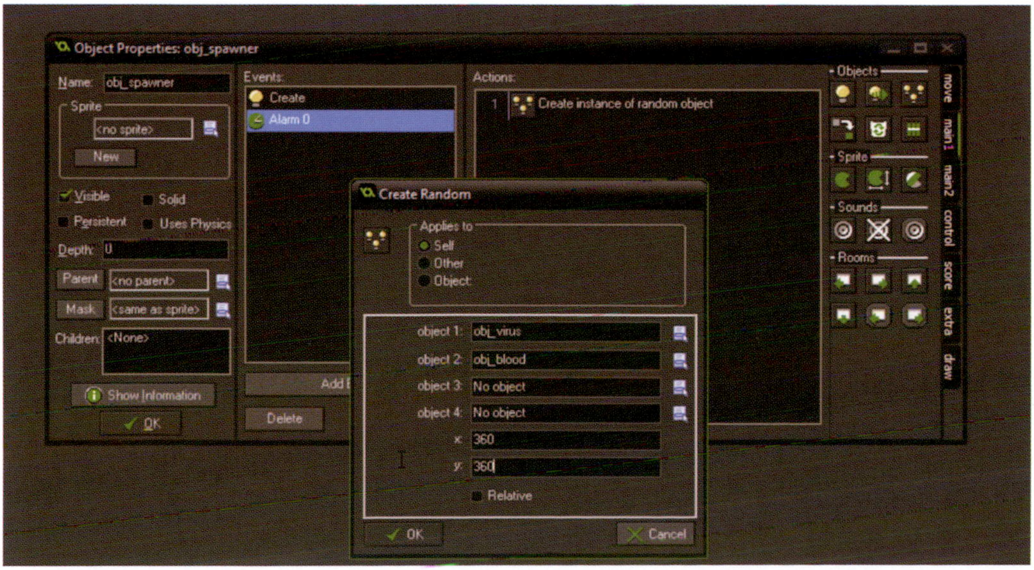

FIGURE 6.9

Adjusting Object Animation Speed and Direction

Step 1: Open the **obj_blood** object and add a **Create** Event.

Step 2: In the **Create** Event add a **Set Variable** Action and set the following:

Variable: image_angle
Value: irandom(360)

Step 3: Drag in a **Change Sprite** Action below the **Set Variable** Action and set the following:

Sprite: spr_blood
Subimage: 0
Speed: 0.5

When the objects are now created they will spawn facing a random direction and will animate at half their previous speed.

Rotating Objects Based on the Player's Movements

Step 1: Add another **Keyboard: Left** and **Keyboard: Right** Event to the **obj_blood** object.

Step 2: In the **<Left> Keyboard** Event add a **Change Variable** Action and set the following:

Variable: image_angle
Value: 1
Relative: checked

Step 3: In the **<Right> Keyboard** Event add a **Change Variable** Action and set the following:

Variable: image_angle
Value: –1
Relative: checked

Destroying the Animation

Once an animation event has ended the animation event needs to be destroyed. To do this we will add an **Animation End** Event for the blood cell and the virus objects.

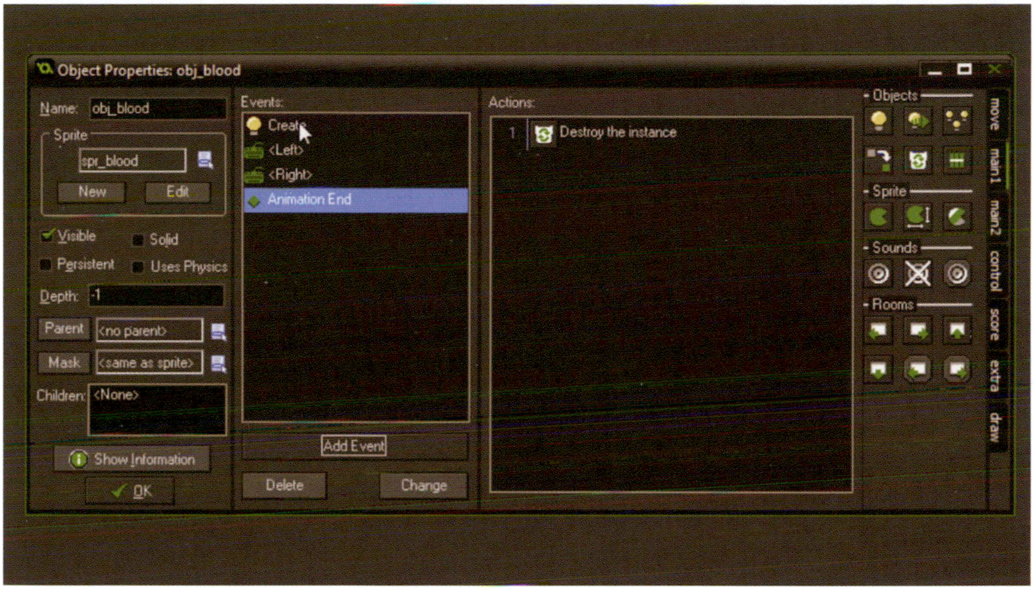

FIGURE 6.10

Step 1: Add an **Other: Animation End** Event to the **obj_blood** object.

Step 2: Drag in a **Destroy Instance** Action.

Step 3: Open the **obj_virus** object and add a **Create** Event.

Step 4: In the **Create** Event add a **Set Variable** Action and set the following:

Variable: image_angle
Value: irandom(360)

Step 5: Drag a **Change Sprite** below the **Set Variable** Action and set the following:

Sprite: spr_virus
Subimage: 0
Speed: 0.5

Step 6: Add another **Keyboard: Left** and **Keyboard: Right** Event.

Step 7: In the **<Left>** Event add a **Change Variable** Action and set the following:

Variable: image_angle
Value: 1
Relative: checked

Step 8: In the **<Right>** Event add a **Change Variable** Action and set the following:

Variable: image_angle
Value: −1
Relative: checked

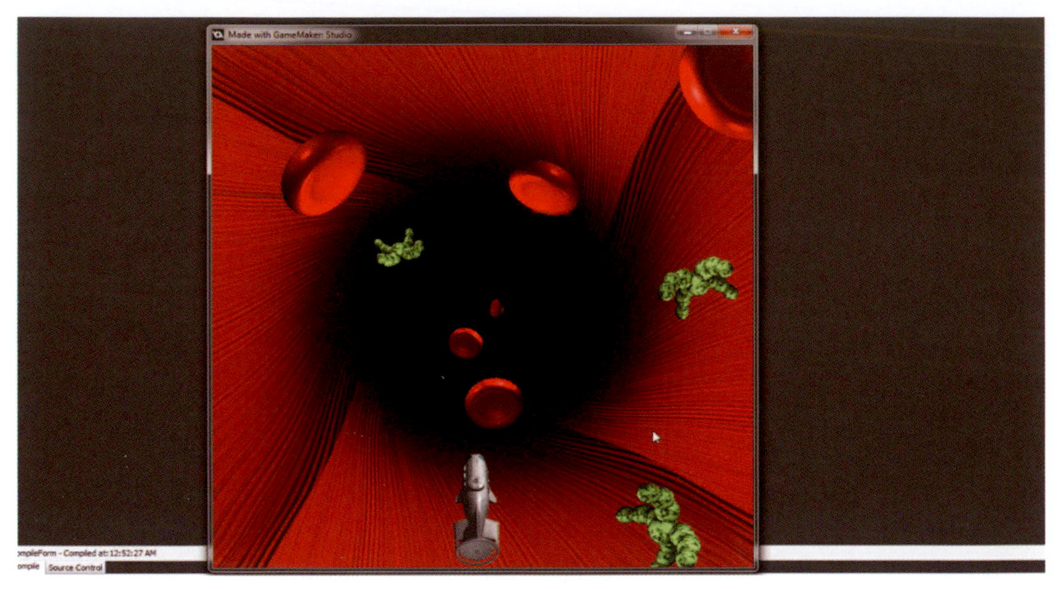

FIGURE 6.11

Step 9: Add an **Other: Animation End** Event and drag in a **Destroy Instance** Action.

As you test the game now the objects should rotate with the room when the player presses the left and right arrow keys. The objects should continue straight along their individual designated paths when no buttons are pressed.

Colliding Objects with the Player's Ship

While testing your game you should have noticed that nothing happens to the objects as they collide with the ship. The objects will need to be destroyed when they come in contact with the ship. This will allow the player to ram the virus shapes to destroy them but this action will also cause the destruction of a healthy blood cell if one comes in contact with the ship.

Step 1: Open the **obj_blood** object and add a **Collision** Event with the **obj_ship** Event.

Step 2: Drag in a **Play Sound** Action and set the following:

Sound: snd_ blood_explosion
Loop: false

Step 3: Drag in a **Destroy Instance** Action below the **Collision** Event**,** then close the **obj_blood** object.

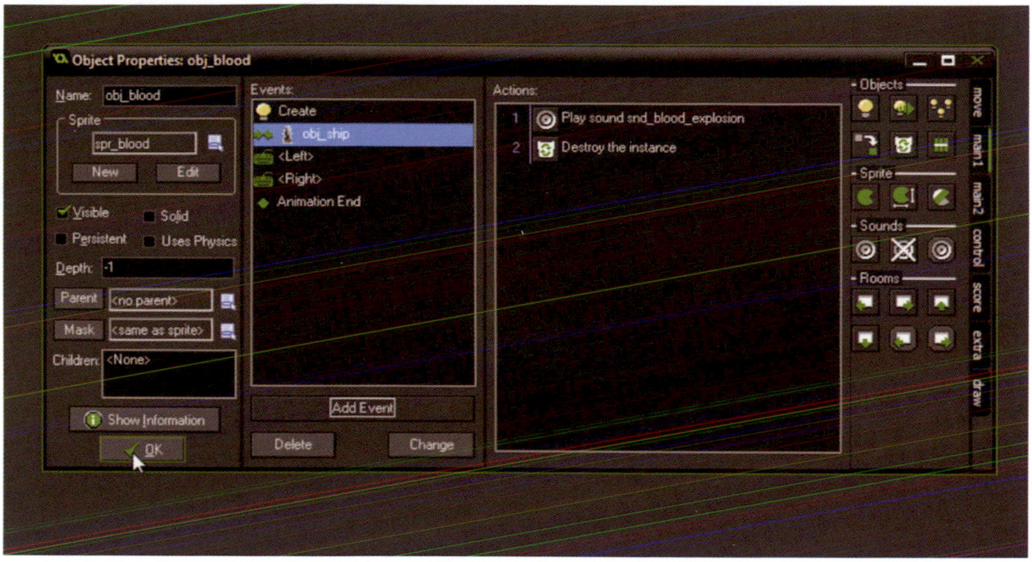

FIGURE 6.12

Step 4: Open the **obj_virus** object and add a **Collision** Event with the **obj_ship** Event.

Step 5: Drag in a **Play Sound** Action and set the following:

Sound: snd_virus_explosion
Loop: false

Step 6: Drag in a **Destroy Instance** below the **Collision** Event and close the **obj_virus** object.

Test the game and attempt to ram as many objects as you can. As you hit the virus objects and the healthy blood cell objects, they should disappear and an explosion should be heard for both.

Creating a Health Bar

Although our game is shaping up nicely we do not wish for the player to destroy everything in the blood. The player's objective in this game is to destroy the virus objects while at the same time avoiding the healthy blood cells. To reinforce this objective the game will have a health bar at the top to gauge how successful the player is at avoiding healthy cells and destroying viruses. The health of the individual the player is attempting to save will go up when a virus is destroyed and go down when a virus gets past the ship. The visual representation of this will be the health bar at the top of the screen consisting of two colors. The green color will increase and the red color will decrease when a virus is destroyed. The player will want to increase the green portion of the bar by destroying viruses until the red portion of the bar is completely gone. However, each time the player lets a virus leave the screen or if the player accidentally destroys a healthy blood cell the green portion of the bar will decrease while the red will increase, indicating that the health of the person being saved is going down. If the green portion of the bar is completely eliminated the player loses the game. If the red portion of the bar is completely eliminated the player will win the game. There will be times in which a player will have to choose to destroy a healthy cell in order to destroy multiple viruses. This strategy causes a temporary setback for a larger gain in the future.

Step 1: The Health Bar will incorporate two different sprites that are layered one on top of the other. This is another illusion designed to trick the brain of the player. The one on top will scale up and down providing the illusion that the one on bottom is doing the opposite. Create a **New Object** and name it **obj_health** and create another **New Object** and name it **obj_damage**.

Step 2: Set the **obj_health** object's sprite to **spr_health** and the **obj_damage** object's sprite to **spr_damage**.

Step 3: Set the **obj_health** object's depth to **−10** and the **obj_damage** object's depth to **−9**. This will allow the health object to always be on top of the damage object.

Step 4: Open the **room_gameplay** room and place the **obj_damage** object and the **obj_health** object into the top left corner of the room as shown in **Figure 6.13**.

Step 5: Close the **room_gameplay** room and open the **obj_health** object.

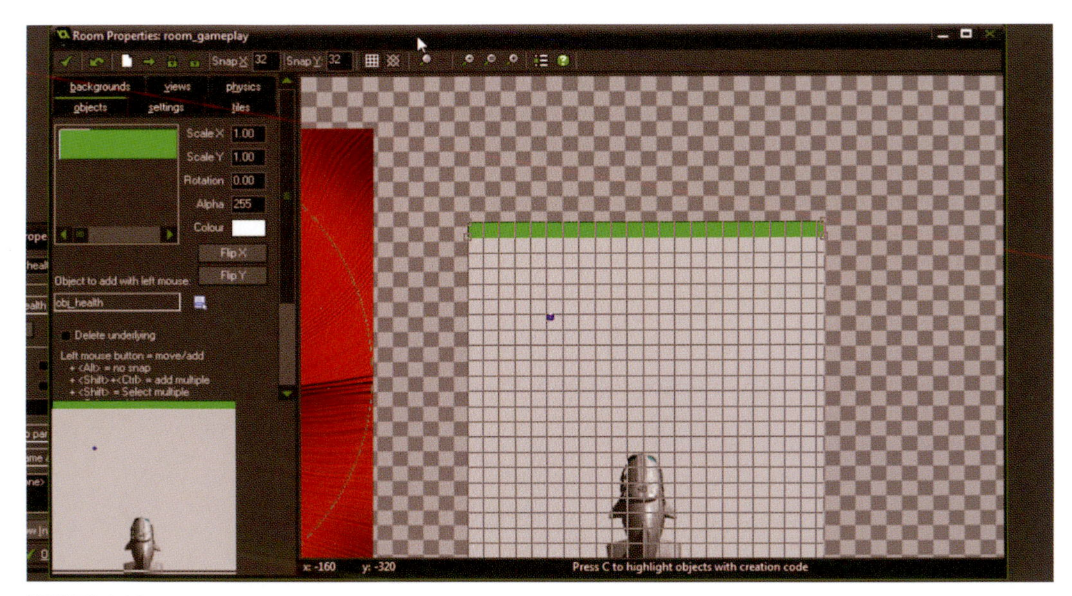

FIGURE 6.13

Step 6: Add a **Create** Event and drag in a **Set Variable** Action and set the following:

Variable: image_xscale
Value: 0.5

This will scale the image in half when the game starts. When the player starts the game they will see the health bar at the top which will be half red and half green. This indicates to the player that they are neither loosing nor winning the game as the health of the person they are trying to save is just as healthy as it is infected. We will now set the actions so that as the game is played the **image_xscale** variable will be used to track the player's progression. If the **image_xscale** reaches **zero** the player will lose the game and conversely if the **image_xscale** reaches **one** the player will win the game.

Testing If the Player Has Won or Lost the Game

Step 1: Add a **Step: End Step** Event and drag in a **Test Variable** Action and set the following:

Variable: image_xscale
Value: 1
Operation: greater than or equal to

Step 2: Drag a **Start Block** beneath the **Test Variable** Action and drag in a **Different Room** Action below the **Start Block** and set the following:

Room: room_gameplay

This will actually be a place holder that we will be changing later in the chapter as more rooms are created.

Step 3: Drag in an **End of the Block** below the **Different Room** Action. This action will test to see if the player has won the game.

Step 4: We now need to test to see if the player has lost the game. Add another **Test Variable** below the **End of a Block** and set the following:

Variable: image_xscale
Value: 0
Operation: less than or equal to

Step 5: Drag in a **Start of a Block** beneath the **Test Variable**.

Step 6: Beneath the **Start of a Block,** drag in a **Different Room** Action and set the following:

Room: room_gameplay

Again this is a place holder that we will be changing later as more of the game is developed.

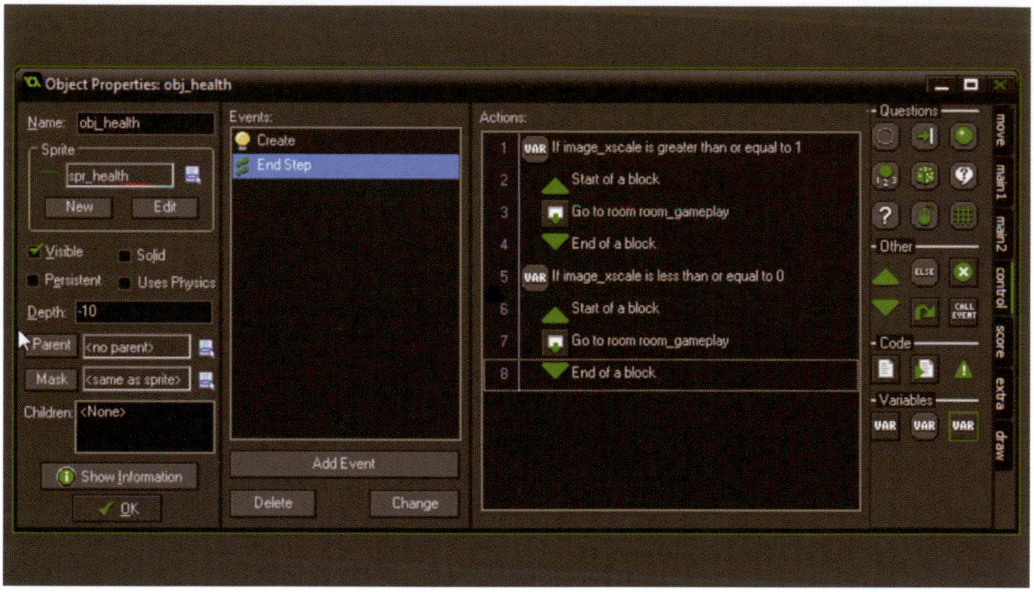

FIGURE 6.14

Step 7: Drag in an **End of a Block** below the **Different Room** Action and close the **obj_health** object.

Setting the obj_health xscale

Step 1: Open the **obj_virus** object and select the **Animation End** Event. If the virus animation ended that means it was able to get past the ship. Therefore the player will lose health.

Step 2: Add a **Set Variable** Action to the event and set the following:

Applies to: obj_health
Variable: image_xscale
Value: –0.05
Relative: checked

Step 3: The player will increase the person's health if they succeeded in destroying the virus. To set this select the Collision Event with **obj_ship** and add a set variable action and set the following:

Applies to: obj_health
Variable: image_xscale
Value: 0.05
Relative: checked

FIGURE 6.15

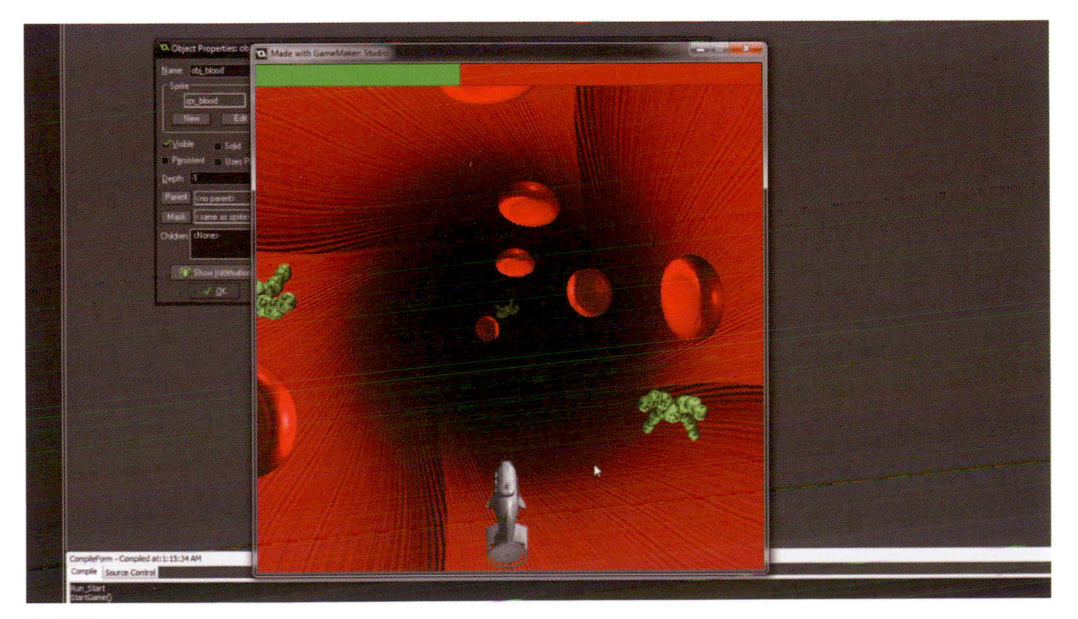

FIGURE 6.16

Step 4: Close the **obj_virus** object and open the **obj_blood** object. In the collision with the **obj_ship** Event select the collision with the **obj_ship** Event and add a **Set Variable** Action to it and set the following:

Applies to: obj_health
Variable: image_xscale
Value: –0.05
Relative: checked

The player will now lose health when colliding with the healthy blood cells.

Test the game to assure the changes made modify the health bar at the top of the screen.

Creating Bullets

Our ship at present can only destroy things by ramming into them. Although this can be fun it does not allow the ship to destroy any viruses that are far away. By allowing the ship to shoot antiviral charges (aka bullets) the player will be able to strategize which virus objects to shoot and which are better to ram with the ship. Either of the options will benefit the player as they both will destroy viruses. Yet by adding the antiviral charges the player can eliminate viruses that are farther away, which will give the player time to navigate around incoming healthy blood cells.

Step 1: First we need to tweak the sprite a bit to make the collision follow the bullet and change the origin. Open the **spr_bullet** sprite and set the origin to:

x: 8
y: 0

Step 2: Click the **Modify Mask** option and check the **Precise** option in the **Shape** section.

Step 3: Create a **New Object** and name it **obj_bullet** and set the sprite to **spr_bullet.**

Step 4: The **obj_bullet** will need to be destroyed when the animation ends. Create an **Other: Animation End** Event and drag in a **Destroy Instance**.

Step 5: The bullets will also need to rotate with the background. Create **a Keyboard: Left** and a **Keyboard: Right** Event.

Step 6: In the **<Left>** Event drag a **Set Variable** in and set the following:

Variable: image_angle
Value: 1
Relative: checked

Step 7: In the **<Right>** Event drag a **Set Variable** in and set the following:

Variable: image_angle
Value: –1
Relative: checked

Step 8: To set the Collision Events with the healthy blood cells add a **Collision** with **obj_blood** Event and add a **Destroy Instance** and set the following:

Applies to: other

Step 9: Add a **Play Sound** Event and set the following:

Sound: snd_blood_explosion
Loop: false

Step 10: Add a **Set Variable** and set the following:

Applies to: obj_health
Variable: image_xscale
Value: –0.05
Relative: checked

Step 11: Add a **Destroy Instance** Action. The bullet is now programmed to destroy the healthy blood cells, play a sound, reduce the player health bar, and destroy the bullet. We will be doing similar steps for when a bullet hits a virus but with a few changes.

Step 12: Add a **Collision** with the **obj_virus** Event and add a **Destroy Instance** and set the following:

Applies to: other

Step 13: Add a **Play Sound** and set the following:

Sound: snd_virus_explosion
Loop: false

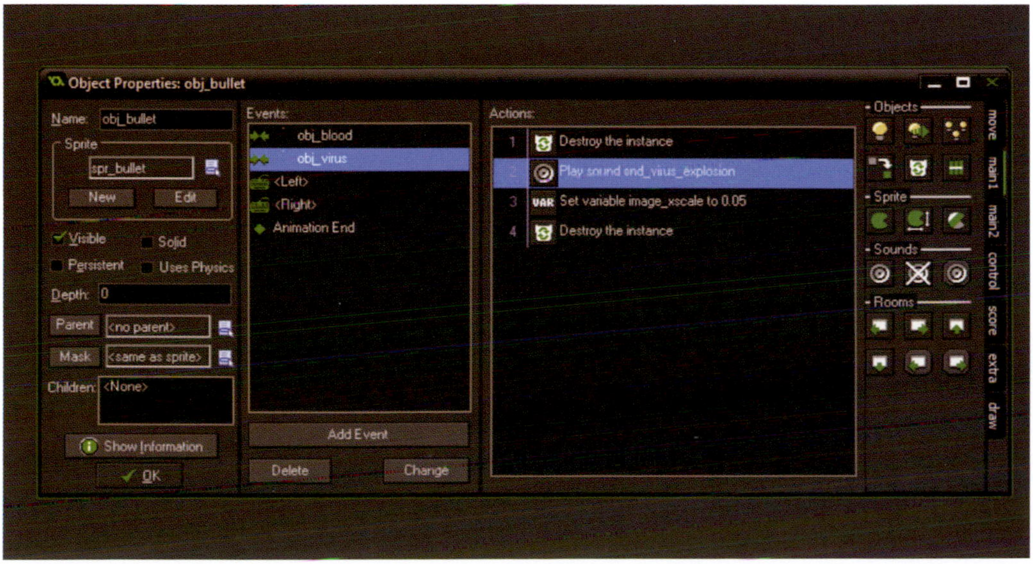

FIGURE 6.17

Step 14: Add a **Set Variable** Action and set the following:

Applies to: obj_health
Variable: image_xscale
Value: 0.05
Relative: checked

Step 15: Add a **Destroy Instance**. The bullet is now also programmed to destroy the viruses and increase the player's health if a virus is hit and destroyed.

Shooting Bullets

The antiviral charges are now ready to be unleashed upon the viruses. It is time to set up the ship so that it can fire them.

Step 1: Open the **obj_ship** object and add a **Key Press: Space** Event.

Step 2: Add a **Create Instance** and set the following:

Object: obj_bullet
x: 360
y: 360

Step 3: Add a **Play Sound** Action below the **Create Instance** and set the following:

Sound: snd_bullet
Loop: false

Test the game to make sure the bullets cause the health bar to decrease when a healthy blood cell is hit and to increase when a virus is hit. Also make sure to move the ship around to check that the bullets are rotating in the environment as they should.

Adding Crosshairs

Although the game already looks like a 3D game, players may still think they can shoot at objects located at the top of the screen rather than at objects coming from the center of the game. We will now employ another simple trick to reinforce the impression that this is a 3D game by placing a crosshair graphic in the center of the screen. This will remind the player that the bullets are traveling away from the player toward the center of the screen rather than traveling up toward the top of the screen as would be more typical in a 2D game.

Step 1: Open the **spr_crosshair** sprite and click the **Center** button, then close the sprite.

Step 2: Create a **New Object** and name it **obj_crosshairs**.

Step 3: Open the **room_gameplay** room and place the **obj_crosshairs** anywhere in the room. Again, trying to get these in the exact center of the room would be tedious and letting the game do this for us is much easier.

Step 4: Open the **obj_crosshairs** object and add a **Create** Event.

Step 5: Add in a **Jump to Position** Action and set the following:

x: 360
y: 360

Creating Title Screens

The gameplay is now complete and the Title Screen, Win Screen, and Lose Screen can now be added.

Step 1: Create **Three New Rooms** and name them **room_title, room_loss,** and **room_win**.

Step 2: For the **room_title** room set the background as **bg_title**. For the **room_win** room set the background as **bg_win**. For the **room_loss** room set the background as **bg_loss**.

Step 3: Close the rooms for now as we need to create the navigational buttons that will allow the player to start or quit the game.

Step 4: Create two **New Objects** and name them **obj_play** and **obj_quit**.

Step 5: Set both objects' sprites to **spr_collider**.

Step 6: In **obj_play** add a **Mouse: Left Button** Event then drag in a **Different Room** Action and set the following:

Room: room_gameplay

Step 7: Open the **obj_quit** object and add a **Mouse: Left Button** Event and drag in an **End Game** Action.

Step 8: Open all three title screen rooms and place the buttons over the graphics using the **Scale** feature. The final results should look similar to **Figure 6.19**.

Step 9: Arrange the **Rooms** in the **Rooms Folder** so they look similar to **Figure 6.20**.

Step 10: Earlier in the chapter we mentioned that we were putting in a place holder in the **obj_health** object. Now that our win room and lose room are complete we can replace the place holder with the correct rooms. Open **obj_health** and select the **Step** Event.

Step 11: Open the first **Different Room** Action and set the following:

Room: room_win

Step 12: Open the second **Different Room** Action and set the following:

Room: room_loss

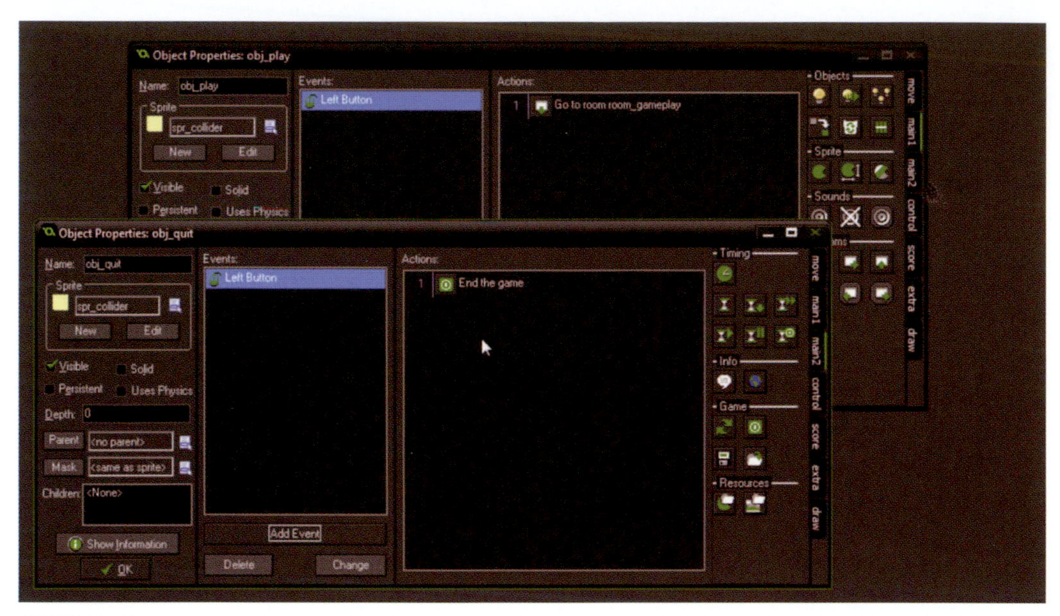

FIGURE 6.18

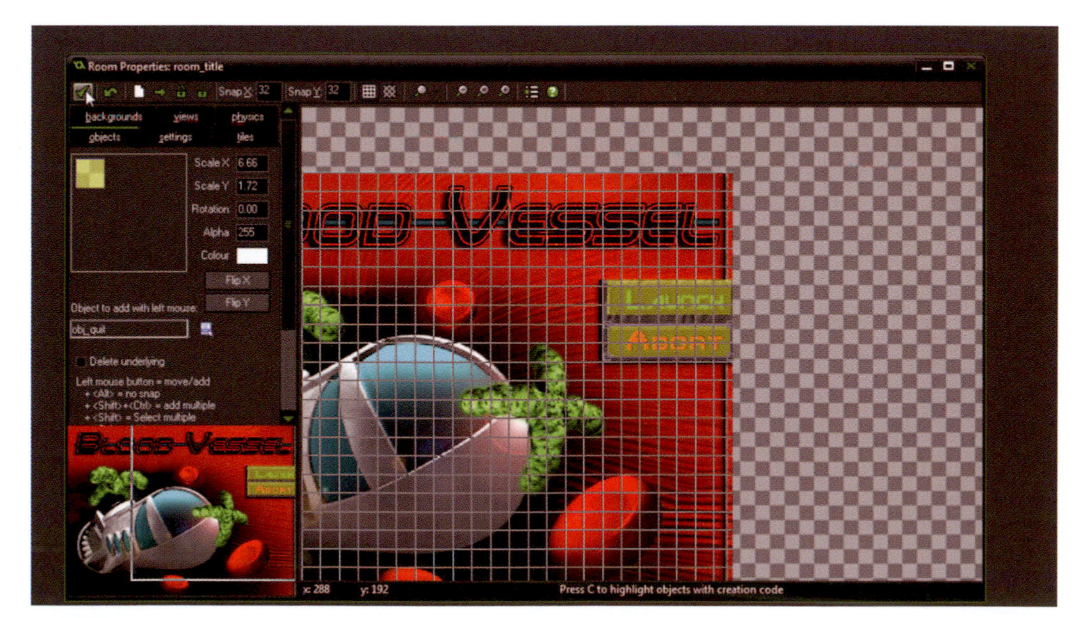

FIGURE 6.19

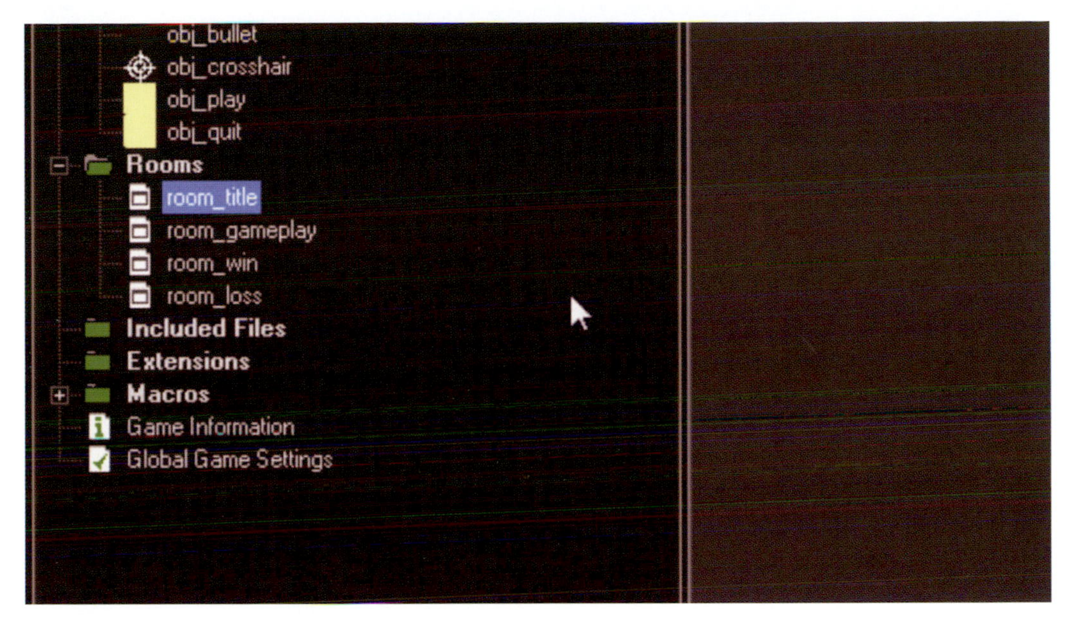

FIGURE 6.20

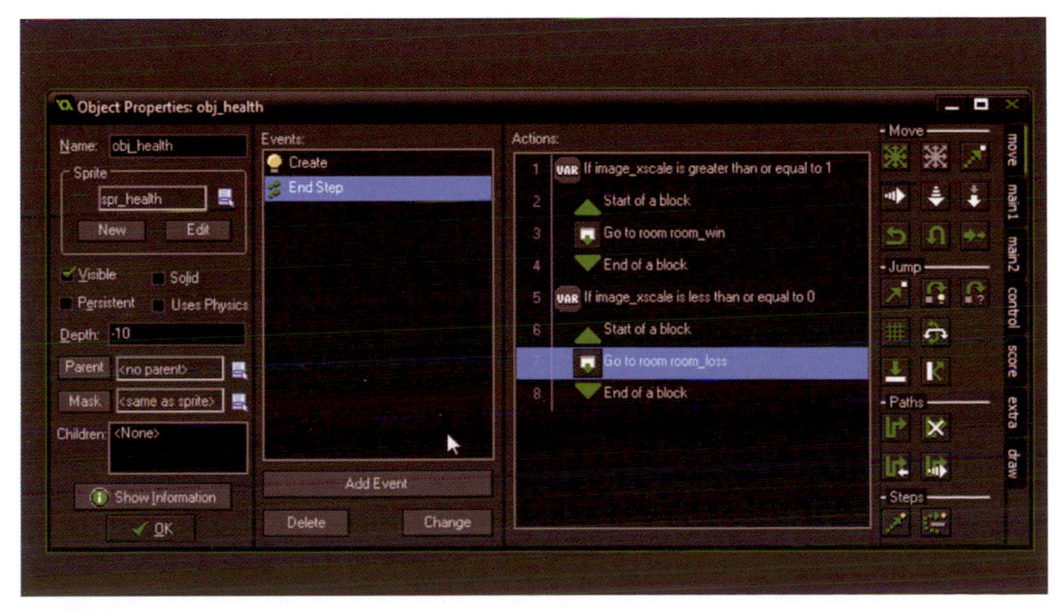

FIGURE 6.21

Adding Background Music

Step 1: Create a **New Object** named **obj_music** and check the **Persistent** option.

Step 2: Add an **Other: Game Start** Event and add a **Play Sound** Action and set the following:

Sound: snd_music
Loop: true

Testing the *Blood Vessel* Game

We hope by now that you have noticed the pun in the title of the game. The game is about a vessel that travels in the blood. When you test your game it should look as though the ship is able to move out of the way of blood cells. However, rather than the ship moving across the screen, it remains in the same position and the whole environment moves instead. Knowing how the eye sees objects in space and identifies which objects are closer or farther away, we have been able to trick the player into thinking three-dimensional objects are traveling toward them when in fact the screen they are playing on is flat, and the objects in the game are all two-dimensional sprites rather than 3D objects. Continue to have others test your game to see if there are any bugs you may have missed. You may wish to see if your friends would classify your game as a two-dimensional game or a three-dimensional game. This would be a trick question, of course, since the game is actually considered a 2.5D game.

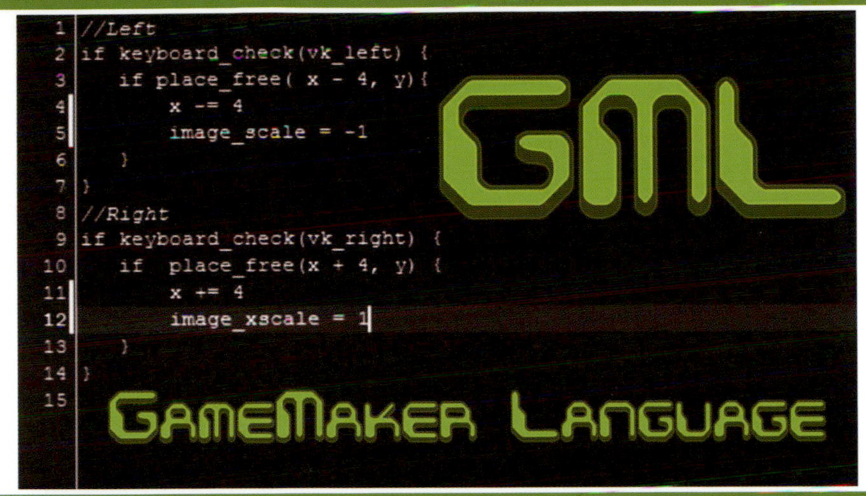

Game Maker Language (GML)

Learning Objectives—Upon completion of Chapter 7 readers will be able to:

- Define GML and how it can be used to supplement game design in GameMaker
- Write scripts using GML
- Identify commonly used variables and their uses
- Use GML to change object behaviors
- Use GML as a shortcut tool for game creation

Project Overview: Redesigning *Lost Dog* Using GML

In Chapter 3 we created a traditional side-scroller game using the drag-and-drop features in GameMaker. Although we were able to successfully create our game, we could have cut the time it took to create our game significantly by coding portions of the game. The coding language GameMaker uses is called Game Maker Language or GML for short. In this chapter we will create the *Lost Dog* game from Chapter 3 again, but this time using GML to replace many of the steps we used previously. We now have an understanding of what these steps we applied did in the game so by recreating the same game using GML, we can apply the knowledge we already have on how the game should work and create the same steps using

GML in a much shorter period of time. This will provide an opportunity to truly comprehend what the coding is actually doing rather than simply retyping text from a page. Knowing what the finished product is supposed to look like will help in building our game development skills from exclusively using the drag-and-drop method to incorporating custom code. We will go into further detail on how coding will replace the steps we used in Chapter 3 as we add each code segment to the game. First we will want to download the **Lost Dog GML** asset files from www.thegamemakerstandard.com/LostDogGML. After downloading the assets folder read over the updates.pdf document which contains any changes since the publication of this book.

Creating a New Project and Importing Assets

Step 1: Create a new project and name it **lostdogGML**

Step 2: Import the assets from the **LostDogGML** asset folder.

Step 3: Rename the assets so they appear similar to **Figure 7.1**.

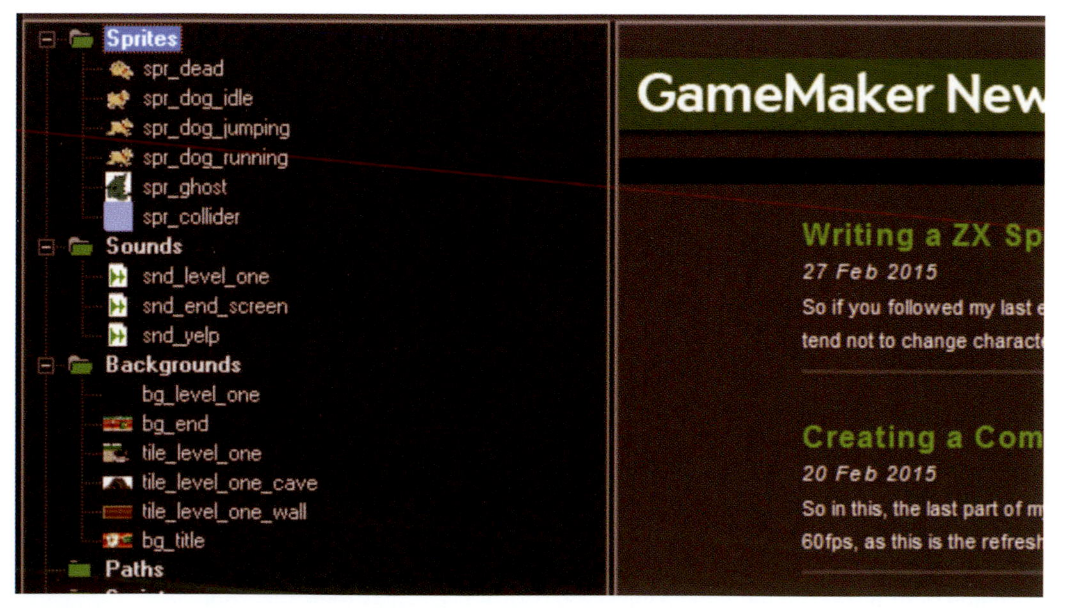

FIGURE 7.1

Setting Up the Player's Collision Box

The player will control a dog in this game by using the keyboard to move back and forth and jumping to avoid obstacles. Our dog will need to jump on top of objects without falling through them; therefore, our dog must be solid so it can collide with other solid objects.

Step 1: Open the **spr_dog_idle, spr_dog_running,** and **spr_dog_jumping** sprites.

Step 2: In each of these sprites click the **Modify Mask** box.

Step 3: Click the **Manual** option and enter the following for each of the sprites:

Left: 15
Top: 20
Right: 64
Bottom: 55

Step 4: Press the **Center** option for all the dog sprites including **spr_dead** and then close the sprites.

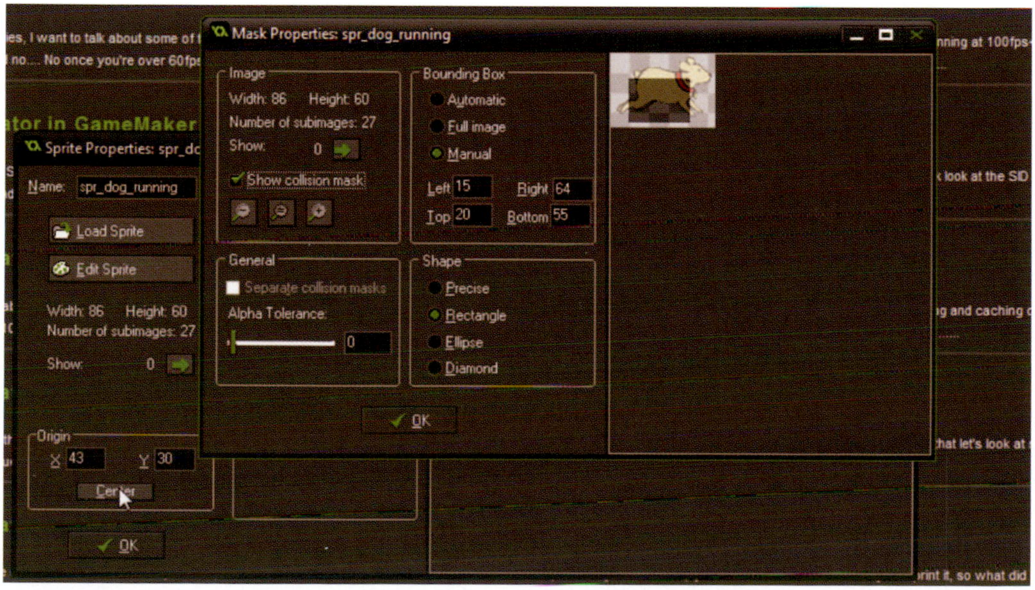

FIGURE 7.2

Creating the Dog and Collider Objects

Step 1: Create two **New Objects** and name them **obj_dog** and **obj_collider**.

Step 2: Set the **obj_dog** object's sprite to **spr_dog_idle**.

Step 3: Set the **obj_collider** object's sprite to **spr_collider**.

Creating a Testing Room

In order to test the functions we will be implementing we will want to create a room for our dog and the collider objects.

Step 1: Create a **New Room** and name it **room_level_one**.

Step 2: Set the **Room Speed** to 60.

Step 3: Place the **obj_dog** object in the center of the **room_level_one** room.

Step 4: Place a few colliders around the dog so that your room looks similar to the one shown in **Figure 7.3**.

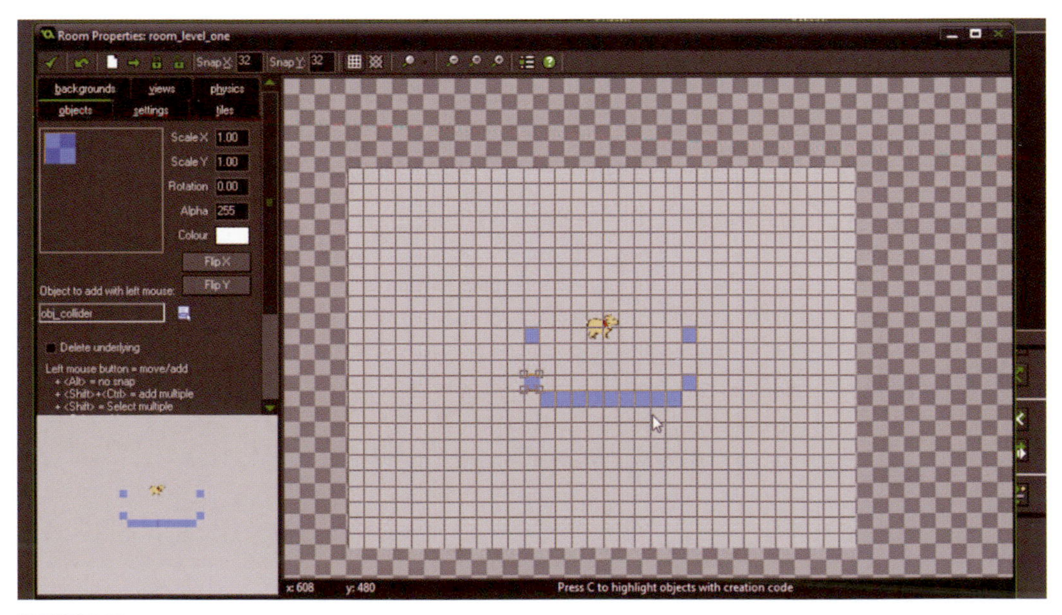

FIGURE 7.3

Coding the Playable Character's Movements

When we initially created this game we used keyboard events to tell the game what keys to use for specific movements. This time we will be creating code that will tell the dog to move left and right.

Step 1: Open the **obj_dog** object and add a **Keyboard: Any Key** Event.

Step 2: Add an **Execute Code** Action to the event.

Step 3: A window will pop up which will allow you to type in the specific code. Type in the following:

```
//Left
if keyboard_check(vk_left) {
  if place_free(x—4, y){
    x-= 4
  }
}
//Right
if keyboard_check(vk_right) {
  if place_free(x + 4, y) {
    x += 4
  }
}
```

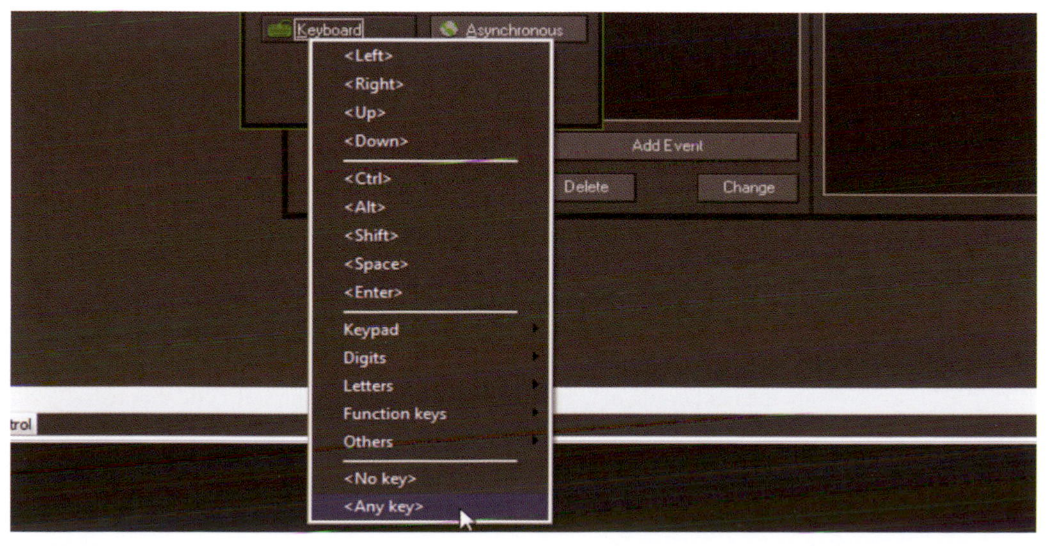

FIGURE 7.4

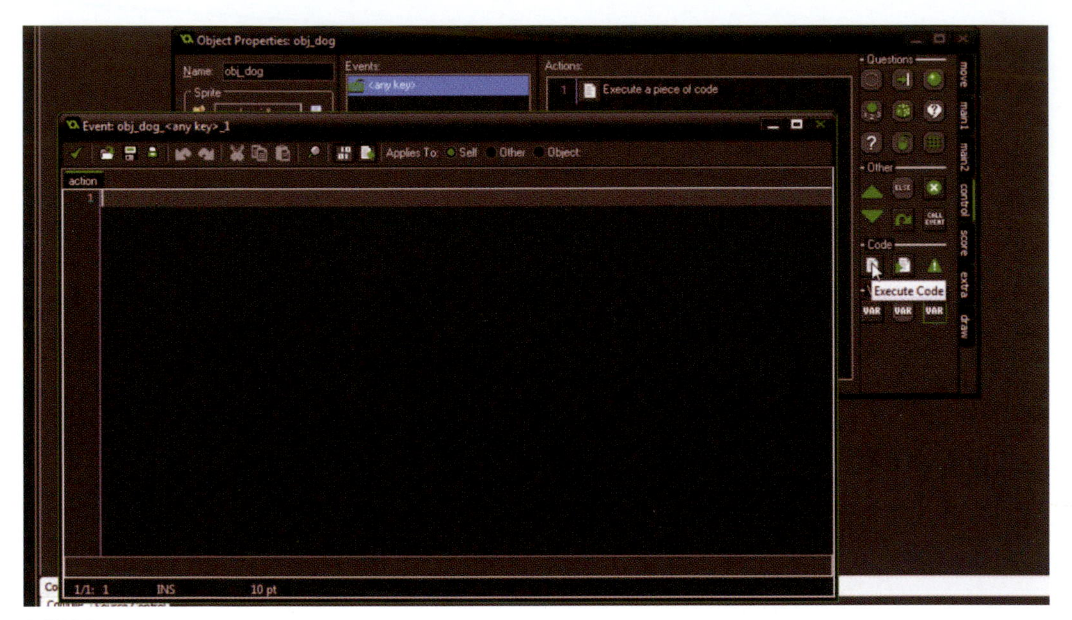

FIGURE 7.5

Deciphering GML Code

Coding languages use symbols to represent certain actions that are understood by the program. The first code symbols we typed in were two right-leaning slashes also known as forward slashes. Whenever GameMaker encounters two forward slashes in the GML code it understands that what follows is a comment and is intended as a reminder to the designer of what the code is doing. GameMaker will then ignore anything after the two forward slashes until it encounters another symbol indicating it should do something different. Comments are useful to designers because they not only remind a single designer what the following code is used for, but they can also be used to track down bugs and relate to another designer reading the code what the code should be doing. This later part is helpful when a team of designers are working on one project together.

After the two forward slashes we typed the word **left**. This reminds us that the following code is designed to tell GameMaker to check if the **left key** is being pressed. The next group of text we typed in was the actual GML code that tells GameMaker to check if the **left key** is being pressed. The code we typed was: **if keyboard_check (vk_left)**. This is essentially asking GameMaker to run a **check** to see **if** the **left key** on the **keyboard** is pressed. An "if" statement can be used to check for virtually anything in a game such as 1+1=2. As you look at that line of code it should start to make sense knowing what the intended result should be. The next portion of the code reads as follows: **if place_free(x—4, y){x-= 4}**. In this particular line of code the open parenthesis before the letter **x** has a paired close parenthesis after the **y**. With coding, parentheses always come in pairs. The same holds true for the brackets around the **x-=4** text. Forgetting to type the second parenthesis or bracket in a line of code is a common mistake and unfortunately results in an error that prevents the intended action from being executed. The intended action in this case is for GameMaker to **check** to see if there are **four free spaces** to the **left** of the dog in which a **solid object** does not appear. If there are **four free spaces** then GameMaker will place the dog **four spaces** to the **left** in the game. The rest of the code we typed tells GameMaker to do the same thing but this time to **check** the **right** side of the dog for a **solid object**.

Converting the Collider into a Solid Object

The code is instructing GameMaker to search for any solid objects four spaces away from the dog. In order for the collider to register as a solid object we will need to convert it into one.

Step 1: Open the **obj_collider** object and check the box labeled **Solid**.

FIGURE 7.6

Step 2: Test the game and move the dog left and right using the left and right keys. The dog will not be able to pass the colliders.

Coding the Dog Image to Switch Directions

The dog is doing pretty well considering it is having to move backward when the left button is pressed. To change this we will add another code to instruct the dog's image to flip so that it is looking in the same direction it is moving.

Step 1: Open the **obj_dog** object.

Step 2: In the **<Any Key>** Event open the **Script** again.

Step 3: In the first **keyboard check**, below the **x-= 4** line, type:

> **image_xscale = -1**

Step 4: In the **second keyboard** check, below the **x += 4** line, type:

> **image_xscale = 1**

```
Event: obj_dog_<any key>_1
Applies To: Self Other Object
action
1  //Left
2  if keyboard_check(vk_left) {
3     if place_free( x - 4, y){
4         x -= 4
5         image_scale = -1
6     }
7  }
8  //Right
9  if keyboard_check(vk_right) {
10    if  place_free(x + 4, y) {
11        x += 4
12        image_xscale = 1
13    }
14 }
15
12/15: 24    INS    Modified   10 pt
```

FIGURE 7.7

Deciphering the Image Switching Code

Run the game again to test that the player character turns to face left and right. The two lines of code we typed in were identical except for the end where the first line has a positive number one and the second line which has a negative number one. These numbers indicate which direction the dog image is facing. The positive number one has the dog face one way while the negative number one tells the dog image to flip horizontally on the x axis so that it is the exact reverse of the positive number one image.

Coding Gravity

The player will want to jump onto solid objects and jump over obstacles. In order for the player to jump, the game must contain a system of gravity. The next section of code we will be writing will add gravity to the game and allow our dog to jump.

Step 1: Create a **Step: Step** Event.

Step 2: Add an **Execute Code** Action.

Step 3: Type the following:

```
if place_free(x, y + 1) {
  gravity = 0.5
  gravity_direction = 270
}
else {
  gravity = 0
}
```

Deciphering the Gravity Code

The first part of the code we added should look similar to the code we added earlier that checked for solid objects to the right and left of the dog. This new code is also checking the **y axis** this time. We learned early on that the y axis is the vertical axis so we know that this code is checking something either above or below our character. The **positive number one** in the code is telling GameMaker to test if there is a **solid object one space below** the player. The rest of the code tells GameMaker what to do if there is **not** a **solid object one space below** the character. If there is not a solid object below the character, GameMaker will set the **gravity to 0.5** and give it a **direction of 270,** which is **down**. The **else** part in the code is only called when the **if** statement is **false** meaning the **else** portion would get called if there **is a solid object one space below** the dog. If there is a solid object beneath the dog then GameMaker will **set the gravity to zero**.

Catching and Returning the Character

If the game were to be run now the player character would fall through the colliders. Another batch of code is needed that will instruct GameMaker to catch the player character and move it back to the location where it collided with the collider.

Step 1: Add a **Collision** Event with the **obj_collider** Event for the **obj_dog** object.

Step 2: Add an **Execute Code** Action.

Step 3: Type the following:

```
move_contact_solid(direction, -1)
vspeed = 0
```

Deciphering the Catching Code

This bit of code will ensure that the player is **on the colliders** and **sets its vertical speed** or **vspeed** back to **zero**. Test the game to check that the dog object collides with the colliders below it correctly.

Coding the Character's Jump Movement

Step 1: Select the **<Any Key>** Event in the **obj_dog** object and open the **Execute Code** Action.

Step 2: Type the following code at the bottom of the window:

```
//jump
if (keyboard_check_pressed(vk_up)) {
  if !place_free(x, y+1) {
    vspeed- = 12
  }
}
```

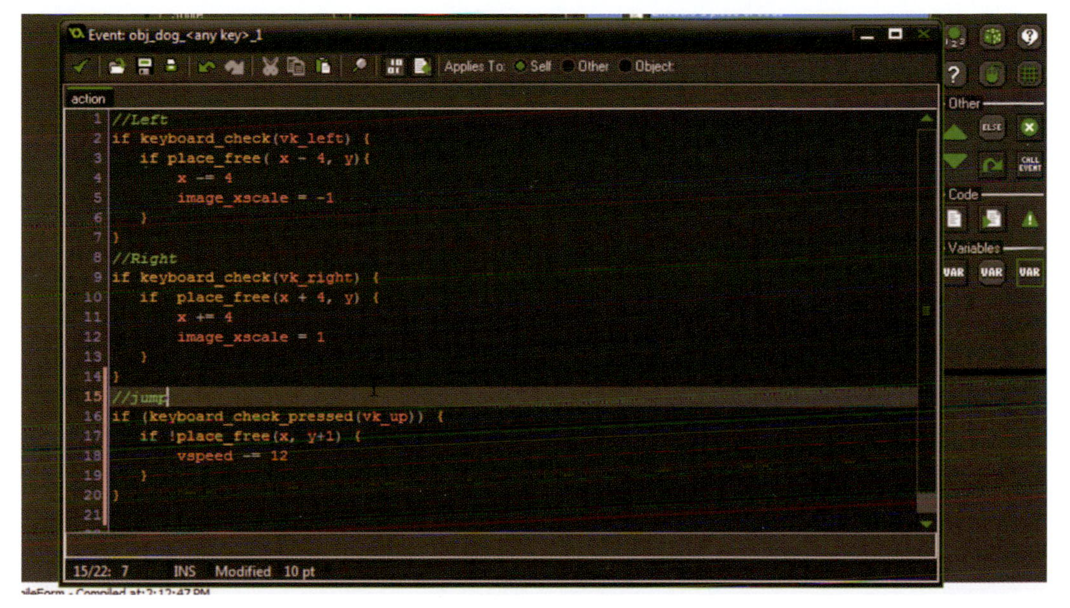

FIGURE 7.8

Deciphering the Jump Movement Code

The code we just added will **check** to see if the **up key was pressed**. This portion of the code should look familiar as it is similar to what we have coded before. The next portion checks if there is a **solid object below** the dog. The code **!place_free** is the same as saying "the place is Not free." Exclamation points are used to represent **NOT**. This will then change the **vspeed** of the dog to **–12** which will launch It up into the air.

Troubleshooting Coding Errors

It is common to mistype something when writing code. The most common coding errors are misspelled words or misplaced parenthesis or brackets. If you get a coding error and need to troubleshoot it, start by comparing each line of the code as it is in the book with each line of the code you typed. There may be a difference in the code you typed in and the code in the book that you are overlooking. This is when you may wish to have someone else look at both sets of code to see where the difference is. Oftentimes a fresh pair of eyes will find a difference in a line of code that someone else has compared several times.

Coding the Player Character's Animations

We will also create the player character's animations differently than we did the first time we created this game by using code.

Step 1: Select the **Step** Event in the **obj_dog** object.

Step 2: Open the **Execute Code** Action.

Step 3: In the **Place Free Section** we know the dog is in the air so here will be a good place to change the current sprite into the jumping sprite. Below **line 3** press **Enter** and type:

sprite_index = spr_dog_jumping

The dog will need to change back to the idle or running sprite when it is colliding with the colliders. The best place to do this is in the same action below **line 7** because we already know the dog is touching a collider.

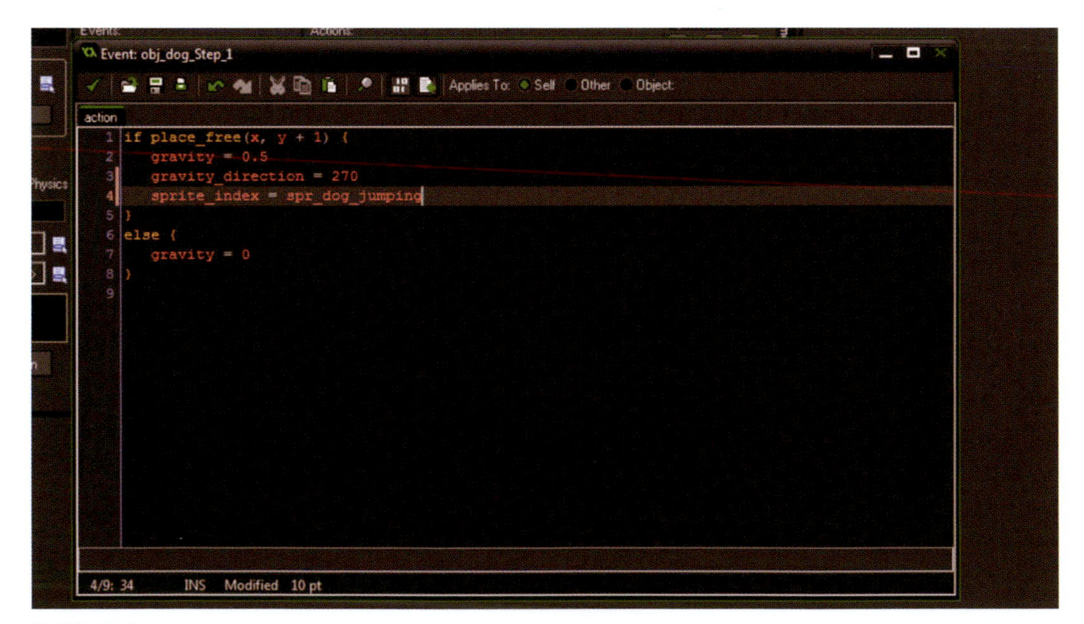

FIGURE 7.9

Step 4: Below **line 7** type the following:

```
if (keyboard_check(vk_left) || keyboard_check(vk_right)) {
    sprite_index = spr_dog_running
  }
  else {
    sprite_index = spr_dog_idle
  }
```

This will check to see if the left or right key is being pressed. If either of the keys are being pressed, the sprite will change into the running sprite. If either of the keys are not being pressed, the image will change into the idle sprite. The two vertical lines separating the keyboard checks are used to represent **OR**. The **&** symbol is used to represent **AND**.

Coding the Room to Follow the Player Character

Step 1: With the dog animations complete, the room can now be set up. Open **room_level_one** and **Delete** the **obj_collider** objects and the **obj_dog** object we placed in the room.

Step 2: Change the room settings to:

Height: 544
Width: 4800

Step 3: Click the **Views** tab.

Step 4: Click the **Enable the Use of Views** box and set the following:

Visible when room starts: checked
View in room:
x: 0 W: 1024
y: 0 H: 544

Port on screen:
x: 0 W: 1024
y: 0 H: 544

Object Following:
Obj_dog
Hbor: 512 Hsp: –1
Vbor: 32 Vsp: –1

Setting the Background Images

Now that the room will follow the dog object, we will set the background images that will be used as tiles.

Step 1: Open **tile_level_one.**

Step 2: Check the **Use As Tile Set** box.

Step 3: Do the same for **tile_level_one_cave** and **tile_level_one_wall**.

Step 4: Open **room_level_one**.

Step 5: Set the background to **bg_level_one**.

Now we can add the detail to our room. Using what you learned from Chapter 3, use the tile sets to create the level. When you're done it should look similar to **Figures 7.10** and **7.11**.

Step 6: To make the collider invisible, open **obj_collider** and uncheck the Visible option.

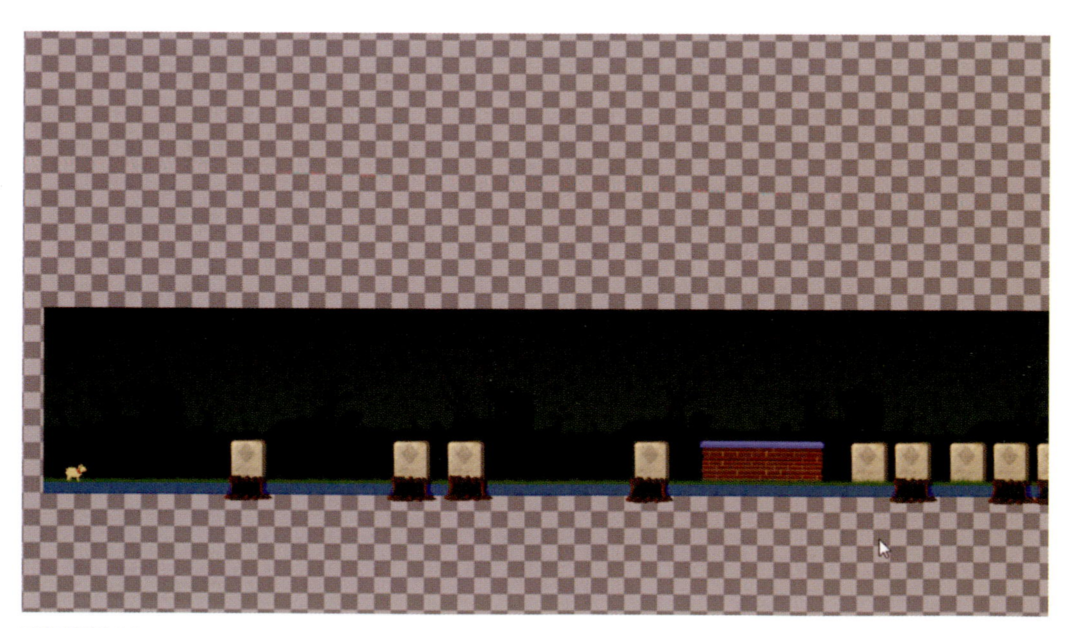

FIGURE 7.10

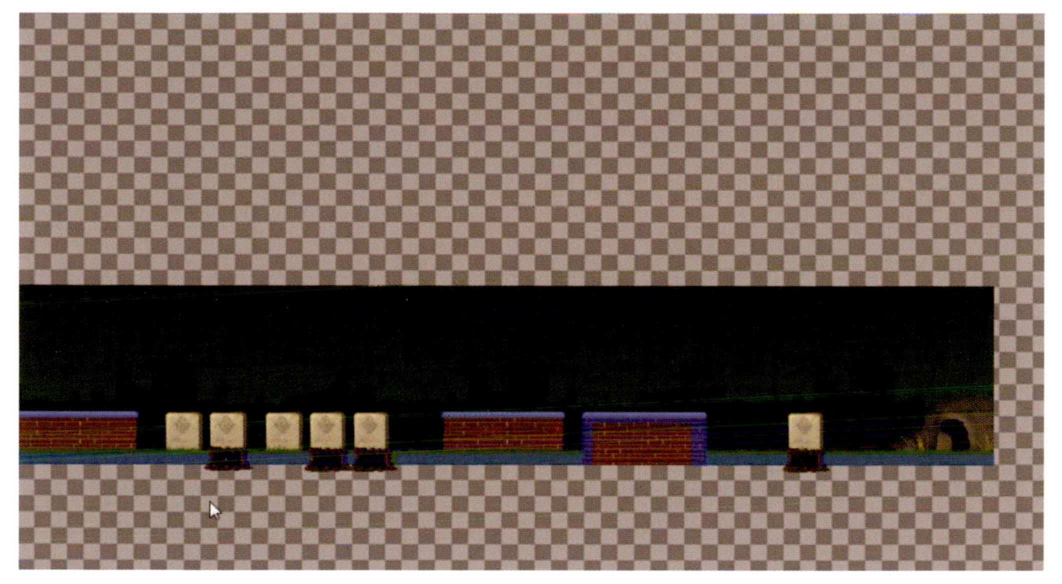

FIGURE 7.11

Coding Simple Artificial Intelligence

We will now populate our level with the ghosts. The ghosts in this particular game would be considered to have very low artificial intelligence (AI). With the AI of the ghost at such a low level, it is debatable if coding would actually prove to be quicker in this instance. We will code the ghosts simply to illustrate how the coding method would be used to create the ghosts. Before we create the object, we will first need to fix the sprite.

Step 1: Open the **spr_ghost** object and press the **Center** button.

Step 2: Click the **Modify Mask** option and check the **Precise** checkbox.

Step 3: Change the **Alpha Tolerance** to **32**.

Coding the Ghost Object AI

Step 1: Create a **New Object** and name it **obj_ghost** then set the sprite to **spr_ghost**.

Step 2: Add a **Create** Event.

Step 3: In the **Create** Event add an **Execute Code** Action.

Step 4: To move the ghost to the left we will type:

```
motion_set(180, 2)
```

This will set the ghost moving in **direction 180,** which is **left** at a speed of **2**.

Step 5: To make the ghost turn and move in the opposite direction after **360,** we will call **Alarm 0** by typing:

```
alarm[0] = 360
```

Step 6: To make sure the ghost stops animating unless we tell it to stop type the following below the previous line: **image_speed = 0**

Step 7: To create the **Alarm 0** Event, close the script and create an **Alarm: Alarm 0** Event.

Step 8: In this next script we will program the ghost to move in the opposite direction and flip its image. Add an **Execute Script** Action then type:

```
if direction = 180 {
motion_set(0, 2)
}
else {
motion_set(180, 2)
}
```

This will test to see if the ghost is moving in **direction 180**. If the ghost is moving **left** the script will set a new motion going in **direction 0,** which is toward the **right**. If the direction was **not 180**, meaning it is **0**, it will set a new motion going in the **direction 180**.

Step 9: To flip the image so it is facing the direction it is moving, place the cursor below **motion_set(0, 2)** and type:

```
image_xscale = -1
```

and below **motion_set(180, 2)** type:

```
image_xscale = 1
```

Step 10: To repeat this process we will write the code that will re-call this alarm every 6 seconds. At the bottom of the script type:

```
alarm[0] = 360
```

Step 11: This will complete the ghost object. Place some ghost objects throughout the level.

Next we need to set up the dog colliding with the ghost, falling out of the map, and completing the level.

Coding the Playable Character's Death

When the dog collides with particular objects such as the ghosts, the dog will die and fall off the screen. We will produce this effect by creating a dead dog object.

Step 1: Create a **New Object** named **obj_dog_dead** and set the sprite to **spr_dead**.

Step 2: When the dog dies it will go into the dead state for 3 seconds before the game transitions to the Game Over Screen. An Alarm Event will need to be created for this. Create an **Alarm: Alarm 0** and a **Create** Event on the **obj_dog_dead** object.

Step 3: In the **Create** Event add an **Execute Code** Action and type the following:

```
alarm[0] = 180
gravity = 0.5
gravity_direction = 270
vspeed-= 8
audio_play_sound(snd_yelp, 10, false)
```

This will trigger the **Alarm 0** Event in **3 seconds,** which equals **180 steps,** causing the object to bounce up in the air before falling off-screen. Look over this code again to see if you can now decipher the code specifics yourself.

Step 4: Select the **Alarm 0** Event and add an **Execute Code** Action to it and type the following:

```
//room_goto()
```

We hope you noticed that this information is added as a comment to the game developer. We will leave this as a comment for now and come back and edit it when we have a room for the player to end up in when they lose.

-close obJ_dog_dead

Setting Up the Events That Will Kill the Player Character

Step 1: Open the **obj_dog** object.

Step 2: Add a **Collision** with **obj_ghost.**

Step 3: Add an **Execute Code** Action and type the following:

```
instance_change(obj_dog_dead, true)
```

This will change the **obj_dog** object into the **obj_dog_dead** object and perform the events.

Step 4: Add an **Other: Outside Room** Event.

Step 5: Add an **Execute Code** Action to it and type the same line as before:

```
instance_change(obj_dog_dead, true)
```

Setting Up Additional Rooms

In order to proceed further we will need to set up the rooms first.

Step 1: Create two **New Rooms** and name them **room_title** and **room_end.**

Step 2: Set the **room_title** room's background to **bg_title** and set the height to **544.**

Step 3: Set the **room_end** room's background to **bg_end** and set the height to **544.**

Step 4: Arrange the rooms so they appear similar to **Figure 7.12**.

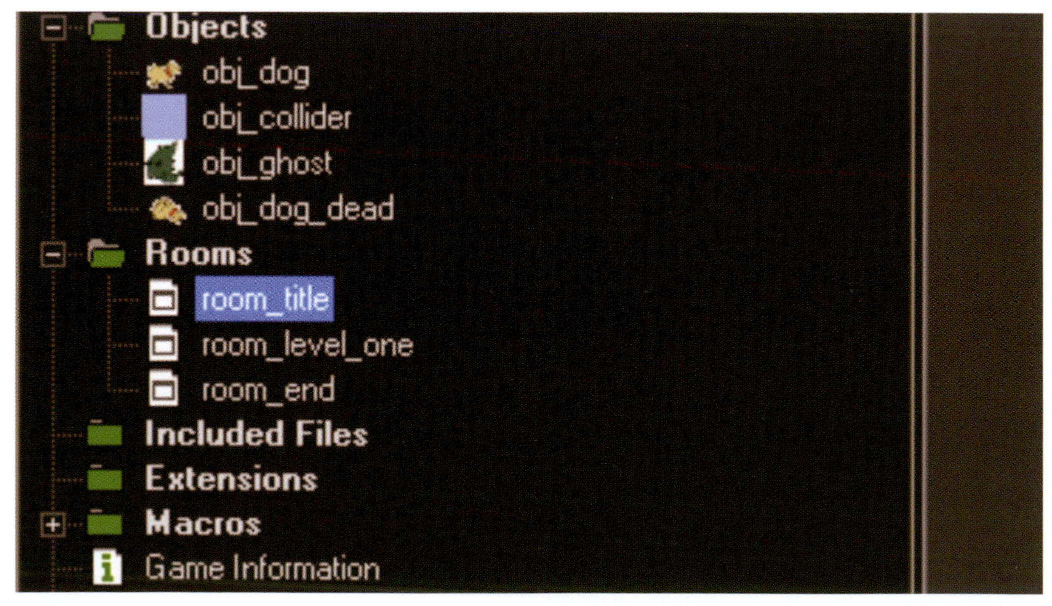

FIGURE 7.12

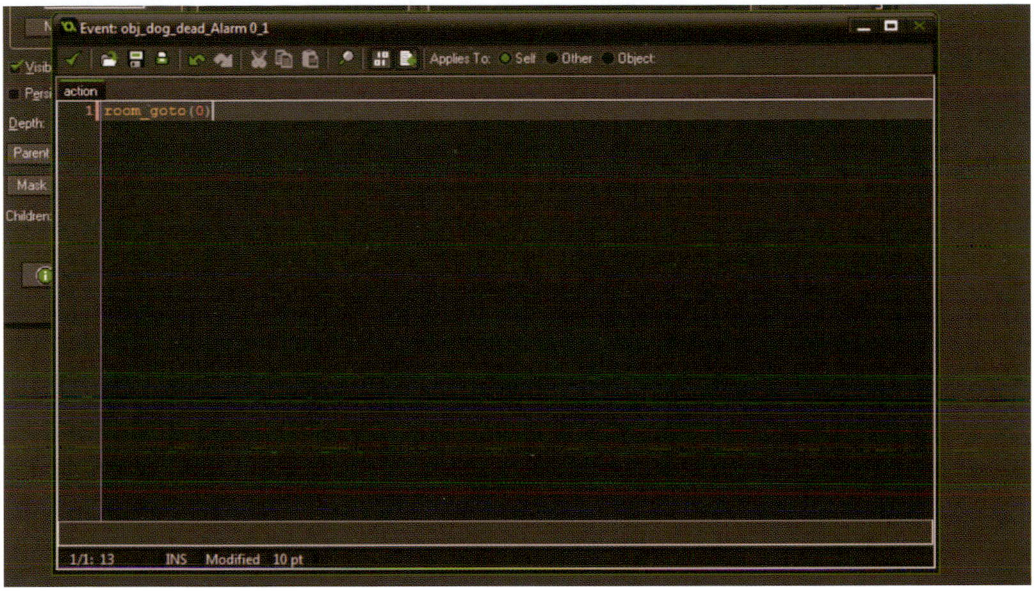

FIGURE 7.13

Coding the Return to Title Screen Action

When the player loses, the game will need to transition back to the Title Screen.

Step 1: Open the **obj_dog_dead** object and select the **Alarm 0** Event.

Step 2: Open the **Execute Code** Action and remove the two forward slashes at the start of the line and add a **0** in between the parentheses.

This will program the game to load the level in **Slot 0** of the room's folder, which is the Title Screen. Level numbers in GameMaker start at zero and go up. The **room_title** room is **0**, the **room_level_one** room is **1,** and the **room_end** is **2**.

Coding the Win Game Transition

Before adding the buttons to the Title Screen and End Screen a new object will need to be created so the dog can collide with it and win the game.

Step 1: Create a **New Object** named **obj_next_level** and set the sprite to **spr_collider.**

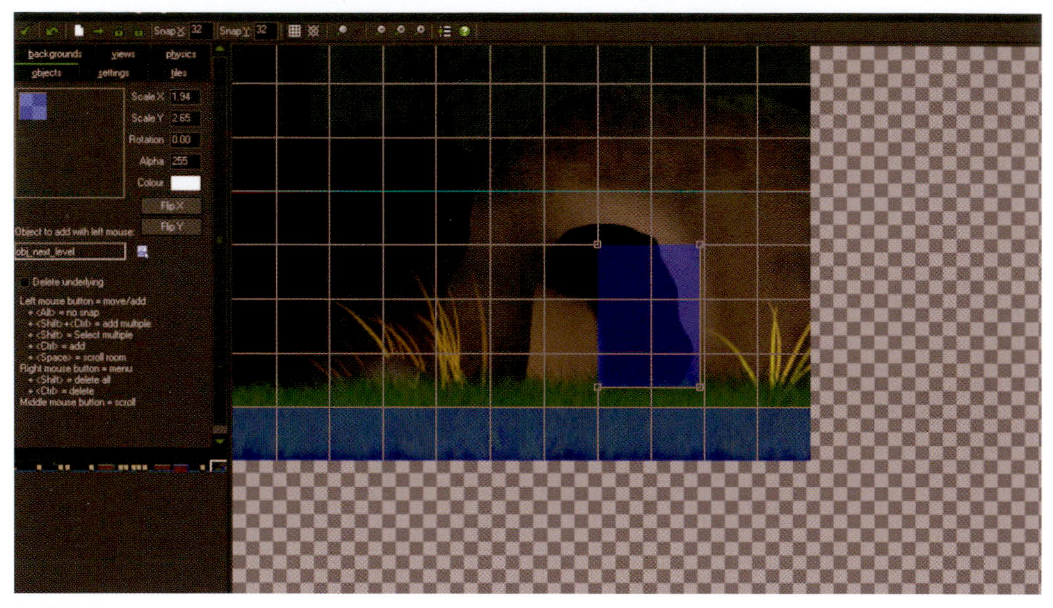

FIGURE 7.14

Step 2: Place the object in **room_level_one** at the end of the level in the cave tile as shown in **Figure 7.14**.

Step 3: We will now set up the Collision Event in **obj_dog.** Open **obj_dog** and create a **Collision** Event with **obj_next_level.**

Step 4: Add an **Execute code** and type in:

```
room_goto_next()
```

Step 5: The action of this code should be pretty obvious, it will load the next level in the list.

Coding the Title Screen Buttons

Step 1: Create two **New Objects** and name them **obj_play** and **obj_quit**. Set the sprites for both objects to spr_collider. **Uncheck** the **Visible** option for **Both** objects.

Step 2: In the **obj_play** object add a **Mouse: Left Button** Event.

Step 3: Drag in an Execute Code Action and type: **room_goto(1).**

This will load room 1 on the list, which is our level one.

Step 4: Reopen the **obj_quit** object and add a **Mouse: Left Button** Event.

Step 5: Add an **Execute Code** Action and type the following: **game_end().**

FIGURE 7.15

This will exit the game.

Step 6: Open the **room_title** room and the **room_end** room and place the buttons in the appropriate places.

Coding Background Music

Step 1: Create a **New Object** named **obj_level_music** with **no sprite.**

Step 2: Add a **Create** Event.

Step 3: Add an **Execute Code** Action.

Type:

```
audio_play_sound(snd_level_one, 9, true)
```

Step 4: Add an **Other: Room End** Event and add an **Execute Code** Action and type the following:

```
audio_stop_all()
```

Step 5: Place this object in **room_level_one.**

Step 6: Create a **Second Object** named **obj_end_music** with no sprite.

Do the same thing for **obj_level_music** but in the Create Event type this instead:

```
audio_play_sound(snd_end_screen, 9, true)
```

GML Terminology

This chapter on GML introduced new terminology that may not be familiar to individuals that have not tried coding before. There are various other types of coding languages and GML is just one of them. **GML** stands for **Game Maker Language** as it is the coding language that GameMaker understands. Other game engines use different languages. Learning GML can assist you in learning other coding languages as many of them have similar structures. For a complete list of build-in GML variables, click on the Help tab in the GameMaker program, then go to Contents>Reference>GML Language Overview. Another term we used in this chapter is **scripting**. Just as a script for a movie tells what will happen in the film, a script in a video game tells the game what will happen. We also saw several references to **vspeed,** which indicates the vertical speed an object is traveling, and references to **image_xscale,** which told the game what direction a sprite was facing on the x-axis. Many of these terms and references may have seemed foreign to you as you began this chapter, but now that you have created a game that required typing code, we hope the odd-looking code snippets are starting to make sense. Coding is a language and the best way to learn any new language is to practice it frequently and by learning new expressions. Using code as a game developer can not only save time but also allow designers greater flexibility for the actions of the objects in the game.

CHAPTER 8

Role Playing Games

Learning Objectives—Upon completion of Chapter 8 readers will be able to:

- Incorporate mini-missions within a game
- Create a store for players to purchase game items
- Pick up weapons and gold
- Create a persistent object for all levels which will store values such as coins picked up
- Add inventory items to the HUD
- Add dialog boxes that direct the player where to go
- Create multiple instances of the same room to create the illusion that the room is the same but elements have changed

Project Overview: *Keeper of the Oracle*

Role Playing Games (RPGs) are adventure games that tell a story through gameplay and allow players to change instances about their character. These instances can be changing the character's wealth, weapons, or appearance. An entire book could be written on creating RPGs as different types of games include various elements. For this chapter we will be concentrating on the core aspects of creating an RPG. Fundamental aspects included in most RPGs include:

- A store in which the player can purchase items for their character
- Pick-up items such as weapons or coins that the player can use in the game
- A system of keeping track of what items a character has and illustrating them in the HUD
- A simple yet captivating story that drives the player to continue playing the game
- Dialog boxes which give the player information needed to know for what to do next
- Increasing challenges in which players must strategize to complete

In the list above the abbreviation HUD was used, which stands for Heads-Up Display. A HUD is an onscreen interface that shows the player various stats from the game. In previous chapters the game HUD showed a player's score and lives. In this game the HUD will be used to keep track of how many coins the player has and what weapon is currently being held.

In *Keeper of the Oracle*, the player receives instructions from the oracle via dialog boxes. The player then goes on a series of mini-missions to complete the tasks assigned. Each mission changes what the player is carrying. The first mission allows the player to pick up a weapon. The second mission provides the player with coins. The third mission introduces the character to the store where they will purchase a new, more powerful weapon with the coins picked up in the previous mission. The last mission has the player using their new weapon to defeat a powerful enemy and win the game. Additional information on each mission will be provided throughout the chapter to provide context why we are adding certain elements to the game. We will start by downloading the game assets for *Keeper of the Oracle* from www.thegamemakerstandard.com/oracle. After downloading the assets folder read over the updates.pdf document, which contains any changes since the publication of this book.

Creating a New Project

Step 1: Create a new project and name it **Oracle**.

Step 2: Import the **Keeper of the Oracle** assets from the **Oracle** assets folder.

Step 3: Organize the player sprites in the **Sprite Folder** with **Subfolders** so that they appear similar to **Figure 8.1**.

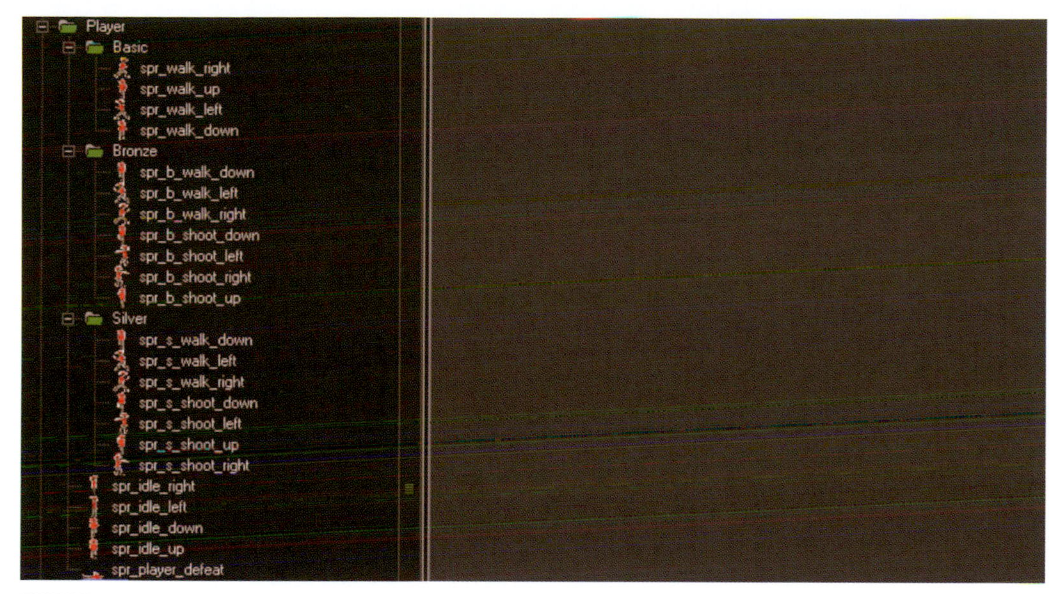

FIGURE 8.1

Setting the Character Sprites

Step 1: Open all the player sprites and **Center** them.

Step 2: Modify the **Collision Mask** using the **Modify Mask** button and set it to the following:

Bounding Box: Manual
Shape: Rectangle
Left: 19 Right: 41
Top: 18 Bottom: 73

When you are done the items following **Sprites** should all be modified:

Walking Sprites:

spr_walk_right, spr_walk_left, spr_walk_down and spr_walk_up

Idle Sprites:

spr_idle_up, spr_idle_down, spr_idle_right and spr_idle_left

Bronze Dagger Sprites:

spr_b_walk_down, spr_b_walk_left, spr_b_walk_right, spr_b_shoot_down, spr_b_shoot_left, spr_b_shoot_right and spr_b_shoot_up

Silver Dagger Sprites:

spr_s_walk_down, spr_s_walk_left, spr_s_walk_right, spr_s_shoot_down, spr_s_shoot_left, spr_s_shoot_right and spr_s_shoot_up

Creating the Player Object

Step 1: Create a **New Folder** in the Objects section and name it **Player Objects**.

Step 2: Create a **New Object** named **obj_player_default** and place it in the **Player Objects** folder.

Step 3: Assign the sprite **spr_idle_right**.

Coding the Player Movement and Animations

We will be using code to create the player movements and animation. This code will be called when a key is held down and it will check the key and go through a series of ifs and else ifs to find the key. Once it finds the key it will check to make sure there is not any colliders in the destination. If no colliders are detected the player will then move. The code will also check to see if the appropriate sprite animation is playing and if it is not, the code will set the sprite and set the animation speed to 0.2. After the animation speed is set the code will then set the variable **myDirection** to the direction the player is facing.

Step 1: Add a **Create** Event and place a **Set Variable** Action in it and set the following:

Variable: myDirection
Value: 0

Step 2: Add a **Keyboard: Any Key** Event.

Step 3: Add an **Execute Code** Action and type the following:

```
if keyboard_key = vk_left {
  if place_free(x - 4, y) {
    x - = 4
  }
  if sprite_index ! = spr_walk_left {
    sprite_index = spr_walk_left
```

```
            image_speed = 0.2
            myDirection = 180
        }
    }
    else if keyboard_key = vk_right {
        if place_free(x + 4, y) {
            x + = 4
        }
        if sprite_index ! = spr_walk_right {
            sprite_index = spr_walk_right
            image_speed = 0.2
            myDirection = 0
        }
    }
    else if keyboard_key = vk_up {
        if place_free(x, y - 4) {
            y - = 4
        }
        if sprite_index ! = spr_walk_up {
            sprite_index = spr_walk_up
            image_speed = 0.2
            myDirection = 90
        }
    }
    else if keyboard_key = vk_down {
        if place_free(x, y + 4) {
            y + = 4
        }
        if sprite_index ! = spr_walk_down {
            sprite_index = spr_walk_down
            image_speed = 0.2
            myDirection = 270
        }
    }
```

The animation will need to be set back to idle when the character has stopped moving. The direction of the player will need to be checked so the correct idle sprite will load. We will set this up for each of the four directions the player can move: **Right**, **Up**, **Left,** and **Down**. We will start with the **Right** direction in which the value will be **0**.

Right:

Step 4: Add a **Keyboard <No Key>** Event.

Step 5: Add a **Test Expression** Action and set the following:

Variable: myDirection
Value: 0
Operation: Equal to

Step 6: Add a **Change Sprite** Action below it and set the following:

Sprite: spr_idle_right
Subimage: 0
Speed: 0

Up:

Step 7: Add a **Test Expression** Action and set the following:

Variable: myDirection
Value: 90
Operation: Equal to

Step 8: Add a **Change Sprite** Action:

Sprite: spr_idle_up
Subimage: 0
Speed: 0

Left:

Step 9: Add a **Test Expression** Action:

Variable: myDirection
Value: 180
Operation: Equal to

Step 10: Add a **Change Sprite** Action:

Sprite: spr_idle_left
Subimage: 0
Speed: 0

Down:

Step 11: Add a **Test Expression** Action:

Variable: myDirection
Value: 270
Operation: Equal to

Step 12: Add a **Change Sprite** Action:

Sprite: spr_idle_down
Subimage: 0
Speed: 0

Creating the Collider Object

Step 1: Create a **New Object** named **obj_collider**.

Step 2: Set the sprite to **spr_collider**.

Step 3: Check the **Solid** option.

Step 4: Uncheck the **Visible** option.

Setting Up the First Oracle Room

The **Oracle Room** is the room in which the player first appears and receives instructions from the **Oracle,** which is represented by a pool of water with a giant eye in the center of the pool. We will be creating multiple versions of this room to create the illusion that each time the player returns to the room that it is the same room but the oracle is saying something different and a new gate is open. In actuality the player will be entering a new room that looks identical to the original room, except this time the background image has a different gate open and the dialog box says something different. We will have a different Oracle Room for each time the player appears to return to the Oracle Room. The player will return to the **Oracle Room** three times; therefore, we will eventually have four different **Oracle Rooms**, the original and

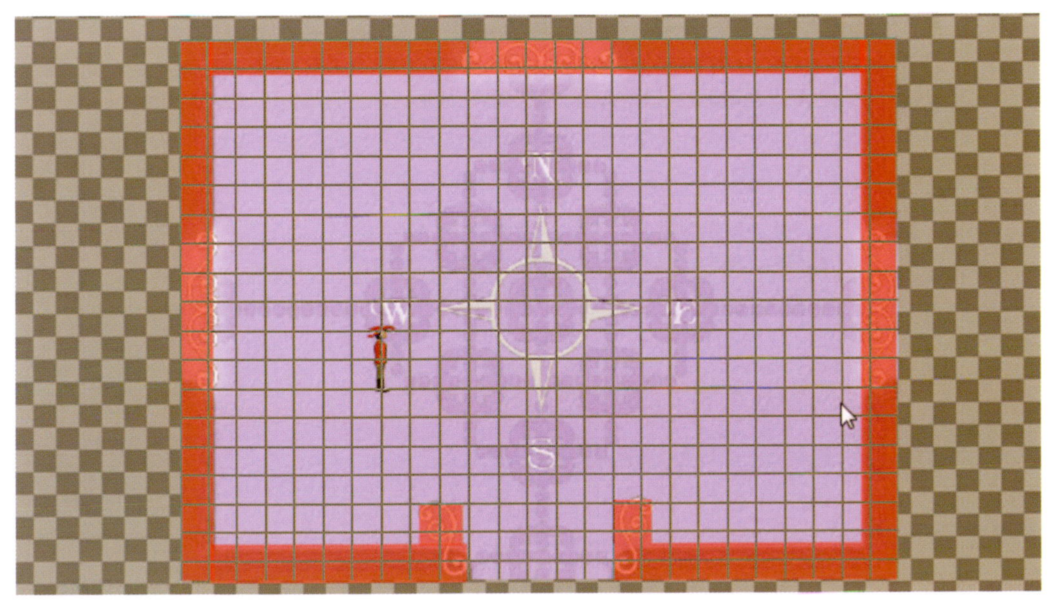

FIGURE 8.2

three copies. This may seem a little confusing at first, but as we create each duplicate room, it will begin to make more sense as to why we are doing so.

Step 1: Create a **New Room** named **room_oracle_one**.

Step 2: Change the **Width to 800** and the **Height to 600**.

Step 3: Set the **Background** to **bg_oracle_one**.

Step 4: Place the **Player Object** anywhere in the room.

Step 5: Place **Colliders** along the walls similar to those shown in **Figure 8.2**.

Testing Player Movement

Now that our first room is created and our player character is placed in the room, we will want to run the game and test that the player animates, moves, and collides with the walls correctly.

Setting Up the Additional Oracle Rooms

Step 1: Create a **New Folder** in the **Rooms** section and name it **Oracle Rooms**.

Step 2: Drag the **room_oracle_one** room into the **Oracle Rooms** folder.

Step 3: Create **Three New Rooms** and name them: **room_oracle_two**, **room_oracle_three,** and **room_oracle_four** and place each of them into the **Oracle Rooms** folder.

Step 4: Set the **Width to 800** and **Height to 600** for all three rooms.

Step 5: Assign the following backgrounds:

room_oracle_two	to	**bg_oracle_two**
room_oracle_three	to	**bg_oracle_three**
room_oracle_four	to	**bg_oracle_four**

Game Progression and Room Hierarchy

The progression of the *Keeper of the Oracle* game appears as follows:

Title Screen > **Oracle One** > **Level One** > **Oracle Two** > **Level Two** > **Oracle Three** > **Shop** > **Oracle Four** > **Boss Level** > **Title Screen**

As the above hierarchy shows, the game will start with the **Title Screen**. When the player presses the **Start Button,** the **Oracle One** room will load and the player will see the hero character in the room. The player will be given a task from the **Oracle,** which appears as a Dialog Box. Essentially the **Oracle** is telling the player to go through the **South Gate** and pick up a dagger. When the player goes through the gate, the **Level One** room will load.

Level One has the player avoiding fireballs that are being shot from masks on the wall. Once the player has gotten through the fireball obstacles and made it to the bottom of the room, they will pick up the dagger which has been placed there. The moment the dagger is picked up, the masks begin to shoot fireballs in a much faster progression, making it impossible for the player to get back to the doorway the same way they walked in. This is a cue to the player to use the dagger which shoots blades. The player will then shoot blades at the masks. As each mask is destroyed, the fireballs emitted from it ceases. With the fireball danger gone, the player can then exit through the door the same way they entered the room.

When the player exits the room it will appear as though they have been taken back to the **Oracle One** room, but this is actually a game designer trick. The player has actually now entered the **Oracle Two** room that looks almost identical to the **Oracle One** room. The **Oracle Two** room now has the **South Gate** closed so the player cannot enter the **Level One** room again as that mission is now complete. The **East Gate** is now open and the Oracle instructs the player to solve a riddle and enter the **East Gate** to pick up some treasure.

When the player steps through the **East Gate,** the **Level Two** room loads. The **Level Two** room contains floor tiles with different letters on each of them. If the player has solved the riddle correctly, they will know which tiles they can walk on and which ones will destroy them. The player cannot idle too long as ice sawblades will be flying out from the walls to motivate the player to move. Fortunately the player has the dagger and can shoot at the sawblades to destroy them. Once the player makes it across the room and picks up the treasure, they will see that their gold supply has been increased. This also allows them to leave through the doorway where they entered the room just as the dagger did in the previous level. The player will still want to walk on the appropriate tiles but will no longer need to worry about the ice sawblades.

When the player exits the **Level Two** room it will appear that they have returned to the **Oracle Two** room, however, they are now in the **Oracle Three** room. The **Oracle Three** room has the **East Gate** closed and the **North Gate** open. The player is instructed to go through the **North Gate** to purchase a new dagger with the coins they just picked up.

When the player enters the **North Gate,** the **Shop** level will load. The view is now from the player character's perspective, meaning we are looking through the player character's eyes and therefore cannot see the player character. The player can then try to select items they cannot afford, which will give them a message that they need more coins. The only item they can afford is the silver dagger. When they select the silver dagger the **Oracle Four** room will load. This room has all the gates closed except for the **West Gate**. The **Oracle** will then tell the player to go through the **West Gate**.

When the player enters the West Gate, the **Boss Level** will load. In the **Boss Level** they will see a **Totem Pole** which represents the **Boss** for this game. Some games have what are called **mini-bosses** at the end of each level and a **Final Boss** at the end of the game. The Totem Pole would be the **Boss** for this game since we do not have any additional levels. If the game had a lot more levels, the **Totem Pole** would be considered one of many **mini-bosses** and at the end of the game would be a powerful **Final Boss**. The **Totem Pole** contains multiple heads that shoot fire and ice. The player will need to use the obstacles in the room to hide from the fire and ice projectiles. They will use their new dagger which is more powerful than the original dagger to destroy each of the totem pole heads individually. When all of the heads are destroyed, a gem will appear. When the player picks up the gem, a new **Dialog Box** will appear telling the player they have completed the game. This will then load the title screen again after a few seconds.

Preparing the Remaining Game Rooms

Step 1: Create five New Rooms and name them: **room_title**, **room_level_one**, **room_level_two**, **room_shop**, **room_finalboss**.

Step 2: Set the **Width to 800** and **Height to 600** for all the rooms.

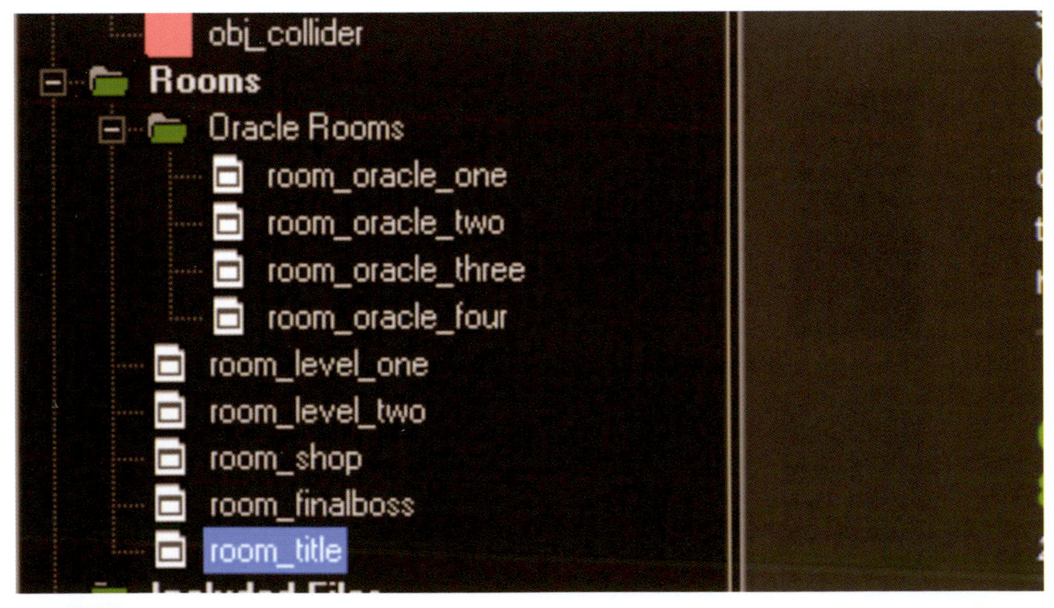

FIGURE 8.3

Step 3: The background of the rooms should be self-explanatory by now. Set up the backgrounds for each room and then arrange them so your room's folder looks similar to **Figure 8.3**.

We will move the Title Room to the top of the list after setting up the Play and Quit buttons.

Creating a Persistent Object

For the remainder of this chapter we will be creating each room in the order that it will appear when played. The first object we need to create is an object that will persist through all the rooms. This object will be used to store values; for example, it will keep track of how many coins the player has obtained so that the player does not lose them when they change rooms.

Step 1: Create a **New Object** named **obj_control**.

Set the sprite to spr_hud

Step 2: Add a **Create** Event and add a **Set Variable** Action. Set the following:

Variable: global.myCoins
Value: 0

Step 3: Add a **Set Variable** Action and set the following:

Variable: global.myWeapon
Value: 0

Step 4: Add a **Set Variable** Action and set the following:

Variable: global.hasGem
Value: 0

Step 5: Add a **Set Sprite** Action and set the following:

Sprite: spr_hud
Subimage: 0
Speed: 0

Step 6: Add an **Other: Room Start** Event.

Step 7: Add a **Change Sprite** Action and set the following:

Sprite: spr_hud
Subimage: global.myWeapon
Speed: 0

This will make the HUD display the appropriate subimage for the weapon.

Step 8: Check the **Persistent** checkbox.

Step 9: Place the **obj_control** object in the top right of **room_oracle_one**.

Displaying Coins in the HUD Display

The game will now display in the **HUD** which weapon if any the player character is carrying. We will also want the **HUD** to display the amount of coins the player character has at any given moment in the game.

We will create a **Persistent Counter Object** that will be placed beside the image of the coin bag. For the purposes of this game and tutorial, the player will never have over 60 gold pieces so the counter will stop at the number 90 and only count in multiples of 10.

Step 1: Create a **New Object** and name it **obj_counter**.

Step 2: Set the Sprite to **spr_counter**.

Step 3: Check the Persistent option and set the depth to −1.

Step 4: Add a **Create** Event.

Step 5: Add a **Set Sprite** Action and set the following:

Sprite: spr_counter
Subimage: 0
Speed: 0

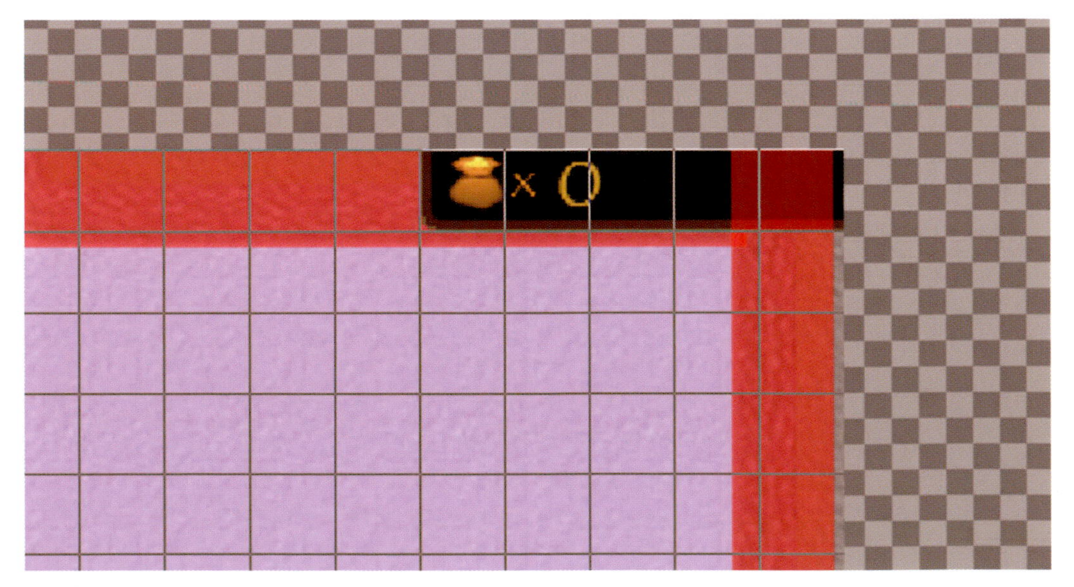

FIGURE 8.4

If the coins go up at any point, we will have the object that changes the coins also change the counter image.

Step 6: Place the **obj_counter** object at the top of right of **room_oracle_one** beside the coin bag **X** symbol.

Creating the Oracle Object

The **Oracle** object is the entity that gives our player information on what to do and where to go in the game. This could actually be any type of character such as a person, animal, or magical being. In the case of this game, it is a pool of water.

Step 1: Create a **New Object** named **obj_oracle** and set the sprite to **spr_oracle.**

Step 2: Check the **Solid** option and set the **Depth** to **1**.

Step 3: Open the **spr_oracle** sprite and click the **Modify Mask** option and set the shape to **Precise**.

Step 4: Open all of the **Oracle Rooms** and place **obj_oracle** in the middle of the room so it appears similar to **Figure 8.5**.

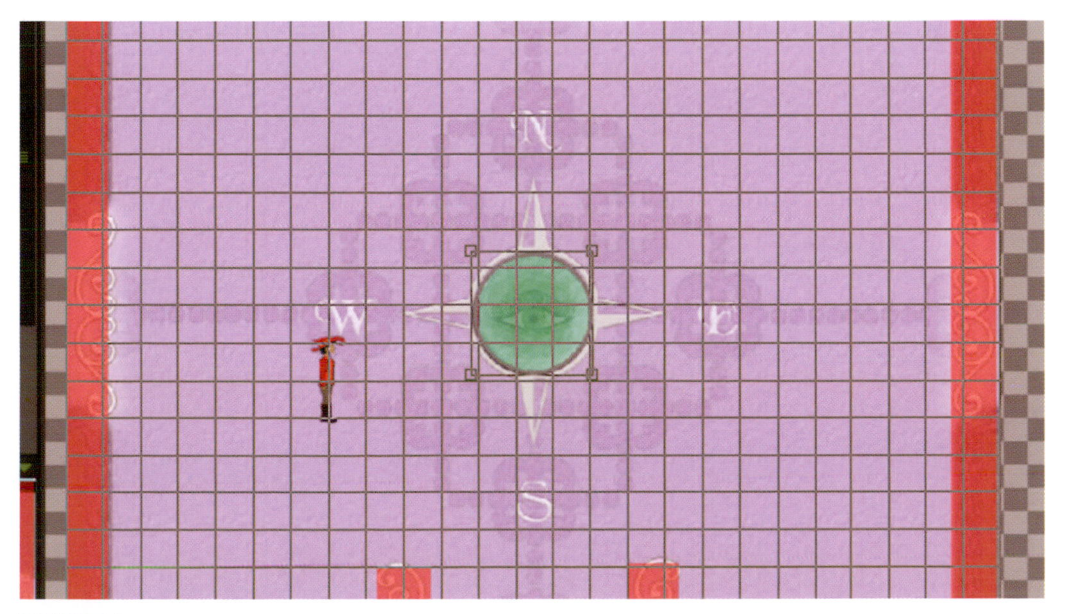

FIGURE 8.5

Creating the Scrolls

The Oracle will give instructions to the player via **Dialog Boxes** that appear as scrolls on the screen 3 seconds after the character enters any of the **Oracle Rooms**.

Step 1: Create a **New Object** and name it **obj_scroll_one**.

Step 2: Set the sprite to **spr_scroll_one**.

Step 3: Uncheck the **Visible** option.

Step 4: Add a **Create** Event and add a **Set Alarm** Action then set the following:

> Number of steps: 90
> In alarm no: Alarm 0

Step 5: Add an **Alarm: Alarm 0** Event.

Step 6: Add a **Set Variable** Action and set the following:

> Variable: visible
> Value: true

Step 7: Place the scroll object in the top left corner of the room so that it appears similar to **Figure 8.6**.

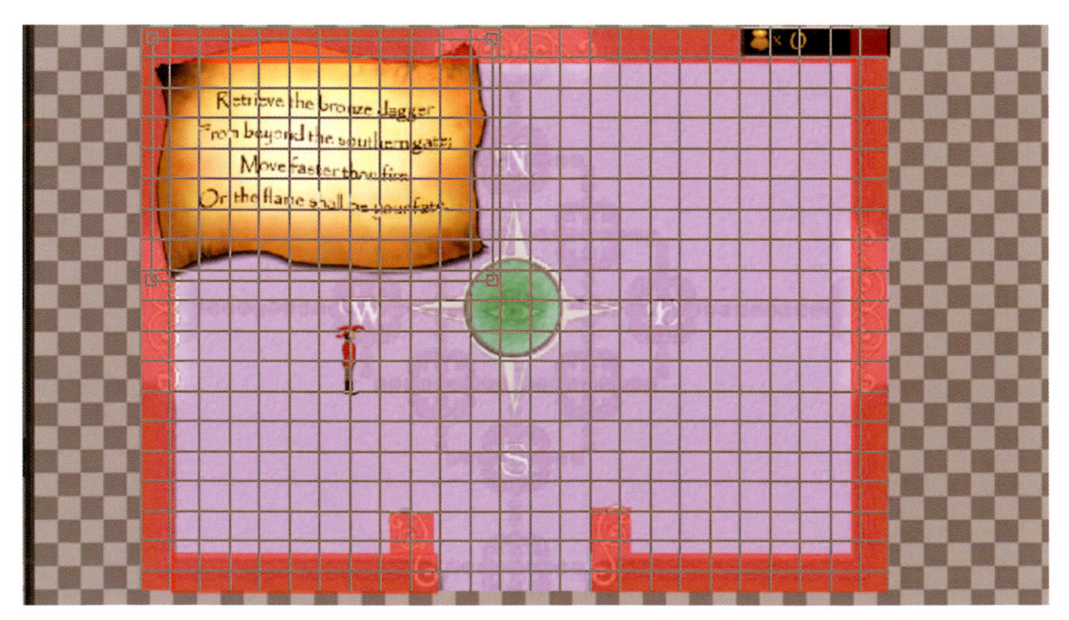

FIGURE 8.6

Creating Next Level Triggers

A trigger is an object that triggers some sort of event in a game. Triggers can be used to spawn enemies, change music, or in this case load the next level.

Step 1: Create a **New Folder** named **Level Triggers**.

Step 2: Create a **New Object** named **obj_nlt_one**. The abbreviation **nlt** stands for "next level trigger."

Step 3: Set the sprite for the **obj_nlt_one** object to **spr_nlt**.

When a player enters a new level the **Triggers** will be **Solid** until the player meets the requirements to move to the next level. This way it can also work like a collider keeping the player in the room until the objective is met.

Step 4: Add a **Collision** with the **obj_player_default** object.

Step 5: Add a **Different Room** Action and set the following:

Room: room_level_one

Step 6: Place the **obj_nlt_one** object just outside the room where the open gate is located in **room_oracle_one** so that it looks similar to **Figure 8.7**.

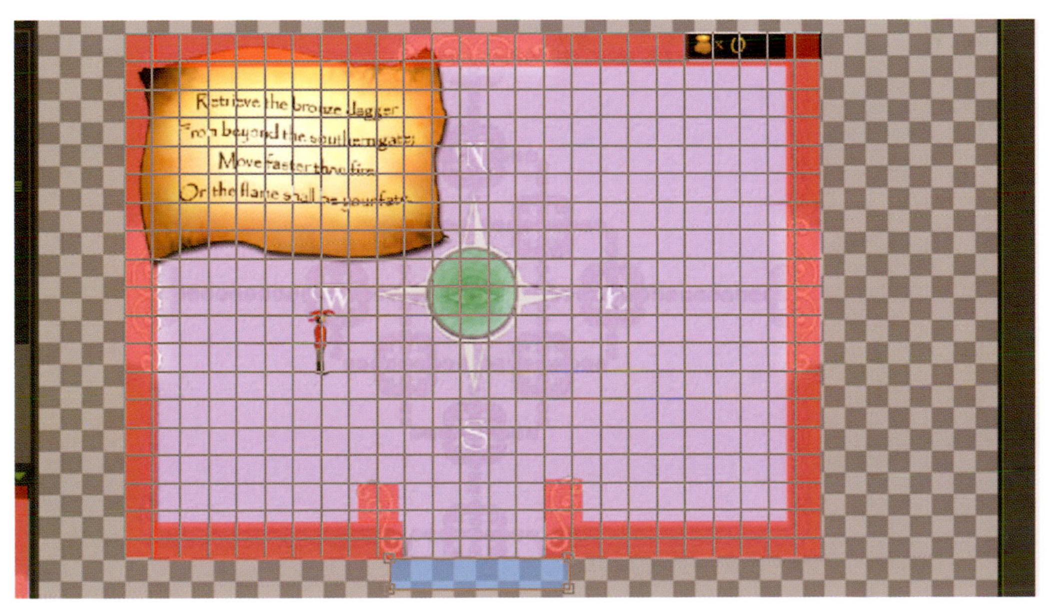

FIGURE 8.7

Building the First Level

Level One will have stone walls that the player cannot pass through. These stone walls can be used to create a maze for the player to navigate through. This is also the level with the fireball shooting masks. The player will need to navigate the maze while at the same time avoid the fireballs. The player at this point in the game does not have any weapons, which increases the difficulty of the level.

Creating the Stone Objects

Step 1: Create a **New Object** named **obj_stone** and set the sprite to **spr_stone.**

Step 2: Check the **Solid** checkbox and set the **Depth** to **2**.

Step 3: Create a **Second Object** named **obj_stone_two**. This second stone object will not be destroyed when the player collects the dagger. The player will be able to use this stone as a barrier to hide from the fireballs.

Step 4: Set the sprite to **spr_stone_two** and check the **Solid** option and set the **Depth** to **2**.

Creating the Masks

Step 1: Create **Three New Objects** and name them **obj_mask_left**, **obj_mask_right,** and **obj_mask_down.** To keep track of them you may wish to put these objects in a folder named **Masks**.

Step 2: Assign the following sprites:

obj_mask_left	to	**spr_mask_left**
obj_mask_right	to	**spr_mask_right**
obj_mask_down	to	**spr_mask_down**

The masks can be placed anywhere on the top wall and side walls. The appropriate mask will need to be used depending on which wall it is on. This will be where the fireballs will shoot out of, so the masks and walls should be placed in such a way that it is difficult but not impossible for the player to navigate to the bottom of the level. We will now add the shooting feature to all three of the masks.

Step 1: For each of the mask objects add a **Create** Event**.**

Step 2: In the Create Event for each mask add a **Set Variable** Action and set the following:

Variable: mySpeed
Value: 90

This variable will be used to adjust the rate in which the masks fire. The masks will shoot at a reasonable speed until the player picks up the dagger. Then the masks will shoot at a much faster speed so the player has no choice but to destroy the masks in order to escape.

Step 3: Add a **Set Alarm** Action in the Create Event for each mask. Set the following:

Number of steps: 1
In alarm no: Alarm 0 (we will be adding the alarm event later).

Creating the Fireballs

Step 1: Open the sprite **spr_fireball** and press the **Center** button.

Step 2: Click the **Modify Mask** option and select the **Precise** checkbox.

Step 3: Create a **New Object** and name it **obj_fireball**.

Step 4: Set the sprite to **spr_fireball**.

Step 5: Add a **Create** Event.

Step 6: Add a **Play Sound** Action to it and set the following:

Sound: snd_fireball
Loop: false

Step 7: Add an **Other: Outside Room** Event.

Step 8: Add a **Destroy Instance** Action.

Step 9: Add a **Collision** Event with **obj_stone** and **obj_stone_two,** then place in a **Destroy Instance** Action.

Step 10: Close the **obj_fireball** object and open the **Three Mask Objects**.

Step 11: Add an **Alarm 0** Event for each mask and also add a **Create Moving** Action then set the following:

Object: obj_fireball
x: 0
y: 0
Speed: 8
Direction: (**0** for Right Mask, **270** for Down Mask, and **180** for Left Mask)
Relative: checked

FIGURE 8.8

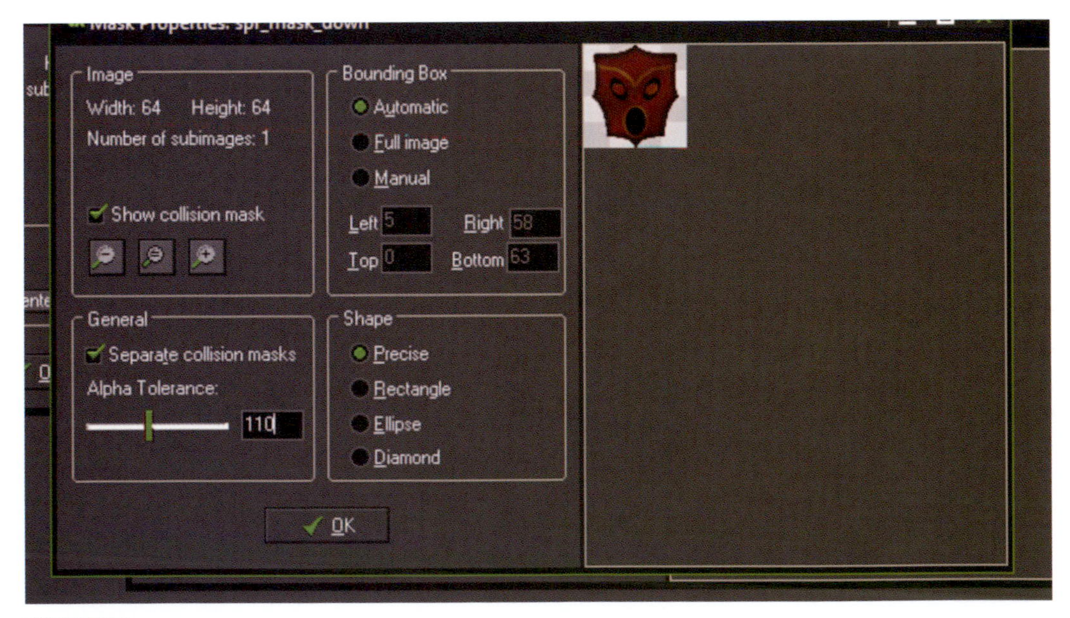

FIGURE 8.9

Step 12: Add a **Set Alarm** Action and set the following:

Number of steps: mySpeed
In alarm no: alarm 0

The mask sprites need to be adjusted so it will appear that they are shooting the fireballs from their mouths and that they contain proper collision. To make sure the fireball looks like it comes out of the mask, the mask needs to appear above the fireball.

Step 13: Set the **Depth** for the **Left Mask** and **Right Mask** to **–1**.

Step 14: Set the **Depth** for the **Down Mask** to **1**.

Step 15: Open the **Three Mask Sprites** and click the **Preview** images so the crosshairs are over the mouth similar to **Figure 8.8**.

Step 16: Open the **Modify Mask** option for each mask and check the **Precise** button, then in the **General** section change the **Alpha Tolerance: to 110.**

Creating the Dagger Object

Step 1: Create a **New Object** and name it **obj_dagger** and use the **spr_bronze_collider** as the sprite.

When the player collides with the dagger, the player character will change into an object holding the dagger weapon and will be able to shoot a projectile a few feet in the direction they are facing. For this a new player object holding the dagger will need to be created.

Step 2: Right-click the **obj_player_default** object and press the **Duplicate** option.

Step 3: Name the new object **obj_player_bronze.** This name refers to the bronze-colored dagger so as not to be confused with the silver dagger the player will be able to purchase later in the game.

Step 4: Create a **New Object** and name it **obj_bronze_projectile.** This projectile will be the dagger that the player shoots.

Step 5: Set the sprite for the **obj_bronze_projectile** object to **spr_bronze_projectile.**

Step 6: Open the **spr_bronze_projectile** sprite and **Center** it then set the **Modify Mask** to **Precise.**

Showing the Player Character Holding the Weapon

Step 1: Open the **obj_player_bronze** object.

To show that the player has picked up the dagger, the player character should be shown holding the dagger from this point of the game onward until they get a new weapon. We will now set up the animations for the player holding the dagger.

Step 2: Select the **<Any Key>** Event and open the **Execute Code** Action and make the following modifications:

Lines 5 and 6: **spr_walk_left** should be changed to **spr_b_walk_left.**
Lines 15 and 16: **spr_walk_right** should be changed to **spr_b_walk_right.**
Lines 35 and 36: **spr_walk_down** should be changed to **spr_b_walk_down.**

When testing the animations for the player character holding the dagger, remove the default player object from room_oracle_one and replace it with the obj_player_bronze. After testing the animations, switch the obj_player_bronze back with the default player object.

1 if keyboard_key = vk_left {
2   if place_free(x - 4, y) {
3   x -= 4
4   }
5   if sprite_index != spr_b_walk_left {
6   sprite_index = spr_b_walk_left
7   image_speed = 0.2
8   myDirection =180
9   }
10 }
11 else if keyboard_key = vk_right {
12   if place_free(x + 4, y) {
13   x += 4
14   }
15   if sprite_index != spr_b_walk_right {
16   sprite_index = spr_b_walk_right
17   image_speed = 0.2
18   myDirection = 0
19   }
20 }
21 else if keyboard_key = vk_up {
22   if place_free(x, y - 4) {
23   y -= 4
24   }
25   if sprite_index != spr_walk_up {
26   sprite_index = spr_walk_up
27   image_speed = 0.2
28   myDirection = 90
29   }
30 }
31 else if keyboard_key = vk_down {
32   if place_free(x, y + 4) {
33   y += 4
34   }
35   if sprite_index != spr_b_walk_down {
36   sprite_index = spr_b_walk_down
37   image_speed = 0.2
38   myDirection = 270

FIGURE 8.10

Shooting the Projectile

Step 1: Add a **Key Press <Space>** Event.

Step 2: Add a **Create Moving** Action to it and set the following:

Object: obj_bronze_projectile
x: 0
y: 0
Speed: 12
Direction: myDirection
Relative: checked

Step 3: We will make a quick script change to the sprite of the player character so it looks like it is shooting. Add an **Execute Code** Action and type:

```
if myDirection = 0 {
  sprite_index = spr_b_shoot_right
}
if myDirection = 180 {
  sprite_index = spr_b_shoot_left
}
if myDirection = 90 {
  sprite_index = spr_b_shoot_up
}
if myDirection = 270 {
  sprite_index = spr_b_shoot_down
}
```

This script will check the player's **myDirection Variable** and choose the correct sprite. We will next make the projectile face the direction it's flying and then have it disappear after a brief moment.

Step 4: Open the **obj_bronze_projectile** object.

Step 5: Add a **Create** Event.

Step 6: Add **a Set Variable** Action to it and set the following:

Variable: image_angle
Value: direction

Step 7: Add a **Play Sound** Action and set the following:

Sound: snd_shoot
Loop: false

If you find the sounds are too loud, you can open the specific sound in the Sounds folder and adjust the volume bar.

The dagger will now point in the direction that it is moving.

Step 8: Add an **Alarm 0** Event.

Step 9: In the **Create** Event add a **Set Alarm** and set the following:

Number of steps: 10
In alarm no: Alarm 0

Step 10: In the **Alarm 0** Event, add a **Destroy Instance** Action.

This would be a good time to test that all of the changes are working without bugs.

Updating the Character and HUD Appearance

To create the illusion that the player picked up the bronze-colored dagger a Collision Event will need to be created that will swap the default player appearance into the bronze-dagger version and update the HUD to show the bronze dagger.

Step 1: Open the **obj_player_default** object.

Step 2: Add a **Collision** Event with the **obj_dagger** object.

Step 3: Add a **Change Instance** Action and set the following:

Object: obj_player_bronze
Perform events: yes

Step 4: Add a **Play Sound** Action:

Sound: snd_dagger_pickup
Loop: false

Step 5: Add a **Change Sprite** and set the following:

Applies to: obj_control
Sprite: spr_hud
Subimage: 1
Speed: 0

Step 6: Add a **Set Variable** Action:

Variable: global.myWeapon
Value: 1

Step 7: Add a **Destroy Instance** and select the **Other** checkbox. This will make it appear that the player picked up the dagger and is now holding it, while the image of the dagger on the ground will disappear at the same time. As we mentioned earlier, other events will also be triggered when the dagger is picked up. We will start by destroying the blocks.

Destroying the Blocks

Step 1: Open the **obj_player_default** object.

Step 2: Select the **Collision** with **obj_dagger** Event and add a **Destroy Instance** and select the **Object** option and choose **obj_stone**.

Increase Enemy Fire Speed

With the blocks destroyed it would be much easier for the player to leave the room. However, the next trigger that will occur when the dagger is picked up is that the fireballs will now start shooting at a faster rate. This will make leaving the room by avoiding the fireballs impossible.

Step 1: Open the **Three Mask Objects**.

Step 2: For **Each Mask** add a **Step: Step** Event.

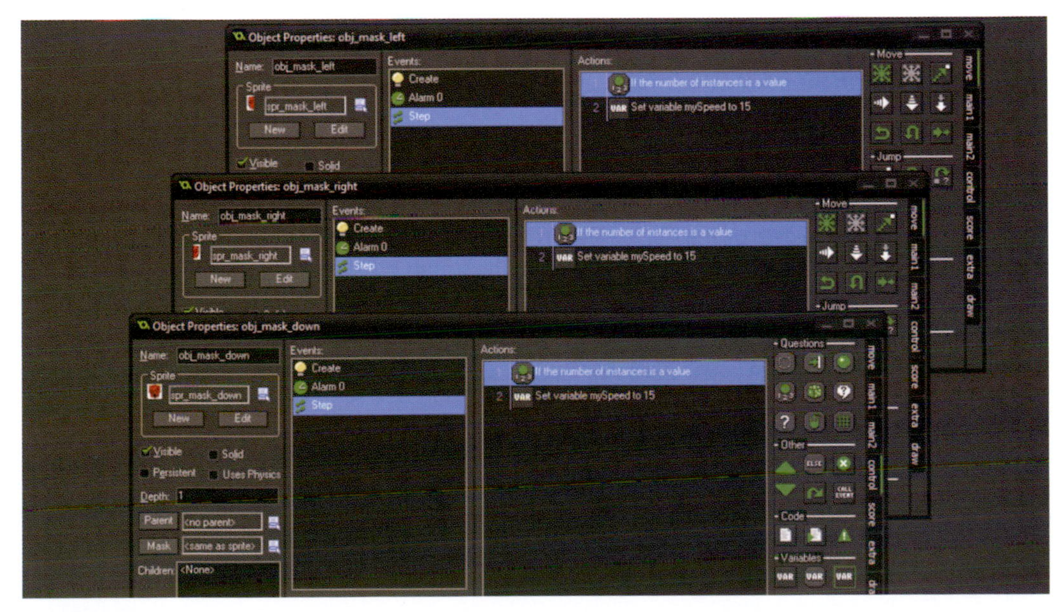

FIGURE 8.11

Step 3: In the **Step** Event for **Each Mask** add a **Test Instance Count** and set the following:

Object: obj_stone
Number: 0
Operation: equal to

Step 4: For **All Three Masks** add a **Set Variable** Action below the **Test Instance Count** and set the following:

Variable: mySpeed
Value: 15

At this point when the player collides with the dagger, the blocks will be destroyed and the masks will shoot in rapid fire, thus forcing the player to attack them in order to escape.

We'll need to set up the actions to detect when the player attacks the masks.

Destroying the Masks

Step 1: Open the **spr_explosion sprite** and center it.

Step 2: When each mask is destroyed, it will explode to let the player know it has been deactivated. Create a **New Object** named **obj_explosion** and set the sprite to **spr_explosion.**

Step 3: Add a **Create** Event.

Step 4: Add a **Play Sound** Action.

Sound: snd_explosion
Loop: false

Step 5: Add an **Other: Animation End** Event and drag in a **Destroy Instance** Action. This will destroy the **obj_explosion** object after the explosion animation is complete. We will now have the masks turn into the explosion when they are hit by a dagger.

Step 6: Open **All Three Mask** objects and for each add a **Collision** Event with the **obj_bronze_projectile** object.

Step 7: For **Each Mask** add a Change Instance Action and set the following:

Object: obj_explosion
Perform events: yes

Step 8: Add a **Destroy Instance** and select the **Other** option to destroy the dagger as well.

This will allow the player to destroy the masks.

Creating the Player Defeat Object

When a fireball collides with the player, the player character object will convert to the player defeat object.

Step 1: Open **spr_player_defeat** and set the origin to **x: 52 y: 81**.

Step 2: Create a **New Object** and name it **obj_player_defeat**.

Step 3: Set the sprite to **spr_player_defeat**.

Step 4: Add a **Create** Event.

Step 5: Add a **Set Sprite** Action and set the following:

Sprite: spr_player_defeat
Subimage: 0
Speed: 0.5

Step 6: Add a **Play Sound** Action and set the following:

Sound: snd_death
Loop: false

Step 7: Add an **Other: Animation End** Action to it.

Step 8: Add a **Restart Room** Action.

Step 9: Open the **obj_player_default** and **obj_player_bronze** objects and add a collision to both with the **obj_fireball** Event.

Step 10: In both add a **Change Instance** Action and set the following:

Object: obj_player_defeat
Perform event: yes

Activating the Next Level Trigger

Step 1: Create a **New Object** named **obj_nlt_two**.

Step 2: Check the **Solid** checkbox.

Step 3: Set the sprite to **spr_nlt.**

Step 4: Add a **Collision** with **obj_player_bronze**.

Step 5: Add a **Different Room** Event and set the following:

Room: room_oracle_two

Allowing the Player to Exit the Room

When the player picks up the dagger the Solid option will need to become unchecked allowing the player to exit the room.

Step 1: Open the **obj_player_default** object.

Step 2: In the collision with **obj_dagger** add a **Set Variable** Action and set the following:

> Object: obj_nlt_two
> Variable: solid
> Value: false

Arrange the Room Objects

All of the Level One room objects are set up and ready to be placed in the room. The stone wall objects can be used to create a maze for the player to navigate through. Two separate stone objects can be used to create the maze. The first stone object will disappear when the player reaches the dagger but the second stone object, which we named **obj_stone_two,** will remain and can be used by the player as a barricade to avoid being hit by the fireballs. The masks can be attached to the top and side walls so

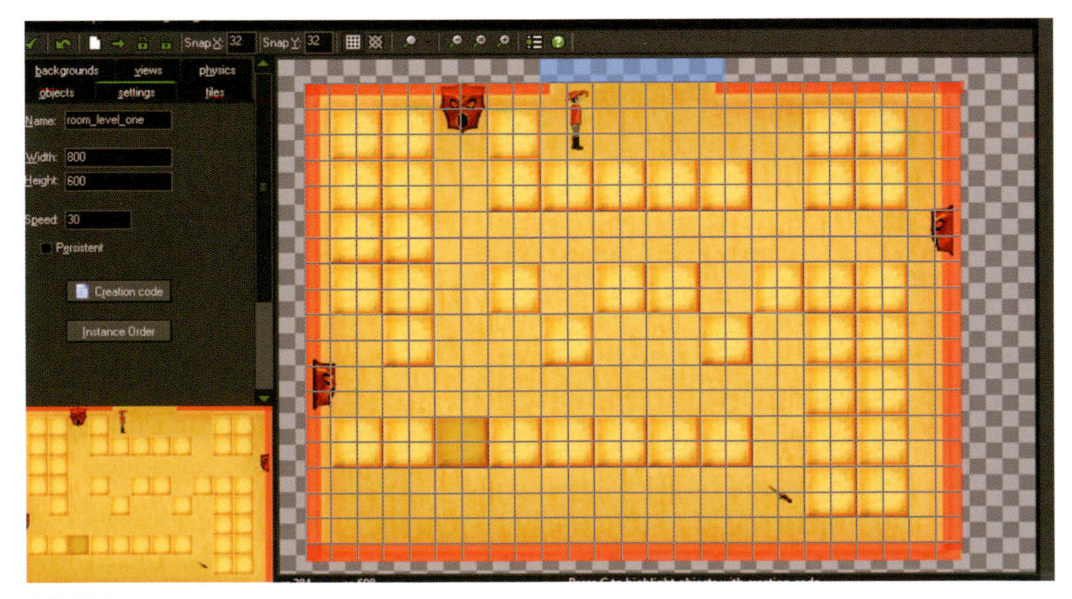

FIGURE 8.12

the player will have to dodge shooting fireballs and the dagger can be placed at the bottom of the room as the player's goal. Arrange the room with the objects to create your own maze configuration. You may wish to use **Figure 8.12** as a guide.

Creating the Oracle Room Two

Step 1: Place the **obj_player_bronze** object just above the **South Gate,** which will now appear closed.

Step 2: Place **Colliders** along the walls similar to those placed in the **First Oracle Room**.

Step 3: Create a **New Object** and name it **obj_nlt_three**.

Step 4: Assign the sprite **spr_nlt** to it.

Step 5: Add a **Collision** with the **obj_player_bronze** object.

Step 6: Add a **Different Room** Action and set the following:

Room: room_level_two

Step 7: Place the **obj_nlt_three** object in the gap between the **East Gates** similar to how we did for the **First Oracle Room.**

Step 8: Create a **New Object** and name it **obj_scroll_two**.

Step 9: Set the sprite to **spr_scroll_two**.

Step 10: Uncheck the **Visible** option.

Step 11: Add a **Create** Event.

Step 12: Add a **Set Alarm** Action and set the following:

Number of steps: 90
In alarm no: Alarm 0

Step 13: Add an **Alarm: Alarm 0** Event.

Step 14: Add a **Set Variable** Action and set the following:

Variable: visible
Value: true

Step 15: Place the scroll object in the top left corner of the room.

Creating Level Two

The player has been instructed to solve the following riddle:

"What appears once in every minute, twice in every moment but never in one hundred thousand years?"

The answer to the riddle is the letter **M**.

When the player enters **Level Two** they will find that the entire floor is made up of tiles that have what appears to be roman numerals carved into them. Each tile has a separate letter. If the player has figured out the riddle, they will see that if they controlled their character to walk only on the tiles with the letter **M** on them that the character could make it all the way across the room to reach a treasure chest. If this was the only obstacle in the room, the level would be too easy. In order to make it more challenging, we will have flying sawblades made of ice hurling toward the player so that they will either need to move quickly or shoot quickly to destroy the sawblades. To create **Level Two** we will be using a tile set.

Using a Tile Set to Create the Level Two Floor

Step 1: Open the **Background** named **tile_room_two**.

Step 2: Check the **Use as Tile Set** box.

Step 3: The tiles are now ready to be placed throughout the room. Open **room_level_two** and select the **Tiles tab** and pick **tile_level_two**.

FIGURE 8.13

Step 4: Place the tiles in the level similar to **Figure 8.13**. This configuration will allow the player to walk along the tiles with the letter **M** on them and move across the room without walking on any tiles that have other letters on them.

Adding a Kill Zone Object

In game design terms a **kill zone** is any area in a game that kills the player's character instantly when the character enters the area. Kill zone objects are placed in games where there are hazards such as fire or lava or virtually any other type of hazard that would kill a player's character instantly. We will be creating a kill zone and placing it on all of the tiles in **Level Two** that are not marked with the letter **M.** If a player were to step on an incorrect tile, it would trigger the player character's defeat animation and the player would return to the previous room.

Step 1: Two sets of colliders are needed for this room in addition to the next level trigger. Create a **New Object** and name it **obj_killzone**, assign the sprite **spr_killzone** to it, and **Uncheck** the **Visible** option.

Step 2: Open **obj_player_bronze** and add a **Collision** Event with the **obj_killzone** object.

Step 3: Add a **Change Instance** Action and set the following:

Object: player_defeat
Perform events: yes

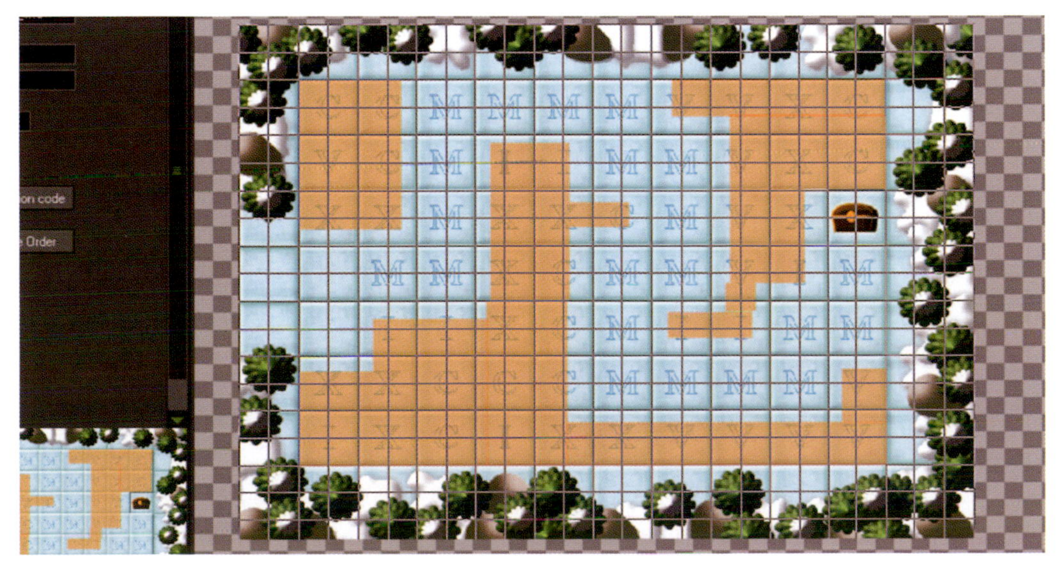

FIGURE 8.14

Step 4: Reopen the **room_level_two** room and fit the **obj_killzone** objects over all the tiles that do not have the letter **M** carved into them. You may wish to use **Figure 8.14** as a guide.

If the player were to step on a tile that does not have the letter **M** on it, the player character would go into the player defeat animation and the game would restart the room so the player would get another chance to complete **Level Two**. If the player navigated the room correctly, they would be able to pick up the contents of the treasure. We will now create a trigger for when the player collides with the treasure.

Creating a Trigger for the Treasure

Step 1: Create a **New Object** named **obj_chest_trigger** and set it to the **spr_collider** sprite.

Step 2: Open the **obj_player_bronze** object and add a **Collision** Event with the **obj_chest_trigger** object.

Step 3: Drag in a **Set Variable** Action and set the following:

Variable: global.myCoins
Value: 50
Relative: checked

The value of 50 will add 50 coins to the player's coin inventory.

Step 4: Add a **Set Sprite** Action and set the following:

Object: obj_counter
Sprite: spr_counter
Subimage: 5
Speed: 0

This will display 50 coins in the HUD.

Step 5: Drag in a **Destroy Instance** Action below the **Set Variable** Action and check the **Other** checkbox.

Activating the Next Level Trigger

When the player collides with the chest the Next Level Trigger needs to be activated.

Step 1: Create a **New Object** and name it **obj_nlt_four**.

Step 2: Check the **Solid** checkbox.

Step 3: Open the **obj_player_bronze** object and add a **Collision** with the **obj_nlt_four** object.

Step 4: Drag in a **Different Room** Action and set the following:

Room: room_oracle_three

Step 5: Select the **Collision** with the **obj_chest_collider** object event.

Step 6: Add a **Set Variable** Action to it and set the following:

Object: obj_nlt_four
Variable: solid
Value: false

The player is now able to have their character enter the level, follow the right path to the treasure, gather the coins, and leave the room. We are not going to make it that easy for the player, however. We will now add the flying sawblades made of ice to the level.

Creating the Sawblade Object

Step 1: Open the **spr_sawblade** sprite then **Center** it and set the **Mask** to **Precise**.

Step 2: Create a **New Object** and name it **obj_sawblade**.

Step 3: Add a **Create** Event.

Step 4: Add a **Play Sound** and set the following:

Sound: snd_saw
Loop: false

Step 5: Add a **Collision** Event with the **obj_player_bronze** object.

Step 6: Add a **Change Instance** to the **Collision** Event and set the following:

Check the **other** option
Object: player_defeat
Perform event: yes

Step 7: Add a **Create** and an **Alarm 0** Event.

Step 8: In the **Create** Event add a **Set Alarm** and set the following:

Number of steps: 360
In alarm no: Alarm 0

Step 9: In the **Alarm 0** Event add a **Destroy Instance** Action.

Since the sawblades are created off screen we needed to add a time that would destroy them after being active for a while.

Creating Sawblade Spawners

Step 1: Create two **New Objects** and name them **obj_sb_down** and **obj_sb_up**.

Step 2: Add a **Create** Event and an **Alarm 0** Event to the **obj_sb_down** and the **obj_sb_up** objects.

Step 3: In the Create Event for **Both Objects** add a **Set Alarm** Action and set the following:

Number of steps: irandom(60) + 15
In alarm no: Alarm 0

Step 4: In the **Alarm 0** Event for **Both Objects** add a **Create Moving** Action and set the following:

Object: obj_sawblade
x: 0
y: 0
Direction: (**90** for up, **270** for down)
Speed: 8
Relative: checked

Step 5: Add a **Set Alarm** Action for both objects and set the following:

Number of steps: irandom(180) + 30
In alarm no: Alarm 0

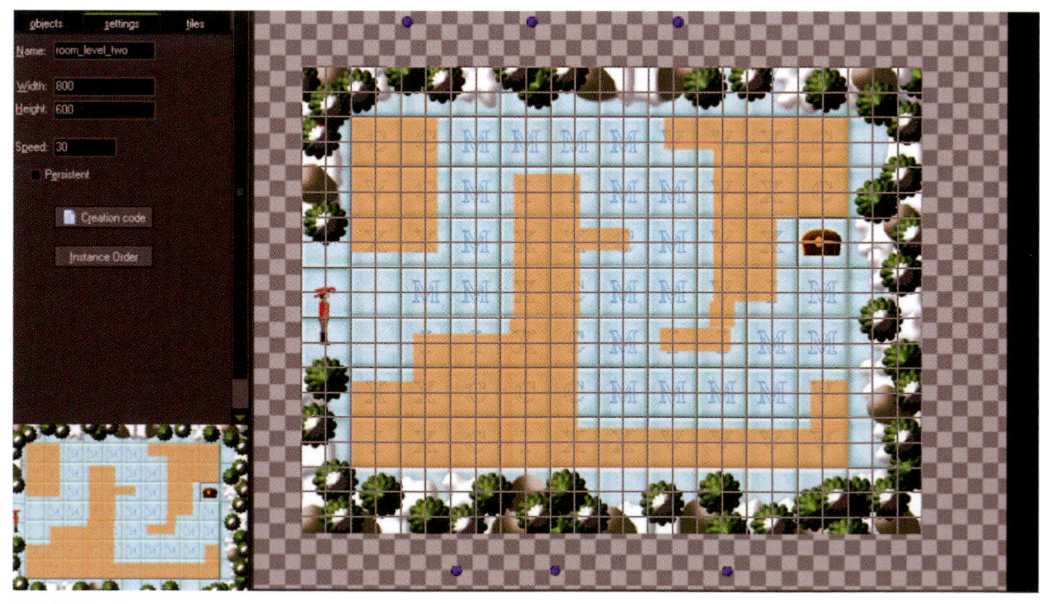

FIGURE 8.15

Step 6: Add **obj_player_bronze** to the level at the **Left** entrance.

Place the spawners at the top and bottom of the room similar to those shown in **Figure 8.15**.

Creating the Oracle Room Three

Step 1: Place the **obj_player_bronze** object just to the left of the **East Gate,** which will now appear closed.

Step 2: Place **Colliders** along the walls.

Step 3: Create a **New Object** and name it **obj_nlt_five**.

Step 4: Assign the sprite **spr_nlt** to it.

Step 5: Add a **Collision** with the **obj_player_bronze** object.

Step 6: Add a **Different Room** Action and set the following:

Room: room_shop

Step 7: Place the **obj_nlt_five** object in the gap between the **North Gate**.

Step 8: Create a **New Object** and name it **obj_scroll_three**.

Step 9: Set the sprite to **spr_scroll_three**.

Step 10: Uncheck the **Visible** option.

Step 11: Add a **Create** Event.

Step 12: Add a **Set Alarm** Action and set the following:

Number of steps: 90
In alarm no: Alarm 0

Step 13: Add an **Alarm: Alarm 0** Event.

Step 14: Add a **Set Variable** Action and set the following:

Variable: visible
Value: true

Step 15: Place the scroll object in the bottom left corner of the room.

Creating the Shop

When the character enters the shop the viewer's perspective shifts to first person so that player is now looking through the eyes of the player character. One look at the total number of coins the player has picked up shows that the player has only enough coins to purchase the **Silver Dagger,** which is the object we want them to have. Any other object in the store cannot be purchased because the player does not have enough coins. We will start creating our shop by creating three button objects that will be placed on top of three items in the shop's inventory so the player can choose them.

Creating Selectable Button

Step 1: Create **Three Objects** and name them **obj_btn_dagger**, **obj_btn_gloves,** and **obj_btn_potion.**

Since the background already contains the images for the dagger, gloves, and potions we will just use a collider sprite and turn off the visibility in the object. This will work as an invisible button above each item that the player will click on to choose the item.

Step 2: Set the sprite to **spr_collider** and turn off the **Visible** option.

Configuring the Dagger Button

Step 1: Open the **obj_btn_dagger** object.

Step 2: Add a **Mouse: Left Button** Event.

Step 3: Add a **Test Variable** Action and set the following:

Variable: global.myCoins
Value: 50
Operation: greater than or equal to

Step 4: Add a **Start Block** below the **Test Variable** Action.

Step 5: Add a **Set Variable** Action and set the following:

Variable: global.myWeapon
Value: 2

The value of 2 will represent the silver dagger we purchased.

Step 6: Add a second **Set Variable** Action and set the following:

Variable: global.myCoins
Value: −50
Relative: checked

Step 7: Add a **Show Message** Action and set the following:

Message: You have purchased a new dagger.

Step 8: Add an **End of a Block**.

Step 9: Add an **Else** Action.

The **Else** Action will be called if the player does not have enough money.

Step 10: Add a **Show Message** Action and set the following:

Message: You do not have enough coins to purchase this item.

Step 11: Close the **obj_btn_dagger** object.

Configuring the Gloves Button

Step 1: Open the **obj_btn_gloves** object.

Step 2: Add a **Mouse: Left Button** Event.

Step 3: Add a **Test Variable** Action and set the following:

Variable: global.myCoins
Value: 100
Operation: greater than or equal to

Step 4: Add a **Start of a Block** below the **Test Variable** Action.

Step 5: Add a second **Set Variable** Action and set the following:

Variable: global.myCoins
Value: –100
Relative: checked

Step 6: Add an **End of a Block**.

Step 7: Add an **Else** Action.

Step 8: Add a **Show Message** Action.

Message: You do not have enough coins to purchase this item.

Step 9: Close the **obj_btn_gloves** object.

Configuring the Potion Button

Step 1: Open the **obj_btn_potion** object.

Step 2: Add a **Mouse: Left Button** Event.

Step 3: Add a **Test Variable** Action and set the following:

Variable: global.myCoins
Value: 200
Operation: greater than or equal to

Step 4: Add a **Start of a Block** below the **Test Variable** Action.

Step 5: Add a second **Set Variable** Action and set the following:

Variable: global.myCoins
Value: –200
Relative: checked

Step 6: Add an **End of a Block**.

Step 7: Add an **Else** Action.

Step 8: Add a **Show Message** Action.

Message: You do not have enough coins to purchase this item.

Step 9: Close the **obj_btn_potion** object.

Configuring the Exit Shop Function

Step 1: Open the **obj_btn_dagger** object.

Step 2: In the **Mouse: Left Button** Event under the first **Show Message** Action, add a **Different Room** Action and set the following:

Room: room_oracle_four

FIGURE 8.16

The player purchasing the **Silver Dagger** is the criteria for moving to the next level. The **Different Room** Action we just set up will automatically advance the player to the **Oracle Four** Room after they purchase the dagger.

Step 3: Place the buttons in the **room_shop** Room so they appear similar to those found in **Figure 8.16**.

Creating the Silver Dagger Player Object

Step 1: Right-click and **Duplicate** the **obj_player_bronze** object and name the new object **obj_player_silver**.

Step 2: In the **<Any Key>** Event make the following changes to the **Execute Code** Action:

Lines 5 and 6: **spr_b_walk_left** should be changed to **spr_s_walk_left.**
Lines 15 and 16: **spr_b_walk_right** should be changed to **spr_s_walk_right.**
Lines 35 and 36: **srp_b_walk_down** should be changed to **spr_s_walk_down.**

The last sprite changes we need to make are the sprites of the character shooting.

Step 3: Open the **Press <Space>** Event.

Step 4: For all the **spr_b_ . . .** values change the letter **b** to an **s**.

For example, **spr_b_shoot_left** should be changed to **spr_s_shoot_left.**

Creating the Silver Projectile

Step 1: Right-click and **Duplicate** the **obj_bronze_projectile** object.

Step 2: Rename the new object to **obj_silver_projectile.**

Step 3: Set its sprite to **spr_silver_projectile.**

This dagger will be more powerful than the last so we will have it shoot three projectiles at once.

Step 4: Open the **obj_player_silver** object and select the **Press <Space>** Event.

Step 5: Open the **Create Moving** that is already in place and change the object to **obj_silver_projectile.**

Step 6: Add two additional Create Moving Actions and set the following:

For the first action set:

Object: obj_silver_projectile
x: 0
y: 0
Speed: 12
Direction: myDirection −15
Relative: checked

For the second action set:

Object: obj_silver_projectile
x: 0
y: 0
Speed: 12
Direction: myDirection + 15
Relative: checked

Step 7: Open **spr_silver_projectile** and center the sprite, then set the **Modify Mask** to **Precise**.

Creating the Oracle Room Four

Step 1: Place the **obj_player_silver** object just below the **North Gate,** which will now appear closed.

Step 2: Place **Colliders** along the walls.

Step 3: Create a **New Object** and name it **obj_nlt_six**.

Step 4: Assign the sprite **spr_nlt** to it.

Step 5: Add a **Collision** with **obj_player_silver**.

Step 6: Add a **Different Room** Action and set the following:

Room: room_finalboss

Step 7: Place the **obj_nlt_six** object in the gap between the **West Gates**.

Step 8: Create a **New Object** and name it **obj_scroll_four**.

Step 9: Set the sprite to **spr_scroll_four.**

Step 10: Uncheck the **Visible** option.

Step 11: Add a **Create** Event.

Step 12: Add a **Set Alarm** Action and set the following:

Number of steps: 90
In alarm no: Alarm 0

Step 13: Add an **Alarm: Alarm 0** Event.

Step 14: Add a **Set Variable** Action and set the following:

Variable: visible
Value: true

Step 15: Place the scroll object in the bottom right corner of the room.

Creating the Boss Level

The final level in our game is the **Boss Level,** which is through the **West Gate**. The player will need to use the **Silver Dagger** to destroy the many heads on the totem pole one at a time. After all the heads are destroyed, a gem will appear that will trigger a dialog box that tells the player they have completed the game. The totem pole will be shooting ice and fireballs at the player so the player will need to use obstacles in the room to hide behind. The first objects we will create for this room are the fire and ice totem pole heads.

Step 1: Create two **New Objects** and name them **obj_totem_fire** and **obj_totem_ice**.

Step 2: Apply the **spr_totem_fire** sprite to the **obj_totem_fire** object and the **spr_totem_ice** to the **obj_totem_ice** object.

These will be placed on top of each other on the left side of the room to form the totem pole.

Step 3: The boss will be firing ice and fireballs at the player. We have already created the fireball object when we created one for the masks to shoot in **room_level_one**. We only need to create the ice object. Create a **New Object** and name it **obj_iceball** then set the sprite to **spr_iceball**.

Step 4: Add a **Create** Event in the **obj_iceball** object.

Step 5: Add a **Play Sound** Action.

Sound: snd_iceball
Loop: false

Configuring the Sprites

Step 1: Open both of the **spr_totems** sprites and press the **Center** button.

Step 2: Select the **Modify Mask** and check the **Precise** checkbox.

Step 3: Do the same for the **spr_iceball** sprite.

Making the Totem Heads Shoot

Step 1: Open both of the totem head objects.

Step 2: Add a **Create** Event to both objects.

Step 3: Add a **Set Alarm** Event and set the following:

Number of steps: irandom(60) + 15
In alarm no: Alarm 0

Step 4: Add an **Alarm 0** Event.

Step 5: Add a **Create Moving** Action and set the following:

Object: (use the right fireball for the totem)
x: 0
y: 0
Speed: 6
Direction: irandom(360)

The totems heads will now shoot projectiles in a random direction.

Step 6: Add a **Set Alarm** below the **Create Moving** Action and set the following:

Number of steps: irandom(60) + 30
In alarm no: Alarm 0

Colliding with the Projectiles

In order for the projectiles to hit the player a Collision Event will need to be made between the player character and the projectiles.

Step 1: Open the **obj_player_silver** object.

Step 2: Add a **Collision** Event with the **obj_iceball** object and the **obj_fireball** object.

Step 3: In both **Collision** Events add a **Change Instance** Action and set the following:

Object: obj_player_defeat
Perform event: yes

Destroying a Totem Head

Step 1: Open the sprite **spr_ice_explosion** and **Center** the image.

Step 2: Create a **New Object** and name it **obj_ice_explosion**.

Step 3: Set the sprite to **spr_ice_explosion**.

Step 4: Add a **Create** Event.

Step 5: Add a **Play Sound** Action.

Sound: snd_explosion
Loop: false

Step 6: Add an **Other: Animation End** Event and place a **Destroy Instance** Action in it.

Step 7: Open both totem objects and add a **Collision** Event with the **obj_projectile_silver** object.

Step 8: In the **Collison** Event of the fire totem object, add a **Change Instance** Action and set the following:

Object: obj_explosion
Perform events: yes

Step 9: In the **Collison** Event of the ice totem object, add a **Change Instance** Action and set the following:

Object: obj_ice_explosion
Perform events: yes

Building the Totem Pole in the Level

Step 1: Open the **room_finalboss** room.

Step 2: Place the totem head objects in a line so they appear similar to those in **Figure 8.17**.

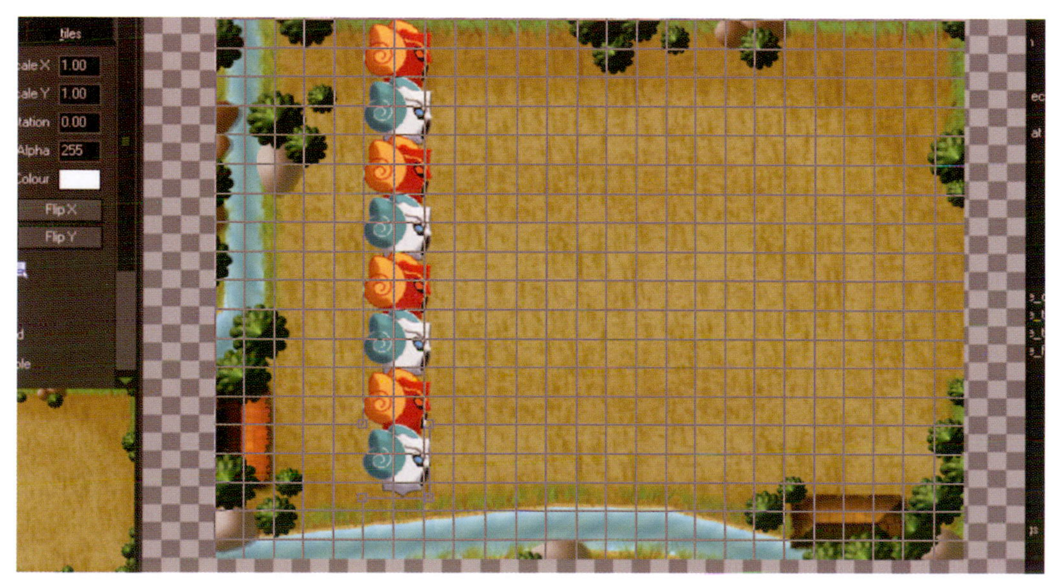

FIGURE 8.17

Providing Obstacles for the Player to Hide Behind

To give the player a fighting chance we will place some objects around the room for the player to move their character behind to avoid the projectiles.

Step 1: Create two **New Objects** and name them **obj_tree** and **obj_rock**.

Step 2: Check the **Solid** option for both of these new objects.

Configuring the Sprites

Step 1: Open the **spr_rock** sprite and the **spr_tree** sprite.

Step 2: For both sprites press the **Center** button and then click the **Modify Mask** option.

Step 3: Open the iceball and fireball objects and add a **Collision** for both with the **obj_rock** object and the **obj_tree** object.

Step 4: In both **Collision** Events add a **Destroy Instance** Action, then place the rocks and trees around the room so the player has objects to hide behind.

Creating the Gem

After the player destroys all of the individual heads on the totem pole, a gem will appear. When the player picks up the gem a dialog box will appear notifying the player that the game is complete.

Step 1: Create a **New Object** and name it **obj_gem**.

Step 2: Set the sprite for the **obj_gem** to **spr_ruby**.

Step 3: Check the **Solid** option and **Uncheck** the **Visible** option.

The player must destroy all the totem pole heads before the gem becomes visible, allowing the player to pick it up.

Step 4: Add a **Step: Step** Event to the **obj_gem** object.

Step 5: Add a **Test Instance Count** Action and set the following:

Object: obj_totem_fire
Number: 0
Operation: equal to

Step 6: Add a **Start of a Block** below the **Test Instance Count** Action.

Step 7: Add another **Test Instance Count** Action and set the following:

Object: obj_totem_ice
Number: 0
Operation: equal to

Step 8: Drag in another **Start of a Block**.

Step 9: Drag in a **Set Variable** and set the following:

Variable: solid
Value: false

Step 10: Drag in a second **Set Variable** and set the following:

Variable: visible
Value: true

Step 11: Drag in two **End of a Block** Actions.

The room will now check to see if there are any ice or fire totem heads remaining in the room. If there are not any left in the room, the gem will become visible so the player can pick it up.

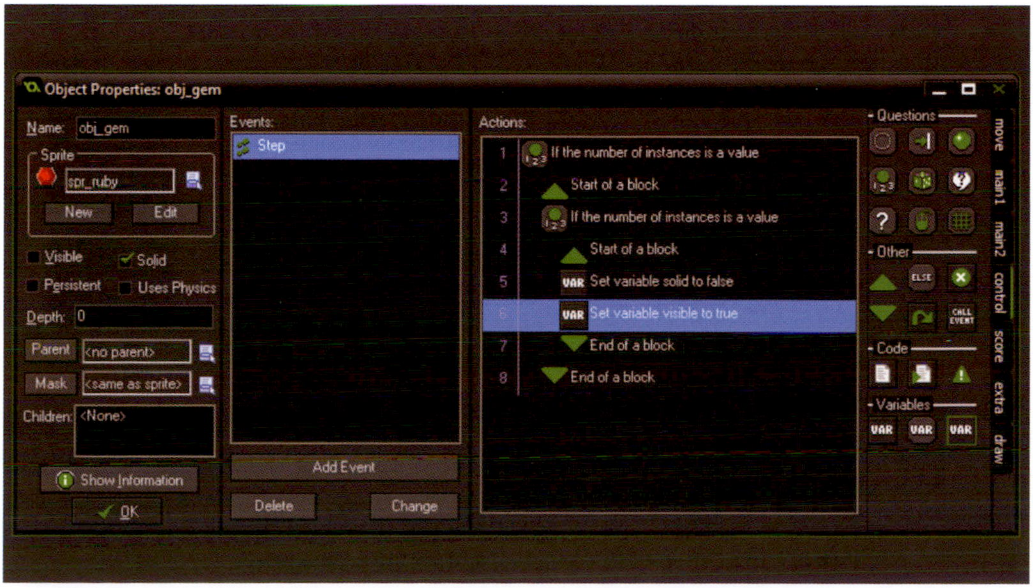

FIGURE 8.18

Allowing the Player to Pick Up the Gem

Step 1: Add a **Collision** Event with the **obj_player_silver** object.

Step 2: Add a **Set Variable** Action and set the following:

Variable: global.hasGem
Value: 1

Step 3: Add a **Destroy Instance** Action.

Step 4: Create a **New Object** named **obj_final_message**.

Step 5: Set the sprite to **spr_scroll_five**.

Step 6: Add a **Create** and an **Alarm 0** Event.

Step 7: In the **Create** Event add a **Set Alarm** and set the following:

Number of steps: 180
In alarm no: Alarm 0

Step 8: In the **Alarm 0** Event add a **Different Room** Action.

Room: room_title

Step 9: Re-open the **Collision** Event between the gem and the player.

Step 10: Add a **Create Instance** Action and set the following:

Object: obj_final_message
x: 352
y: 96

This will make the final scroll appear for a few seconds and then take the player back to the title screen.

Setting Up the Title Screen

Step 1: Open the **room_title** room and check that the background is set to **bg_title**.

Step 2: Create a **New Object** and name it **obj_play**.

Step 3: Set the sprite to **spr_collider**.

Step 4: Uncheck the **Visible** option.

Step 5: Add a **Mouse: Left Button** Event.

Step 6: Add a **Different Room** Action and set the following:

Room: room_oracle_one

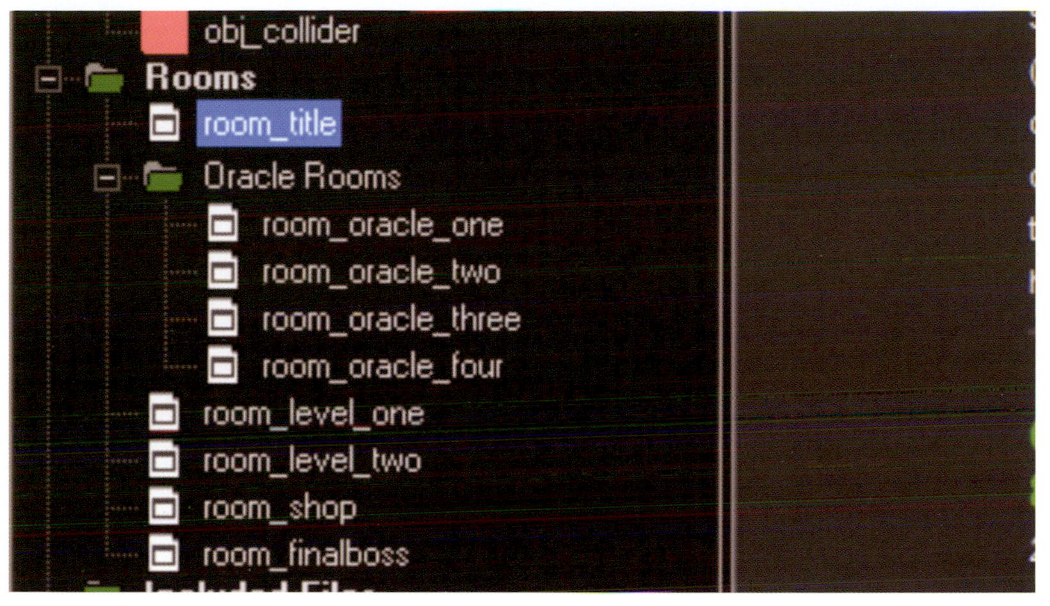

FIGURE 8.19

We will have the player use the escape key on the keyboard to exit from the title screen.

Step 7: Add a **Key Press <Escape>** Event.

Step 8: Drag in an **Exit Game** Action.

Step 9: Place the new button over the Begin Quest text.

Step 10: Organize the rooms folder so the rooms look similar to **Figure 8.19.**

Creating an In-Game Quit Button

Step 1: We will also set up a method for the player to quit while in the game. **Create** a **New Object** and name it **obj_quit_button**.

Step 2: Set the sprite to **spr_quit_button**.

Step 3: Check the **Persistent** option and set the **Depth** to **−2**.

Step 4: Add a **Mouse: Left Button** Event.

Step 5: Add a **Different Room** Action and set the following:

Room: room_title

Step 6: Open the **room_oracle_one** room and place it on the **HUD** so it appears similar to **Figure 8.20**.

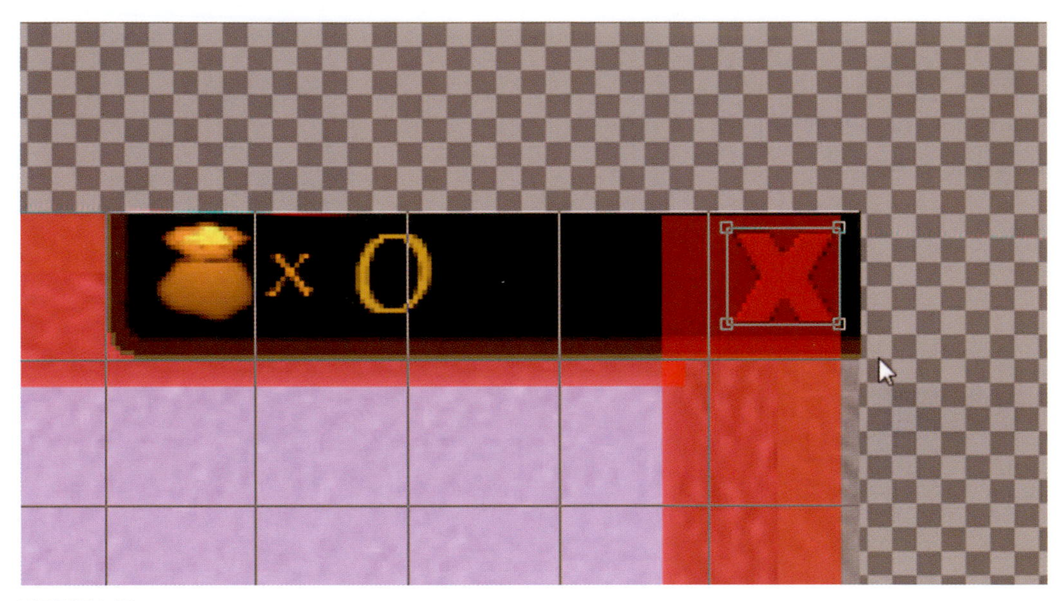

FIGURE 8.20

Adding Background Music

Step 1: We will begin by setting up all the background music for each room. **Create** a **New Object** and name it **obj_music_oracle**.

Step 2: Add an **Other: Room Start** Event.

Step 3: Add a **Play Sound** Action and set the following:

Sound: snd_oracle

Step 4: Add an **Other: Room End** Event.

Step 5: Add a **Stop Sound** Action.

Sound: snd_oracle

Step 6: Place the object anywhere in each of the four oracle rooms.

Setting Level One Music

Step 1: Create a **New Object** and name it **obj_music_south**.

Step 2: Add an **Other: Room Start** Event.

Step 3: Add a **Play Sound** Action and set the following:

Sound: snd_south_room

Step 4: Add an **Other: Room End** Event.

Step 5: Add a **Stop Sound** Action

Sound: snd_south_room

Step 6: Place the object anywhere in **room_level_one**.

Setting Level Two Music

Step 1: Create a **New Object** and name it **obj_music_east**.

Step 2: Add an **Other: Room Start** Event.

Step 3: Add a **Play Sound** Action and set the following:

Sound: snd_east_room

Step 4: Add an **Other: Room End** Event.

Step 5: Add a **Stop Sound** Action.

Sound: snd_east_room

Step 6: Place the object anywhere in **room_level_two**.

Setting the Shop Music

Step 1: Create a **New Object** and name it **obj_music_shop**.

Step 2: Add an **Other: Room Start** Event.

Step 3: Add a **Play Sound** Action and set the following:

Sound: snd_shop

Step 4: Add an **Other: Room End** Event.

Step 5: Add a **Stop Sound** Action.

Sound: snd_shop

Step 6: Place the object anywhere in **room_shop**.

Setting Boss Level Music

Step 1: Create a **New Object** and name it **obj_music_west**.

Step 2: Add an **Other: Room Start** Event.

Step 3: Add a **Play Sound** Action and set the following:

Sound: snd_west_room

Step 4: Add an **Other: Room End** Event.

Step 5: Add a **Stop Sound** Action:

Sound: snd_west_room

Step 6: Place the object anywhere in **room_finalboss**.

Testing the Game

You will want to have several people test this game for you after you have eliminated any initial bugs you find. This RPG game has incorporated several features that were not present in previous games. The more features added to a game, the higher the potential for bugs to occur. We added several features to the game using code which saved time; however, should even one character of code be off, such as a letter is capitalized and should not be, the coded feature will not work. After your game has been tested, you may wish to change the layout of the obstacles or floor tiles of the south, east, and west rooms to make the game more challenging. Remember that a challenging game is fun while an impossible-to-win game is not.

Selling Games and Licensing Fees

Learning Objectives—Upon completion of Chapter 9 readers will be able to:

- Identify consoles capable of running GameMaker games
- Identify export options available in GameMaker
- Compare upgrade options for specific target audiences
- Identify advantages of each exporting option
- Recognize multiple options for selling their game

Exporting Options

GameMaker provides multiple exporting options designers can use to publish games for specific platforms. With various operating systems and game consoles on the market, it is necessary for games to be exported in different formats so that they can be played on a variety of devices. If, for example, you wanted to create a game that will be played on mobile devices, then you would want to export your game one way, whereas if your target audience is using a specific game console, then you would want to export your game specifically for that particular console. Fortunately, these exporting options allow you to create your game one time and then through exporting, the game becomes customized for the different platforms rather than you, as the designer, having to create multiple versions of your game. Let's explore these different exporting options.

Exporting for Different Operating Systems

If you were to ask a couple of friends to name as many different operating systems as they could, many of them would most likely be able to name Windows and Mac. However, without realizing it, they are probably familiar with several other operating systems but never classified them as being in the same category as Windows and Mac operating systems. Android is one example of an operating system commonly used. Although Android is best known for being a cell phone operating system, it has also been used as the operating system for a game console. We will explore that aspect later when we discuss various consoles. Other operating systems your friends may not have guessed would be Ubuntu Linux and Tizen. Although they may not be familiar with the names of these operating systems, there is a good chance they have operated a device that uses them. GameMaker includes game exporting options for all of the operating systems mentioned above as well as additional exporting options for developers to publish their games for specific platforms.

Windows Platforms

While working through the previous chapters of this book, you have already exported to a Windows platform by publishing your game as an executable so that it could be played on other Windows computers that do not have GameMaker installed. Traditionally, this is how many video games were packaged. In the not-so-distant past independent game designers would save their game as an executable, burn it to a CD, put it in a nice CD package with cover art, and sell it. Today's buyers are looking for something different as they may wish to play games on a different device than a personal computer with a CD-Rom. Some buyers may wish to play games on their tablets, which may not have a CD-Rom; others may wish to play games on their mobile devices such as cell phones. Fortunately, GameMaker has exporting options for these buyers, although these options may not be included in the version of GameMaker you are currently running and here is why. The following may sound like a sales pitch of sorts, but the intention is to provide information on which version of GameMaker is best suited for the needs of different game developers. This book is titled *The GameMaker Standard* to reflect that we are using the Standard version of GameMaker: Studio. The Standard version allows game developers to download GameMaker for free in order to learn the software. There are two other versions of GameMaker that can be purchased. Upgrading to one of these other versions opens up more export options in addition to the export to Windows option that we have been using to make our executables. The first of these two options is the GameMaker: Professional version. In this version of GameMaker, developers have access to all of the tools of the Standard version with the addition of being able to export games to the Windows app platform. If your goal is to create games for the Windows PC and app market, then this would be all you needed. Additional export options can be purchased for the Professional version of GameMaker, allowing designers to choose to purchase only the export options they desire. If a designer or a game development company wanted all of the various export options that GameMaker has to offer, then they would want to purchase the GameMaker: Master Collection, which contains all exporting options. As each of these exporting options are discussed in this chapter, keep in mind that each one does not come with GameMaker: Standard but can be purchased individually to work with the Professional version and that all of them come with the Master Collection. For example, another Windows platform export available is the Windows Phone 8 export. This export is available with the Professional version of GameMaker and is designed for buyers wishing to play games on their Windows 8 phones.

Mac Platform

The Mac OS X export allows designers to create games that can be exported for use on machines running Mac OS X. The Mac iOS export is designed for mobile Mac devices such as iPads and iPhones. Before diving into creating games for different platforms, you will want to research additional steps that may be required to publish games to these platforms. To publish games for iPads and iPhones, developers will need a Mac developer's license first. This is also true for developers wishing to publish their games for various game consoles. Additional information on developer licenses is outside the scope of this particular book as this information is constantly changing for various consoles. Developers will want to research what type of developer license, if any, is needed for the console they are wishing to develop for before beginning any project.

Game Consoles

GameMaker also exports to the latest game consoles such as the Playstation 3, Playstation 4, and the Xbox One. Each of these export modules are sold separately for the GameMaker Professional version so developers may wish to research which console their target audience is most likely to be using before purchasing. Other game consoles are also available on the market with more in development. The Ouya game console may be a good option for game developers using GameMaker. The Ouya game console is much newer than both the Playstation and Xbox. Ouya uses Android as its operating system and supports games created with GameMaker. Ouya requires games submitted to be free for users to play or at least contain free components. This may mean developers publish a series of game levels for users to play for free with the option of purchasing more advanced levels. Game developers may instead wish to make the entire game playable for free, but have in-game items that can be purchased such as in-game equipment, outfits, weapons, or vehicles.

Mobile Devices

Earlier the Android Export Module was mentioned. This allows game developers to export their games not only to the Ouya game console, but also for use on mobile devices using the Android operating system. Another export option that opens the door for games to be played on a wide variety of devices is the HTML 5 export. HTML 5 is an acronym that stands for Hyper Text Machine Language and the 5 denotes the version of HTML. HTML is the code language behind many of the websites visited every day online. HTML is a code standard, which means that if browsers such as Google Chrome, Internet Explorer, Safari, and Firefox, among others, want to display websites properly they will want to be HTML 5 compatible. This standard allows game developers to develop games and export them to HTML 5 with the understanding that web browsers will be able to run the game. This opens the door for games to be played on any device with Internet access that has an HTML 5 compatible browser. This includes users running Windows as well as those using a Mac, an iPad, an iPhone, a Windows phone, an Android phone, and the list continues as more devices are being developed to navigate the Internet using web browsers.

Research Before Release

This chapter mentions the various exporting options available to developers using GameMaker. Before upgrading to a different version of GameMaker and purchasing export modules, it may be financially beneficial to review your goals as a game developer.

If you wish to develop your game development skills and share games with family and friends using Windows-based PCs, then you may not have a need to upgrade to a different version of GameMaker. If your goal is to develop games for the Android mobile device market only, then you may wish to invest in the GameMaker Professional version and add the Android Export Module, since upgrading to the Master Collection would be more than you would need. Exploring your future plans and target audience can save you time and money.

Licensing Fees

Different game engines have different licensing fees associated with them. Some game engines allow you to use the engine to create and sell your game without paying a licensing fee until your sales reach a certain amount. Other game engines allow you to purchase the game engine and whatever you create belongs to you and you do not need to pay any royalties or licensing fees (GameMaker falls into this category). When using a game engine to develop your game, it is recommended that you read the licensing agreement before attempting to sell your game. Providing a rundown of different game engines and licensing fees for each would make for a quickly outdated document as new engines are being developed and other engines change their licensing fees periodically. Therefore, keeping up with the current licensing fees for the game engine you are using is paramount in the business of designing and selling games.

Selling Your Game

Once you have your game complete, there is a variety of marketplaces in which you can sell your game. The following examples are listed as some of the ones for YoYo Games and a description of each can be found on the YoYo Games distribution webpage www.yoyogames.com/studio/publish:

- Google Play—Described as the most-visited store for Android apps with 1 billon downloads a month.
- Apple App Store—Marketplace to sell your game to be played by iPad, iPhone, and iPod touch customers.
- Amazon App Store—Allows developers to sell apps on Amazon and Kindle Fire.
- Tizen App Store—Marketplace for games based on HTML 5 for use on multiple devices.
- Opera Mobile Store—Described as one of the leading mobile app stores and digital application distribution platforms for the developers of mobile apps in the world.
- Windows Phone Store—Marketplace for designers creating content for use on the Windows Phone.
- Steam—Provides the ability to distribute games to a community of more than 25 million gamers around the world.
- Ubuntu Software Center—Ubuntu users will be able to view your applications, along with ratings and reviews.
- Facebook—All of the core Facebook Platform technologies, such as Social Plugins, the Graph API, and Platform Dialogs, are available to Apps on Facebook.
- Chrome Web Store—Marketplace for apps designed for the Google Chrome browser.

This list is not all-encompassing as there are many other marketplaces online for games. You may find that you need to distribute your game to multiple marketplaces, and even then you may find other ways to distribute your game to make the income you are looking for.

Earning a Living

Creating and selling games is a highly competitive field and there are not any guarantees that your games will be successful. Testing your game with various audiences and incorporating constructive feedback can help you create better games. You may not succeed on your first try, not many do, but the ones that do succeed are naturally the ones that did not stop trying. Although the game creation field is very competitive, if it were impossible to earn an income you can survive on creating games, there would not be so many people and companies competing. The skills you have learned while working through the chapters of this book will help you on your journey of developing your game development skills. You may wish to continue using this book in the future as a reference source to refresh your skills in a particular area. Additional information associated with *The GameMaker Standard* book can be found at this book's companion website: www.thegamemakerstandard.com.

Resources

"GameMaker: Studio/Distribution." YoYo Games. Accessed February 24, 2015. https://www.yoyogames.com/studio/publish.

"GameMaker: Studio/Multiformat." YoYo Games. Accessed February 24, 2015. https://www.yoyogames.com/studio/multiformat.

Newman, Jared. "Ouya to Enter Gaming Market with $99 Android-Powered Console." *PCWorld*, July 10, 2012. Accessed February 24, 2015. http://www.pcworld.com/article/259026/ouya_to_enter_gaming_market_with_99_android_powered_console.html.

Glossary

2.5D—2.5D uses two-dimensional images in such a way that they create the illusion they are moving in a three-dimensional space. Before computer technology allowed designers to create fully three-dimensional games, 2.5D was a common technique used to simulate a 3D environment.
AI—Artificial Intelligence.
Android—Operating system used on many cell phones and the game console Ouya.
Aspect Ratio—The dimensions of the viewable area of a game as they relate to the height of the game window in comparison to the width.
Assets—Resources used to create a game such as graphics and sounds.
Authoring Tool—A program designers use to create software.
Background—The image behind the action of a game.
Block—Drag-and-drop software that allows designers to drag blocks that represent items of code rather than having to type code.
Bounding Box—The area around a character or object in a game that represents where the object's surface area is.
Browser—Used to search and access web pages on the Internet.
Build—Each new version of a game is called a *build*. As new features are added, a new build of the game is created.
Bullet—A projectile that shoots in a game. Although these projectiles are called bullets, they can actually appear as any type of object in a game.
Canvas—The visual area of the game that players can see in which all game elements are placed.
Check Empty—When the software identifies if a particular area is free of objects or not.
Coding—Computer language that instructs the software what to do.
Collision—When two objects hit one another.
Collision Checking—When the software identifies whether or not two objects have hit each other.
Collision Mask—The surface area of an object that can be hit by another object.
Commercial Games—Games created for entertainment and profit.
Competitive Play—When two players are playing the same game with different goals.
Console—Hardware created to play games specifically designed for the device.
Coordinates—Used to identify where a particular object is located at any time on the canvas.
Designer—Someone who creates games.
Destroy Instance—When a game object no longer exists.
Dialog Box—A message providing the player with information relating to the game.
Different Room—After completing a level, the player will move to a different room that signifies the next level or a title screen.
Drag-and-drop—Selecting objects with the mouse and moving them to a different location.
Draw Score—Used to create a visual representation of the player's score at any time within the game.
Else—The action that takes place if a series of variables is not met.
End of a Block—GameMaker icon that signifies the end of a series of actions.

Event—Tells the game which action should take place when a certain key is pressed or if a particular circumstance occurs, such as an object colliding with another.
Execute Code—A way of adding customized coding to a GameMaker game.
Export—Converting a game to play on a particular device.
Game Engine—Software used to design games.
Game Genres—Just as movies are broken down into genres such as horror or action, games are broken up into genres such as side-scrollers and puzzles in addition to many other types.
GameMaker—Game authoring program used to create games.
GameMaker Versions—This can refer to past versions of GameMaker or to the three versions that are currently a part of GameMaker: Studio.
GML—Game Maker Language.
Gravity—Applying a directional force to an object.
GUI—Graphical User Interface.
Health Bar—Indicates the life force remaining for a character.
Hor.Speed—The speed in which an object travels on the x axis.
HTML 5—Hyper Text Machine Language coding standard used for browsers. The number 5 indicates the current standard.
HUD—Heads-Up Display which illustrates game statistics to the player such as health, score, weapons, or coins.
Icon—A graphical representation that when selected runs a program.
Idle—The default position a character is in when no keys are pressed.
Image Rotation—A function used to move an object on a designated axis.
Jump to Position—Moving a character to a different location in a game.
Key Release—When an action occurs or stops occurring when a particular key on a keyboard is no longer being held down.
Keyboard Event—An action that occurs in a game when a particular key on a keyboard is pressed.
Keyboard Shortcut—When a combination of keys are held on a keyboard to produce a specific action. Typically used to save time from searching menu options.
Kill Zone—An area of a game that will cause a player character to die if they enter the area.
Level—Playable area of a game. Games may contain only one level that continues until a player eventually loses or multiple levels that move from one to the other after the player meets particular criteria.
Licensing Fee—A fee that is paid to a game engine company for using its engine.
Lives—The number of tries a player has in a game to complete it.
Mac OS X—Operating system for Macintosh computers and devices.
Map Keys—Setting particular keys to perform different functions.
Menu—Portion of a game in which players can make selections such as play game or quit.
Multi-Level—Games that contain more than one playable level.
Multiple Instances—More than one of the same object in a game.
Music Loop—When the end of a piece of music starts back at the beginning of the song seamlessly so that the song appears to be infinite in length.
Object—Typically represented as a sprite, an object instructs the sprite how it should appear and act.
Object Spawner—An area or in-game object that creates new instances of another particular object.

Ouya—Android-based game console.
Parent—Object used to control a series of other objects.
Persistent Object—An object that remains no matter what level a player is currently on.
Pick-Up—In-game item the player character can pick up and carry.
Pixel Art—Style of art in which images are created by drawing individual pixels.
Player—The person playing a game.
Player Character—The in-game character a player is controlling.
Pop-Up box—A box that appears with information and can contain selectable options.
Power Up—In-game object that can be picked up by the playable character to enhance their ability.
Puzzle Elements—In-game riddles that players must solve to move on in a game.
Relative—Relating to the position of the player character.
Rooms—Title screens and game levels in a game are represented by different rooms.
RPG—Role Playing Game.
Score Counter—Visual representation of the player's score in a game.
Script—Code that tells a particular object or game element what behaviors to perform.
Shoot 'Em Up—Game genre in which players shoot other objects in a game as the primary mission.
Shop—An in-game store where the playable character can buy in-game items using coins found in the game.
Side-Scroller—Game genre in which the player appears to move sideways across the screen. Typically, the game camera follows the player character so that the background scrolls while the character stays in the same position to create the illusion of the character running through the environment.
Snap X, Snap Y—GameMaker option that allows designers to move items on the game grid.
Sound Effect—Audio file that plays in the game to represent an event.
Spawn—When a new object appears in a game.
Speed—How many steps it takes for an action to complete in a game.
Splash Screen—Sometimes referred to as the tile screen of a game. The splash screen is the first screen a player sees when they run a game.
Sprite—Graphical representation of a game object.
Sprite Depth—How close a sprite is to the player in relation to the depth of other in-game objects. By changing the sprite depth, characters can appear to move in front of or behind other objects.
Sprite Editor—Area in GameMaker in which designers can customize their sprites using basic drawing tools.
Sprite Strip—A series of sprite images that each appear slightly different to give the illusion of movement when played in succession.
Start of a Block—GameMaker icon that signifies the beginning of a series of actions.
Steam—Online retailer and gamer community base.
Subfolder—A folder inside another folder.
Submenu—A menu inside another menu.
Switch States—Changing the visual state of a game object to something different.
Target Audience—Group of people a game is designed for.
Tile—A single graphic from part of a tile set that can be dragged onto the canvas.
Tile Set—Series of graphics that can be dragged onto the canvas.
Title Screen—The first screen a player sees that allows the player to start or end the game.

Trigger—In-game event that when initiated causes something else to happen in the game.
Two Player—Game created for two people to play at the same time.
Ubuntu Linux—Operating system.
Use of Views—Modifying what the player can see inside the room.
Visible—When an object can be seen in a game.
W, A, S, D Keys—Common combination of keys used to control player character movements.
Windows—Operating system used on personal computers.
Xbox One—Game console created by Microsoft.
x axis—Where an object is located between the left and right side of the screen.
y axis—Where an object is located between the top and bottom of the screen.
YoYo Games—Company that owns GameMaker.

Index

A

B

C

D

E

F

G

H

I

J

K

L

M

N

O

P

Q

R

S

V

W

X

Y